I found myself in need of re-reading your Chapter 8. It became even more powerful the second time through. The language is assertive yet so calming and powerful. Lauren was right... your use of words is poetic. It's a chapter that needs to be read and re-read and re-read by your readers, because it keeps calling forth to us, inspiring additional "gains" each time. We can live in knowing what you're saying, but in daily life we (I) start doing more intellectualizing vs. feeling or being. I hope you DO keep the last paragraph. It ties it the chapter together so well, and calls people forth, releasing them in a basic and profound way.

Jeffrie – Life Coach and CEO Scottsdale, Arizona

What an outstanding and profound undertaking you have accomplished!!!! Thanks from those who have yet to learn the lessons you have addressed.

Suzanne – Editor, Sedona, Arizona

Early Acclaim for
Visionaries Thrive In All Times

The spirit of your message is so powerfully alive that it lifts me up and carries me above the page - above the words, above the sentence structure, grammar, verb tense and punctuation. I have to read it several times to get my mind to focus on the form and structure.

My feeling is that you are living what you are writing about and that's why your message is so powerful. Eckhart Tolle says that there is an energetic vibration in words of truth, and that when you read it, you are not just taking words into your mind - you are affected on a very deep energetic level. That happens to me with your book. I'm not just "right with you" intellectually; I'm right with you experientially. I believe that this book will be a life changing experience for many people.
Gayle – Tucson, Arizona

Oh, my God, I LOVE it. While I was reading, it felt like my chakras were activated. I had a ton of questions to ask you and comments to make while reading (not relating to lack of understanding, though), but now they're just running around in my head without form, and I'm sitting here soaking it in. It matches where I am, which obviously helps, and has interesting twists regarding helping others. Chaos theory fits so well in it, and thanks for being non-sexist.
Jeffrie – Life Coach and CEO Scottsdale, Arizona

You have a great writing style - simple yet often poetic and profound. This book is a great accomplishment. I know it will be well received.
Lauren – Author and CEO Toronto, Ontario

Those other two chapters (6 and 7) are awesome. Really. They get the message across succinctly and orderly. They should be read before "Allowing" (Chapter 8). I am so proud of you for getting this far. Have you put any of it out on the Internet yet? It might be the first time I have read a good explanation of negative thoughts affecting (our) outcomes.
Patti – Author Atlanta, Georgia

You are incredible! I love the way you write. Coupled with the fact that I'm passionate about the content of this chapter, I really enjoyed reading it.

It was completely absorbing material which felt very clear, concise and empowering. I especially grinned when I read the sentence which says "...(others) are in their own state of aligning with Source at their own rate of comfort and discomfort" ... Yep, that would be me now, wouldn't it!! And I also believe no one ever arrives 'at' being a visionary but rather continues on their own personal journey AS one, (though) even occasionally getting sidetracked.
Susan – Tempe, Arizona

I wanted to write and let you know how much I appreciate you! You have helped me so much by what you told me on our last phone conversation that I just had to write! I have been keeping my vision totally on my goals and what it is that I am wanting, and at the same time staying afloat allowing things to ride until it hits! Not paying attention to the little negative things. . . . . Always keeping in mind my end results:
>   FREE TIME
>   ABUNDANCE & MONEY
>   (And) FEELING GOOD
>   "THE ONLY THING THAT MATTERS!"
I just wanted to let you know, thanks for coming into my LIFE; you are a true gift to me.
Rae – Arizona

VISIONARIES
THRIVE
IN ALL TIMES

A JOURNEY OF PERSONAL TRANSFORMATION
J. HAMILTON

Published by VisionariesLab Press
2675 W. Hwy 89A, #1101
Sedona, Arizona 86336
www.visionarieslabpress.com

First Edition

Cover design, illustration and book layout by Tony De Luz
Author Photo by Victoria Monize

ISBN 1-4196-0241-1

Library of Congress Control Number: 2005920125

Printed in the United States of America

Comments are welcome
For more information or contact...
info@visionarieslabpress.com

9.6

We have in our lives no more and no less than what comes from our hearts, our minds and what we know to be so.

Our realities are created by our thoughts: conscious, unconscious and subconscious.

And, until recently, fear and doubt have played the biggest part in the creation of our realities.

Contents

PROLOGUE

"Today is the beginning of the rest of your life."

Beginning today, we have far more potential for managing our lives than we ever thought possible. In fact, as we come to understand the capacity for directing our lives, we will discover that we, individually and collectively, have it within us to positively influence the entire course of reality on this planet.

Another adage, of equal age and wisdom —
"The only thing we can change is our mind."

Identifying that the only change possible is that which is internal to ourselves is the first step toward real and lasting change. According to the ancient principle of cause and effect, we are able to create new and differing effects (realities) simply by a shifting of our beliefs and our thinking (cause). This is in distinction to continually attempting to manipulate or change outward circumstances that are, in fact, the end results of one's thinking processes. Certainly, effects are the wrong place to start solving problems or revising realities.

We have dominion over our thoughts, our choices and our aspirations. As we begin to embrace and assume conscious mastery over what we output, we begin a pathway, a trail and a vision that takes us toward dominance over our affairs. Suffice to say, the results we achieve in our lives are exclusively of our own making.

For the purpose of this book, the mind is defined as the collection of our conscious, unconscious and subconscious thoughts and patterns. The mind includes repetitive and habitual patterns of thought, as well as our barely conscious and unconscious "self-talk." The mind also includes our emotions, beliefs, attitudes and perspectives, as well as "what we know to be so." Within this definition, we do not separate the mind from the brain.

In the meantime, we have become inadvertently lazy. We have become accustomed to the conveniences of our mind's automatic and habitual patterns of thinking that direct our outcomes and run our lives with little ongoing refinement and interpretation from us.

We use our minds to "get what we get, want what we want, and end up with what we end up with." In review, we can see that we have much more in our lives from our patterns of thought and focus than we might ever suspect. For everything we have in our lives, we have corresponding thinking, attitudes and perspective, as well as patterns of focus. Ultimately, we will come to see that it can be no other way.

This, then, becomes an exercise in changing our minds and outgrowing systems of thinking that no longer serve us. This will allow us to move in a more intentional direction for the creation of our realities and our outcomes. In the cusp of the 21st century, we are just beginning to move past the fear and doubt that has kept us huddled in the past and afraid of the dark for so very long.

As we become aware of what we each have in our lives and the thinking patterns we hold dear, we begin to see how we might revise our realities by improving the quality of our output. It becomes our goal to recognize our patterns of thinking and the results we achieve and learn how to refine our thought patterns to bring more meaning to our lives.

Our intent, then, becomes to review and revise our lives and realities upwardly and consciously. As we move from painful and doubtful survival methodologies taught by our forefathers and resolve to a more holistic approach, we have the opportunity to radically influence the outcome of our own development. The importance of rapidly (and naturally) moving toward what does work combined with what we teach our children are important keys as we shift and change our lives for the better.

The ability to more effectively communicate with ourselves, and each other, will make the world a better place. It therefore becomes our duty to see of what we are made, to discover our possibilities, and then to become more.

Our life's momentum is the sum of the quality of the choices we make as we go through life. As our momentum and intentionality improve, the order, synchronicity and quality of our experiences improve. As we continue to refine our momentum, our lives take on new meaning and we expand into our possibilities.

It is the intent of this material to provide a blueprint for making our lives more by coming into alignment with Universal Forces. As we come to understand ourselves, we come to understand the world around us, and thus we begin to positively influence our outcomes. And, as we come into a partnership with the order that keeps the planets in their orbits and apples coming from apple seeds, we begin to fulfill our mission as intentional beings in a whole new way.

By the use of new choices and decisions in alignment with Spirit, we effortlessly discover new and exciting vistas. As we become more conscious, we discover a vast correlation between what we put out and what we get back.

Cause and effect is alive and well and, it turns out, well within our grasp! A world of beauty, harmony, resonance and expansion is available to us simply by changing our mind. As creators of not only our output, but also the quality of realities we each live within, life can be everything we have ever imagined it to be – and more.

It turns out that it is up to us.

Acknowledgment

Everybody I have interacted with over the past several years has contributed to this book in one manner or another. Sometimes it is the simplest of remarks, but all have contributed in each their own unique way, and I am grateful. I wish to acknowledge my parents and, in particular, my mother, who, as a product of her own beliefs and momentum, remains one of the people I am closest to.

A pivotal influence in my young adult life was fictional character Jubal Harshaw – attorney, doctor, metaphysican and human extraordinaire – who provided refuge for the man from Mars, Valentine Michael Smith, in Robert Heinlein's *Stranger in a Strange Land.* It was here that I was introduced to my first glimpse of sovereignty, wherein one human being has absolute dominion over his/her affairs. Though Jubal Harshaw was a fictional hero, he nonetheless stands tall in impact and influence.

Another huge influence was Ramtha. While I only met Ramtha several times in workshops in 1986 and 1987, I realized what he had to offer almost instantly. Another teacher of sovereignty, he had a huge impact as I continued to refine the importance of my own nature and the importance of dominion over my surroundings, which are clearly of my own making. To clarify, my surroundings include my mental, emotional and spiritual states and well-being, as well as my physical reality.

In a recent review of *Power vs. Force* by Dr. David Hawkins, Ph.D., I am surprised to realize how very much Dr. Hawkins' material has influenced and supported many of my thoughts and concepts. Much of what is important to me finds support in his work.

Furthermore, I wish to acknowledge and dedicate this book to those who have the courage to question "Is this all there is?" We know there is a great deal more to life because we have the eyes to see and the perception to reveal what is true. According to Dr. Hawkins' work, courage is the single most important factor in the individual and collective rise of an understanding of each our own innate natures and capacity for becoming. Our potential is immense and simply a matter of choice and a bit of courage.

And last, I wish to dedicate this book to you, holding this book in your hands. It is not by default or accident that you find yourself exactly where you find your feet planted in your life and this day in time. That there is more depth to life is no doubt. That you are ready for more is apparent. That you make the choice is up to you.

It is my wish that courage become your watchword and your lifelong partner, and that courage reveal to you how to stand tall as a human being. For in discovering your potential, we all become substantially more. After all, what else is there to do, other than to discover of whom and what we are made, and then go forward secure in our own truth?

Assuredly, as a species, we race toward our perfection, our potential and our solutions – only a matter of a perspective away. As the most fundamental resource on the planet, our individual capacity to create and stretch and grow represents a blossoming that is just beginning to stir all over the planet. And, as a species, we are becoming more distinct and succinct each and every new day. As we discover ourselves, an identity that is truly our own, we become our potential.

Happily, we sit on the front row of exciting and ongoing ever upward change – something we can write home about and say we were a part of – a time of the people of planet Earth beginning to come into their possibilities, a time of humanity beginning to shine. For humanity has never so shined like the millions of voices we are becoming, united in our most fundamental common denominator, something common to us all and something that resides within each of us. It is in our capacity to blossom in partnership with Innate Intelligence that we bring our essence into the open and into the Light.

Be assured that as this transformation continues to expand, our planet, known from a distance as blue and white, will become a planet of blue-and-white brilliance for which the message will travel into deep and far space. We have survived, and we have arrived.

I would like to extend personal thanks to a few friends I've met along the way: Ambaya, Bill Lewis, Bob Crozier, Bob Sittel, Brent Baker, Cecil Barton, Dotty Terzini, Doug and Barbara, Gayle Meadows, George Hasbun, Janina Fisher Balfour, Jeffrie Story, Jerry and Esther Hicks, Judith Olson, Lauren Holmes, Linda von Geldern, Louise Green, Naomi Marie, Ruth Hartung, Sheri Congdon, Sunny Strait, Suzanne Cole, Sydney Pinkerton, Victoria Monize, as well as the rest of the free radicals in the world.

And a special thanks to my editor, Catherine Rourke, who has so capably morphed her talents to my writing style.

Ultimately, this book is dedicated to those with curiosity, courage and a knowing that tells them there is more...

Namasté

INTRODUCTION

I have challenged tradition and the status quo practically since the day I was born – sometimes at great expense, and always at great adventure and interesting outcomes. Following my gut and my instincts and what I knew to be true, I have always had new and interesting perspectives, new and interesting horizons, and, as always, new and interesting alternatives from which to choose.

What has made little sense has given me little reason to submit or commit. And while this is sometimes a lonely endeavor, it has brought me endless exploration and a constant affirmation of my own character. Marching to my own drummer has ultimately proven invaluable to my own sense of worth. It has given me a huge basis for understanding the world around me from my own perspective, for which I continue to experiment and adventure out each and every day.

My strongest attribute has always been a powerful connection with common sense. I grew up through trial and error and paid attention to everything that was important to me. Presently, my background includes 30 years of mediation, which has served me like no other education can. A grounded introduction to one's own inner workings, access to innate wisdom and connection with Innate Intelligence has no par in the outer world. My experiences are mine; my output is mine; and my results are mine. I have come to be entitled to my opinions and perspectives as I flow my truth in front of me. It is with this understanding that *Visionaries Thrive In All Times* is written and offered.

This brings up the subject of security. So many equate security with the size of their wallet and their financial holdings. And while society has accepted financial security as a certain measure of one's value, real security cannot be traditionally measured, nor devalued. True security comes from no place other than your connection with who you really are and what is true for you. True security is stable, ever available, an inside job and something you can take with you when you pass at your physical death. Come to think of it, true security is also the definition of true success.

Visionaries Thrive in All Times was written as a certain type of reporting of the incontrovertible momentum of humanity as I see it. Humanity, a species bestowed with little known secrets and riches and seemingly inexperienced, is doing every conceivable variation of attempting to discover who and what it truly is – something about 100 buttons and pushing all of them, just for the sake of clarity. "Out of contrast comes clarity" is a most basic principle found in all aspects of nature. For it is in the contrast of trial and error that we get clear about what is true, what is right, and how to go forward in our lives.

Speaking of nature, humanity carries within itself the seeds of perfection, the seeds of true success and the seeds of getting it right. *Visionaries Thrive In All Times* reports that humanity has no conclusion other than to get it right. Humanity, as a part of the natural order of things, is innately driven toward success. No matter the size of the mistakes (the bigger the mistake, the bigger the lesson and ultimate clarification), we are innately driven toward perfection, to overcome obstacles, surmount difficulties and to blossom like the life form we truly are. That humanity flirts with its own death is inconsequential as seen in the overall scheme of things.

That this book is written in positive narrative is to be assumed, for after all, all of nature is "written" this way. Therefore, this book is a constant striving, a consistent affirmation, of not only the possibilities, but also the certainties of our very existence. That we might burn ourselves to a cinder is always a possibility, but, even at that, we will be back to try it again. Not so dissimilar to the tender green grass stem making its way through the crack in the summer sidewalk, we are "of the same stuff" and made in that same spirit. Humanity carries a spark that says that no matter what the conflict, the size of the contrast or the length of the difficulty, we will prevail. It is written in our genes, our spirits and our souls.

Read with an open mind, *Visionaries Thrive In All Times* allows a bit more light to penetrate your nervous system, a bit more light to enter the darkness of where you have not yet gone, and a bit more light to shine from your eyes. Anyone can listen to the naysayers; anyone can lay down and say it can't be done. Anyone can wait to see who does it first, or ask, "Does it work"? Someone once said, "Do what other people do, get what other people get." OK, I fess up. I say it all the time. It's really that simple.

Visionaries Thrive In All Times will prompt you to think of possibilities you may never have consciously allowed. *VTAT* may lead you to a rabbit hole more in resonance with your true momentum and more in keeping with your true potential. Know that this book is written as a constant affirmation and contains momentum that will catapult you beyond your horizons of self-limitation and those who say it is not so. Absorb and collect information useful to your comfort, your true security and your soul's growth. And listen to your nervous system, for that is your true teacher. Know that you have choice and that you are responsible for your outcomes.

For it was repeated by a fellow not so much subtler than myself:
Observers thrive in good times
And suffer in bad;
Visionaries thrive in all times.

Namasté

J.Hamilton

Chapter One
SURVIVAL

*T*here is good news, and there is bad news. The good news is that God creates your realities; the bad news is that you are God. I know this might sound confusing, so I will retract the remark for the time being. In its place I will state that instead of part of your realities being created by the devil or God, your neighbors or your boss, all of your realities are created by you: you and your conscious mind, you and your subconscious mind, and you and your unconscious mind.

We also have what may be termed the superconscious mind. The superconscious mind represents an aspect of ourselves that is our connection with Innate Intelligence, the part of us that is always connected to the term that I prefer for God, Source. The superconscious mind is capable of being an excellent partner, though, for the most part, we find that it is unplugged. On the other hand, it has always been and continues to be available as intuition, knowing, insight, etc. It is often described as readily available to us between our thoughts and sometimes defined as the point of stillness between the in-breath and out-breath.

Our superconscious mind is made available to us based on our capacity to listen, and, as we shall come to discover, to feel. Our realities are completely created by ourselves. There is no outside influence or source for our realities - a discovery we will come to acknowledge as our greatest gift.

This might be of surprise to many, but think about it: How many have seen evidence for god(s), or superheroes or mythical beings solving problems on our behalf? How many superheroes are protecting us or holding the tide against evil forces for us? How many of us have ever witnessed anything other than man-made evil, i.e., ignorance, anger, rage, hate, greed, etc.?

How many have seen evidence for God, gods, or superheroes or mythical beings solving problems in our behalf?

How many have witnessed God dropping a million dollars on someone's front porch when we most or least expected it? How many relate to the concept of Satan or evil as taught in our ancient lore? How many have seen graffiti written on any of our most beautiful sunrises or sunsets? It will never happen. There are no outside influences in our lives, and in this lies our power as members of the human race.

The good news is that we are the superior link in the chain of evolution on Earth, and we are likely here for a good reason. According to ancient lore, we were created in the image of God, which is an interesting remark in itself. God is, of course, the Creator, and, as the progeny of God, "we" must be, individually and collectively, creators as well.

Is it possible that as the son of God (plural, male/female), we have more purpose than standing in grocery lines or as recipients of whatever somebody decides gasoline ought to cost? Are we here simply as the beneficiary of some kind of order that is too vast to understand? Maybe we are here as puppets or underlings, similar to the characters in "The Wizard of Oz," for which we are the recipients of someone else's version of what is best for us?

Maybe we are here at the behest of others. Possibly we are the play toys or lab rats of magicians or a galactic race, or a race of giants? Maybe we are here to go to heaven or hell upon our demise after our one-time experience (with no warm-up or practice) of life on Earth? Or, possibly we are here as some kind of cosmic experiment in free will? What we really need to know is who we are in relationship to the world around us and whether we have choice in any of this.

Maybe we are no more than participants in other people's realities, drawn into each other's experiences and swirled around for which we have little to say? Or similar to the ants, stuck in long lines, we appear to constantly work, work, work, with no end in sight? Possibly we exist simply to be the recipients of God's love like big flowers? Are we here simply to bask like big lizards, albeit a bit different from the reptiles?

Why are we here? Possibly we are here to make rhyme and reason of our circumstances? Perhaps we are here to accumulate wisdom and truth and become more? Maybe we are here to step into our potential as the son of God as a species? This is what is so obvious as we look over our past and our ever-so-slow evolving growth. Is it possible we have access to tools and benefits for which we are presently unaware?

How did the skyscrapers and the big cities, with their huge airports, harbors and communications and commerce centers, come to exist? How about the massive strip mining operations with huge dump trucks with tires two stories tall, the shuttle craft that carry astronauts to and from the Moon or the quarter-mile-long supertankers? How did the Gothic cathedrals of Europe, Stonehenge or the Egyptian pyramids or Machu Picchu come to exist? How did America come to exist? What part do we as humanity play in all of this?

How did we as a culture move from the critical importance of priests and fire-keepers and living in caves to driving automobiles that talk to us, guide us with global satellite positioning and offer unparalleled comfort at highway speeds? How did the massive hospitals, computers, the Internet, the Hubble telescope or quantum physics, or any of the other millions of subjects and realities humanity invented and developed, come to exist?

Was all of this just here? Was all of this found under a rock? Or did we create it as tools and representations of our own evolutionary growth path? Does humanity as the son of God create? Plainly, it can be seen that humanity does create and has been creating for quite some time. That humanity is becoming more sophisticated in its creating is a result of an increasing sophistication and wisdom, as evidenced all around us. For, after all, we live in a world of vast conveniences, supersonic flight, trips to the Moon and soon the planets and beyond. The list goes on and on. Humanity as a young creator is just beginning to learn to create with wisdom, integrity and intention, for which its possibilities are absolutely endless.

We are on quite a learning curve, and, as we continue to sort out our identity and our potential, we sort out our responsibilities and our capacities to create. There is a vast opportunity and magnificence in the world for those with eyes to see. Clearly we are becoming responsible for a significant part of the evolution that is life on Earth.

The next time we see a neighbor, acquaintance or stranger, it would behoove us to realize that that individual is of a lineage of creators that comes straight from God. That individual, part of a lineage of creators who are just beginning to get it right, is slowly but surely learning to create in a more conscious and intentional manner. Learning from our mistakes, accumulating and slowly gaining in wisdom and becoming more competent and potent all the time, we are becoming intentional creators who are just beginning to get it right and will get it right.

Inner Space

Where might we be going with all of this? What is to be expected of all of this? The answer is that we are going straight to the stars, but not exactly as we might first suspect. Most believe that the final frontier, as popularized by a well-known science fiction series, is outer space. Outer space is something that humanity can, and, capably and thoroughly, will explore, but we want to talk about the true, and, more importantly, the real final frontier - inner space.

The next time we see an acquaintance or stranger, realize that that individual is of a lineage of creators that comes straight from God.

As a species, we are beginning to explore strange new worlds (cause and effect). We are discovering new life forms (ourselves and our capacities), and we are boldly going where no man has gone before (beyond our fears and doubts) – because our final frontier is inner space. An exploration of our inner universe and the source of our outpourings and our capacity to create is what we are all about. This is where we find the source of our power and all of our possibilities and outcomes.

Interesting concept, our inner universe. Pictorially, we believe/imagine God as outside of ourselves, but it is within us, our inner universe yet to be explored, where we will truly find God and all of our solutions. As the son of God (humanity) imbued with the will of the Creator, we come to understand that our very capacity to exist, to create and to survive is an inside job! Out of our inner nature comes all of our solutions and future direction, as well as all of our potential. It turns out that we are the superheroes, and buried deep inside of each of us is a potential that defies all understanding – that is, until we begin to discover our true nature and begin to settle into our new routines. It will then become quite apparent who we are in the scheme of things.

I propose that the reality that we each live within is a function and expression of what comes from our hearts, our minds and what we know to be so. One hundred percent of our reality is under our dominion and comes from under our scalp and behind the buttons on our shirts. Ultimately, we have 100-percent management and dominion over the direction and outcomes of our lives. And, actually, it can be no other way. It is from this understanding that our capacity for intentional reality creation and the joy and peace that has always been alluded to in our ancient lore becomes available to us.

Additionally, this knowledge and the awareness of our potential is ancient knowledge. This knowledge has been practiced and has survived for eons out in the open, as well as underground as mystery schools and other ancient lineages of study, and has over time risen in waves and come and gone back underground. It likely goes back 12,000 years and more likely, 50,000 years, and possibly far longer. Most recently it arose out of the Dark Ages as the European Renaissance of the 14th through 16th centuries and continues to this day as the Industrial Revolution, the Space Age and Nuclear Age, as well as the communications age and the information revolution of our present time.

How many of us have heard "When the student is willing, the teacher will appear"?

I also propose that dominion over our affairs makes us the source of what we have, get and end up with in our lives. Remember the merry-go-rounds and carousels of amusement parks past? Initially a great deal of fun, the same scenery over and over again eventually becomes boring as we begin to wish for new and different adventures, sights and sounds. Handy being a creator now, isn't it? Of course, the downside is that there is nobody we can blame for our circumstances but ourselves.

This connection between our inner universe (mind) and our outer world (reality) makes us capable of potentially flawless creation. Humanity is capable of creating with perfect acuity by aligning with

Innate Intelligence and principles of truth for which this is just the beginning! Clearly, it is my belief (and your entitlement) that death can be overcome, that poverty can be overcome, that pollution can be overcome, that abuse and manipulation of the less fortunate can be overcome and that there can be a far better world ahead. As we learn to manage reality creation through partnership with Innate Intelligence, i.e., our connection with Source, our realities can so vastly improve that heaven on earth can be the result, for which we would all be well-pleased.

Once this intentional alignment with Innate Intelligence becomes consensus as practiced by enough individuals, our collective outer world begins to take on a new form. Our world becomes representative of our capacity to outflow our connection and partnership with Innate Intelligence and each other – something to which we all have access. Our planet blossoms as the next outpouring of mankind as a whole.

Consensus Reality

There is the story of a group of monkeys not too different from ourselves. Happy, but not too happy, living their lives, making ends meet, and then they are introduced to an idea. The idea revolves around the fact that they are ruining their teeth eating sweet potatoes that are sandy. Scientists are sure that by attempting to teach the monkeys to wash their food, they can eliminate the harmful damage due to the sand and grit in their teeth.

Slowly, some of the younger monkeys began to learn from the scientists and began to clean their sweet potatoes prior to dining. As a certain number of younger monkeys began to practice this technique of gustatory preparation, suddenly all of the monkeys began to do the same thing. What makes the story interesting is that monkeys on other islands began this practice, as well – hence the 100th monkey syndrome. Once a certain proportion of a population begins the practice of a thought or an idea, it suddenly becomes what "everybody" does.

Visionary Mode

Individually and collectively, and some sooner and some later, we move past "survival mode" and otherwise the mere necessities of life and begin to have time to contemplate improvement in our lives. We begin to see a correlation between –
- our minds,
- our thoughts,
- our results, and finally,
- our underlying intentionality.

And, as we begin the pursuit of correlating output with our corresponding realities, we discover access to Innate Intelligence – initially as gut feelings and intuition, and eventually, as whole new qualities of what we know to be so.

There are some who have learned to achieve a no-holds reliance on insight from Innate Intelligence and who are often seen as extraordinary individuals. Though oftentimes not well-understood, they are the essence of which our history and lore is written. And, it is not unusual for such individuals to glean new information, compare notes and share their inner proddings and insight among their peers and compatriots. To discover that humanity has been recording insight into its inner nature, and documenting access to Innate Intelligence attempting to reveal itself since the beginning of time, is a huge hint that somehow we are on the right track.

Having a bit of free time, we begin to get answers that we once did not have the time, nor the inclination, to discern. As a species, we are emerging from an era when, as farmers and immigrants, we spent our waking hours just trying to keep up, much less get ahead. We were so busy with the fundamentals of survival that leisure time was virtually nonexistent. We had little time to contemplate our existence.

We have now grasped the basics of survival, and we are beginning to allow our minds to pursue activities that bring us new and more refined types of survival. This is a reflection of having time of our own and being part of a free society that allows us to explore dominion over our thinking and our corresponding capacity for results – a far more important statement than first meets the eye.

What was initially available to only the few has become available to the many. For thousands of years, knowledge was available only to those who could collect it, catalog it, protect it, seize it or inherit it in some manner. Knowledge was a most specialized resource and maps, books and wisdom were jealously guarded. Challenges to the status quo (primarily the Church) by early individuals were often very painful or cost them their lives. Knowledge was available to only the few and changed very little over the bulk of our past. It wasn't until the advent of the printing press, the telephone, the computer, fax and Internet, i.e., our capacity to readily share information among ourselves, that humanity began to truly wake up and grow up.

Among the many disciplines of science and study available to humanity, an understanding of accessing Innate Intelligence is by far the most important, because this information is most closely aligned to our true nature and the source of our power as individuals. Accessing the potential that is bottled up inside of each of us is

We are all the same far more the same than we are different!

our most important resource and our most interesting and enlivening journey. As long as accessing Innate Intelligence has been sought, it has been documented in myriad manners as a baseline for wanting to understand ourselves better.

A type of quest and knowledge that can be traced back to the beginnings of civilization, and which may be far different than traditional or popular thinking presently teaches or allows, is what we seek. After all, there is a great deal of fear and superstition taught as truth, and there is a great deal of truth that simply isn't taught. And, as we learn to access Innate Intelligence, we are at a point of coming to know the difference. We decide what is true or not true for ourselves in a whole new way.

9

Knowledge about our connection with Source, about our relationship with God and the part we play in the cosmos is about our true potential as human beings. It's about the superhero in all of us – something we innately know about or once did – something that doesn't seem to be supported by the generalities of modern mass-mind thinking, or taught within the universities or displayed by authority figures whom we assume to be our leaders.

Lookin' for Answers

We are living in very special times right now. Choice abounds, wisdom abounds, and access to knowledge abounds. Access to information is everywhere. How many are familiar with Transcendental Meditation (TM) and Maharishi Mahesh Yogi of the 1960s? How many remember that Maharishi was the guru who influenced the Beatles and introduced and popularized meditation to the Western world? How many realize the vast influence the Beatles had through their music, individual personalities and experiences? The Beatles sang about love and mysticism and had a vast popularity and influence because their message resonated within us in a deeply felt way.

And where we came from is Source, and where we are going is Source.

How very far we have come since the 1960s! How is it that we have come to change and advance so rapidly over the past 40 or 50 years? What has caused the fantastic leaps in consciousness that are so evident as we overview our recent past?

By way of example, *A Course In Miracles* (ACIM) has had an enormous influence over the past 30 years. ACIM was a result of collaboration by two Columbia University professors published in 1975 in response to their observation that "there must be another way." This inner dictation and channeled information has now spread all over the world, reaching countless lives and several generations of people.

Many are familiar with the influence of other modern day philosophers, mystics and gurus. They include the Dalai Lama, Thich Nhat Hanh, Gurumayi, Osho, Yogananda, Ram Dass, Timothy Leary, the Seth material, Richard Bach, Shirley McLaine, Arnold Patent's Universal Principles, Marianne Williamson, Deepak Chopra, Wayne Dyer and so many others. What has been the influence of this insight into our very nature and present day and increasingly modern culture? How many of us have heard "When the student is willing, the teacher will appear"?

We must be asking a great many questions, because the teachers are appearing. But this is not the time our mothers told us about; this is the time we innately deep down inside knew about. We resonate with the spiritual advances brought about since the 1960s. But how did we know, and how did this come to be? Why has there come to be such growth in the inner delving of the mind and soul in this day and time? What has brought us to this precipice of a new understanding of ourselves? One would have to admit there is increasing contrast between the old and the fast-approaching new.

It is apparent that society as we once knew it began to radically shift in the mid-1960s and early 1970s. Those born since the late 1940s or since the atomic bomb was dropped in Japan began a radical shift away from a narrow limited consensus of reality. In quest of "there must be more" or "is this all there is?", we began to dig within and respond to Innate Intelligence's budding as we opened up just a bit more.

How much generationally and globally have we leaped by the practice and ideas associated with meditation, or *A Course In Miracles* or the Beatles singing "All you need is love, love, - love is all you need."?[1] Or, the immense influence of a song titled "Imagine" by John Lennon? What do we feel as we read these lines? What does accessing the inner part of ourselves tell us about ourselves and the hope we have for the world of which we are a part? Are we really intact as a generation, and do we have something to say and something to learn? Do we have something to give?

11

We are in the midst of a soft revolution. We are rapidly revamping what we think, what we believe, what we know and what we want to know. A whole new world view in thinking and a whole new knowledge, awareness, and consciousness is expanding right under our very noses! We are right in the middle of a vast planetary change as we learn about right and wrong and better and best. We are a generation asking questions, doubting some of what we have been told, and a great deal of what has been assumed to be so! Our feelings and our gut is telling us there is much more, for which Innate Intelligence is readily available for the asking.

Through the use of science and technology, we are one of the first generations to have the capacity to overview what we have created thus far and make a determination as to how effective we have been. As we review our past, we are for the first time able to think about how we would like our future to be. Consciousness is beginning to peer out of our eyes as we review our surroundings, because we finally have a bit of time on our hands. We are the carriers of new thought and new wisdom. We are the new decision makers and we are the new reality makers. We are responsible for our future (as we are responsible for our past), and we are beginning to understand how we are going to get there. We are discovering that we are capable of becoming responsible for how it is going to turn out. We are becoming visionaries.

Can we see the distinct and far-reaching shifting and expansion of consciousness that has occurred since the 1950s? Can we see the effect and influence of how we have come to think and revalue the world around us? Can we see how much power and awareness we have accumulated in the last 40 or 50 years? And, indeed, in less than one or two generations? Things are moving very fast; much faster than they have ever moved before. It behooves us to pay a little more attention to how we "get what we get," how we "got what we got," and how we "end up with what we end up with."

It won't happen overnight because there is so much old and sticky momentum. And though we are seemingly becoming more powerful faster than we become wise, we are nonetheless moving very rapidly toward our potential. Who fears the Chinese, the Russian or the Korean people? Authority figures tell us that these people are our economic, political and military foes, but the Chinese and the Russian people, whom there are supposed vast ideological and political differences, are more similar to us than we think. How indelibly impressed were we by our commonality as we watched the anonymous student[2] opposing the tanks in Tiananmen Square on June 5, 1989, or became aware of Andrei Sakharov, the Soviet Union's leading physicist turned political dissident and inspiration for Soviet democratic reform and human rights?

It turns out that "those" people across the globe are far more like you and me than our media, leaders and government would have us believe. Why is this? Because, first and foremost, we are all human beings. As human beings, we each have an identical spiritual identity underlying our differences of language, skin color, habits, heritage and differences of upbringing and religion. We are discovering in the Information Age and the communications revolution that we are far more alike than we are different.

To understand survival requires us to look at where we came from, as well as where we are going.

Computers and the Internet are becoming the great equalizers. It won't be long until we all have computers and access to the Internet and Google searches. It won't be long before we can readily translate languages and compare notes at slightly less than the speed of light. We will discover that, first and foremost, we are all human beings. We are all the same – far more alike than we are different!

It won't be long before we discover that we all have the same things in common, including our potential, which springs from our access to

Innate Intelligence – equal in quality and availability to us all. What if spiritual love and spiritual respect became what tied us together, rather than allegiance to a nationality, a flag, fear and doubt or misinformation? What would happen if we didn't need national borders, checkpoints and passports because it turns out we are all the same?

It is no small matter that the tide is turning toward the unfolding of human potential, and turn it must, and turn it will. Just like the grass grows up through the cracks in the sidewalk, life expands – humanity expands; we expand. It is our potential; it is our heritage; it is our outpouring; and we as a species are dependent upon it for our survival. And it is our promise. Not only does our survival as a species depend on our potential, but it is written into our DNA; it is our inheritance; it is our outcome! It is everywhere around us.

Everywhere, life's intent is to expand and grow and become fuller. We are no different. We simply find ourselves in the envious position of being one of life's most sophisticated outlets, with a most sophisticated and enormous capacity for free will that cannot be denied. Life flows through our nervous systems. We are life itself! We have life's purpose within us, and we have the capacity for a newfound expression that is life inventing itself in a new way every day.

We *are* life's most sophisticated outlet. And a result of our evolution is a great deal more joy, peace and love in the world. Chris Griscom of Galisteo, New Mexico,[3] wrote a book titled *Ecstasy is a New Frequency* (1987), suggesting that as we move up the ladder of conscious awareness, ecstasy and joy become part of our legacy as alert, alive, awake and aware spiritual beings merging into our possibilities. We have something to talk about! We have something to look forward to! We have something to strive for, and we have something to become!

Survival and Comfort

The term "survival" has been used several times now. Initially, survival meant keeping out of the way of large, meat-eating animals and "getting through the night." Later, survival came to mean the efficient storage of food for "getting through the winter," and, in present time, survival seems to mean the accumulation of wealth and possessions for "getting through life."

Luckily, today we can add the ingredient of comfort as an aspect of our survival, which speaks to our story more than we know. Interestingly, as we thrive as a society and species and begin to have the leisure of comfort, we are re-evaluating the mad dash for the accumulation of things assumed to represent our survival. Innately, many are beginning to turn away from the simple amassing of wealth and materiality as a method "for getting through life" and beginning to tune in to what might be a more refined approach to the survival issue.

Yet, comfort continues to be a byword in our survival scenario. Survival issues are different than they were in the past, and they are increasingly driven by our need for comfort and security. But now, as we have achieved what we believe would give us our comfort and security, we are discovering that it is not giving us what we expected or innately resonate with.

We are discovering that our comfort and security have deeper meaning and might be more aligned to what can be gained by listening to Innate Intelligence or gained by aligning with life and nature through an understanding of the spiritual aspect of our lives. In fact, by definition, our survival would necessitate an ultimate form of security, and the only place ultimate security comes from is by truly knowing ourselves. Truly knowing ourselves distinctly includes discovering our true nature, i.e., our sacred connection with Innate Intelligence.

Since we have a spiritual aspect that remains mostly unknown, basically unintroduced, and, innately, we seem to be driven in that direction anyway... As an aside, how many remember the life when we were all baby crabs and were born under the full Moon and the idea was to get to the water and swim before the birds got us? That was Innate Intelligence guiding us toward security and survival. It is a little different now, but not much.

Ultimately, our survival and our security means going back and having a look at where we came from, or at least getting in touch with where we came from so we can better understand where we are going. And where we came from is Source, and where we are going is Source. And with just a slight adjustment to our perception, we can see that we were always connected to Source, and will always be connected to Source, no different than an apple growing from a branch of an apple tree.

Is it so hard to see that we all live in a vast, orderly hierarchy of life? After all, the big eat the small; the rains come; the plants grow; fruit continuously comes from fruit trees; etc. Foods of vast variety exist; there are minerals in the ground that become steel, glass and petroleum. Then there's the amazing organization of the planets in their implicit and resonant order, and the spleen not trying to do the lung's job, and on and on. We live in a vast array of order. Clearly order exists, and clearly we are part of it.

Where we come from may not even remotely look like what we have been taught as ancient popularized lore. For the time being, I am not going to attempt to define God other than to say that we live in the middle of a broad collective knowing that we come from something bigger than ourselves and that we go back to something bigger than ourselves (as I speculate that it is a bit early to suggest that God extends itself through us as a species). Our survival requires us to align with Innate Intelligence as we climb the ladder of our own self-realization. And, as we come to a fuller awareness and understanding of our own capabilities and capacities, we will grow into our ever expanding potentials and outcomes. This is life – our life, all of life – individually and collectively.

Ultimately, it is in the refinement of our security and comfort that we continue to refine our natures until we one day know who and what we each truly are. We are then able to assess and integrate "of what we are made," and move forward with more intentionality and a surer footing toward our potential. As we come to know ourselves, our survival becomes easier and more comfortable, and we learn a few tricks along the way.

CHAPTER TWO
PERSPECTIVE

*D*uring the cusp of the 21ˢᵗ century, we are discovering that our survival issues are driven by comfort and ease. As we acquire the fundamentals of food, shelter and automobiles with heated leather seats, as well as home entertainment systems that talk to satellites, our survival, driven by our quest for comfort, leads us toward who we truly are. Ultimately, modern technology, as an extension of ourselves, helps us identify our true nature, similar to science and quantum physics discovering and refining its own truths.

As we work our way within, we are surprised to discover an amazing amount of wreckage. While some of us were achieving comfortable homes and extensive travel to resorts around the world, we were also discovering that putting our physical worlds in order was only part of the challenge of mastering our survival. Along the way, we realized that our mental, emotional and spiritual natures were important ingredients to our long-range goals of survival, as well.

What we are discovering en masse is that even with the comforts of traditional success, we are still not quite happy. One would certainly think that the acquisition of possessions and demonstrations of wealth, comfort and power would be the pinnacles of success. But instead, an expression was coined similar to "Is this all there is?", "There has to be more," or "There has to be another way."

Truly an age-old question and now in massive proportion, the most pervasive movement in the history of the world has begun. The most important step humankind has ever made (other than the importance of doors on caves), and in similar timing to the exploration of our outer universe, is the exploration of our inner universe – en masse.

Tools for the descent into our minds and psyches require that we get a grip on our relatively unknown and unseen mental, emotional and spiritual natures. To the credit of academia and professional counselors, their associated client-base and pioneering and discoveries aside, it is the individual who first began to use the tools of going within that is our focus and the true foundation for change on this planet.

Slowly, individuals began to chart their own course, follow their bliss and otherwise listen to their inner nature beckoning them to uncover their true rhyme and reason. There was no broad-based acceptability, nor few credible assurances that delving within would gain them anything. Nor were the early individuals assured of long-range results. In fact, they were going where few had gone before, at odds with societal acceptability, for which courage and their inner-prompting was their only true sidekick. But there was a sense of connection with an aspect of themselves that needed to be explored.

Individually, we began to discern our inner natures and accept direction and insight that best matched what we believed to be true. There were no assurances that clearing the "within" would give us a happier "without," but it did seem to make sense. First we had to come to grips with our own inner workings and, accordingly, our outer workings might/maybe/ought to/possibly/could/would/should improve.

One of the first realizations to come to these inner travelers was that perception was a matter of the perceiver. It became apparent that a disjointed and fractured inner nature (anger, frustration, guilt, etc.) gave one a perception of an outer world in a similar manner. As we began sort out our inner beliefs and "inner debris and crapola,"[1] our outer worlds began to shift toward more wholeness and peace.

Beginning to understand this phenomenon, we began to have new insights into the nature of our own reality creation. It became apparent that we perceived the outside world through our belief systems, attitudes and emotional states, and that as we refined our inner nature, our outer world improved. People began to feel more whole and more connected, and the promise of the mystics, prophets and poets of our past encouraging humanity to turn within for truer happiness and inner peace was beginning to be felt.

Alternate Realities

During the same time frame, the experimental and recreational use of street drugs of the 1960s and 1970s was on the rise. Many came to realize that an alternative perception of reality could be induced by the ingestion of certain substances, both natural and synthetic. Having been practiced by native cultures for thousands of years and fiercely researched by many governments including the United States and Soviet Union, we were introduced to the fast approach that there was more than one perception of reality.

As children, we are raised with our perceptions taught to us as black-and-white, for which our beliefs and expectations are created accordingly. As youngsters, we accept these truths as established by those who come before us. We are taught the meaning of something that we might otherwise interpret and decide for ourselves. In other words, many of our perceptions and belief systems are given to us.

Humanity has been powerfully influenced in this manner since the beginning of time. Parents, teachers and authority figures instructing us what something means, what to be afraid of, what to watch out for, and what's acceptable and unacceptable. They offer oversight and interpretation to help us fend for ourselves and survive – a method that will always have some validity – on the other hand, a method fraught with ignorance, abuse, misuse, neglect, naiveté and misunderstanding. And, our past is laced with historical or political re-interpretations, and more often than we might expect, boldfaced lies.

Humanity continues to learn and grow and expand, as it always will.

Regardless, humans with a bit of free time on their hands began to experiment with their realities and perceptions. Though tools for transformation were not initially nor formally understood, humanity was none-the-less experimenting with interpretations of reality brought on by psychotropic substances, Eastern mysticism and ancient lore delving into and accessing their mental and emotional realms. We were getting an accumulation of mind-bending (black-and-white reality bending) experiences, for which a wealth of new information was being assimilated and a whole new generation was identifying itself and its values.

Few had been told, nor was it suggested, that there was more than one way of looking at life. But under the influence of discovering the nature of our minds, we were finding whole new worlds and often preferring them to the proverbial black-and-white interpretations as handed down to us. Millions of people safely experienced the effects of marijuana, LSD, mushrooms, psycillibin, mescaline, Ecstasy and peyote, and have come to experience fuller and more complete lives. Admittedly, there has been wreckage by the unwise and abusive use of such drugs by individuals with little understanding and awareness of their own personal boundaries, but humanity continues to learn and grow and expand, as it always will.

Furthermore, many millions of people safely experienced the effects of numerous courses of study of esoteric, mystical and otherwise practical wisdom including *A Course In Miracles*, Arnold Patent's *Universal Principles*, *The Urantia Book*, Religious Science, Unity Church, the est Training, Landmark Education, and Dianetics and Scientology, etc. Instructors included, but were not limited to, Leonard Orr, Werner Ehrhart, Ram Dass, Jose Silva, Maxwell Maltz, Napoleon Hill, Dale Carnegie and Timothy Leary, who were all catalysts for new interpretations of black-and-white.

Tony Robbins' seminars, Silva Mind Control, Lifespring, Atavar, Transcendental Meditation, self-hypnosis, mind development courses and other non-traditional spiritual studies and ancient wisdom teachings all suggested that there was more to life than what appeared at first glance. This widened the crack in the proverbial egg that had been our black-and-white perceptions and existence for so very long. All of this was in response to the chorus of "Is this all there is?" for which Innate Intelligence brought access to new teachers, new techniques, new technologies and new insights and wisdom.

Learning how to focus and review from a higher perspective brings peace and comfort.

Many were discovering their inner worlds in an entirely different manner. Another experimental unfolding of the generation of the 1960s and 1970s was jogging. Though most would not see fit to compare hashish or LSD with jogging, the point is that people found that jogging made them feel better and expanded their mental horizons. Jogging brought them to new and different states of clarity, including emotional highs and relaxation. But more importantly, it gave them fodder for a comparison of before and after the jogging experience.

Jogging was a successful antidote to stress. Jogging filled an outlet for individuals who needed the benefit of self-regulation and habitually disciplined activities that generated patterns of intentional mental and emotional productivity. Joggers saw and achieved results in their inside and outside worlds on a consistent and ongoing basis. They continued to jog, and their worlds continued to expand.

Joggers improved their outer worlds by improving their mental states and inner worlds. And, unbeknownst to joggers at the time, they were traversing this inner/outer connection and gaining the benefits and experience of transformation. They were playing with and enhancing the states of their mind, and their outside world was showing the benefit of it.

Meditation

There are numerous of examples of individuals who attempted to intentionally generate and achieve results in their outside world by delving into their inner world. One of the most profound was through the use of meditation as initially popularized in the early 1960s by Maharishi Mahesh Yogi with the promise of inner peace in one's life. Nothing like it had ever occurred in the West before. People slowly began to invest into and discover the inner workings of meditation. Over a period of years, huge numbers of people began to meditate.

Deepak Chopra, a Western trained doctor from India and early proponent and spokesperson for meditation, brought substantial credibility to the practice of meditation by successfully uniting Eastern and Western philosophies. As individuals began to include meditation in their daily lives, the medical profession slowly acknowledged and substantiated its health effects. Meditation, an introspection that dates back many thousands of years, adapted to meet the needs of the Western world, began to thrive.

In today's time, millions of people meditate with regularity. Consciousness expands with the insights that deep relaxation brings, eventually becoming a reflection in their outer lives. Turning inward at dizzying rates and discovering the influence meditation brought to their daily lives, many began to experience a more fuller life.

Another one of the early stepping-stones of the "soft revolution" came from a cultural dissatisfaction and disillusionment with the Vietnam War. The most visible and vocal opponents were the new generation of poets, musicians and students. There is considerable documentation of the influence of music and its increasingly outspoken opposition to the United States war effort. John Lennon; Crosby, Stills and Nash; Neil Young; Joanie Mitchell; Bob Dylan; and a multitude of other musicians voiced the values of a disenfranchised and increasingly disenchanted generation to an undeclared and ultimately unjust (black-and-white) war.

Do we realize that we are 100-percent responsible for the realities we each have in our lives?

John Lennon's "Give Peace A Chance," "Power to the People" and "Imagine" vocalized the confusion and dissatisfaction of an entire generation. With increasing at-home demonstrations against the Vietnam War and the United States government losing "its" war both domestically and on foreign soil, the United States began to shove back against the American citizenry. As the government attempted to deport John Lennon and put down riots and demonstrations for which a number of students were shot and killed by the U.S. military on American campuses, a great many realized that fighting something so big was fruitless and dangerous.

Out of the contrast of pushing against the United States government and the predictable and expensive results, people began to turn within in droves. That they used hallucinogens, books, teachings, ancient scripture, mysticism or medicinal and healing plants of an earlier time is no matter. People began to redefine their realities, en masse, to console their souls and otherwise, escape the pain of a reality gone too far wrong. New tools began to form, and new methodologies and perceptions came out of the contrast of what wasn't working at the time. The movement toward introspection continues to grow to this day.

A Matter of Perception

A Course In Miracles, comprised of 365 daily lessons, teaches that there is more than one way of looking at things. The course teaches that by changing our mental habits and perceptions, we can find more peace in our lives. ACIM taught that unconditional love was a perception that could be learned, for which we could see peace as an alternative. ACIM also taught that we could access Spirit and inner guidance for refining the outcomes of our lives.

It is in this final delving within and directly accessing Innate Intelligence that we discover our true nature.

Presently, *A Course In Miracles* is taught in a multitude of countries and published in nine languages. It introduces, as its first lesson, "Nothing I see means anything," while its second lesson teaches "I have given everything I see all the meaning it has for me." Later lessons include "There is another way of looking at the world," "I could see Peace instead of this," and "My sinless brother is my guide to Peace." Ultimately, ACIM delivered its students to the doorway of a new way of life and a new understanding of the world around them.

As a student of *A Course In Miracles* at the age of 30, I found the lessons to be hard work. Initially, it was very difficult to accept the idea that everything I knew about a coat hanger or a kitchen table was the result of past thinking. I beheld the coat hanger and (eventually) realized that everything I knew about the coat hanger, I knew from past conditioning. I discovered I was incapable of looking at my outside world in present time. I was therefore unable to experience my outside world in its true expression. I was unable to experience anything in present time, because I dragged everything I knew, or thought I knew, about a subject with me. I was, therefore, unable to enjoy or experience the magic and love of present time because of my preconceived perceptions. My black-and-white conditioning was unable to help me experience present time.

I discovered that I imbued life with properties based on conditioning and knowledge that may or may not have been accurate. The point is that my awareness about a subject at hand was unable to help me ascertain present time reality, because my entire view came from a sort of indoctrination that I had little to say about. This misinformation was coloring my present time experience and limiting its potential outcome – and creating discomfort for me, as well. I was completely in the past, looking at something in the present. It turned out that Innate Intelligence and true reality were unavailable to me while I was in this inside-out perspective. As I began to learn about the world of perception, I realized that I had new choices available to me, and my world began to unfold in a more useful manner.

Eventually, the lessons allowed me to look at life in present time and I was able to give up preconceived notions (judgments) about things for which I may or may not have had accurate information. ACIM was a very powerful teaching tool used by a very courageous aspect of society that brought many to a better understanding of the world around them. It taught that perception based on past conditioning brings confusion about the present.

We miss the love, peace and presence that is at the center of present time. Learning how to focus and review from a higher perspective brings peace and comfort, which, we come to see, has a positive and significant influence on our outer reality and outcomes. As we begin to feel better, we begin to relax. As we relax, we begin to experience present time in a more useful manner. As we side with truth, we don't have to work so hard at maintaining our existing realities.

A generation of people began to discover the use of its inner resources to get ahead. And, don't forget, we were taught that what we need always came from outside of us – God, money, wealth, security, comfort, proper education, etc. In a manner of speaking, we were taught, "If we were good, we would go to heaven," and, "If we were bad, we would go to hell" – always outside of us. One of our most important tools – our spirituality and access to Innate Intelligence – was presented as outside of us, and thus ultimately unavailable. Perception changed this.

If we look around us, everything is in a state of flux. Nature is continually refining and redefining itself. Nature is continually adapting, because its prime directive is survival, its mechanism is adjustment, and its outcome is expansion. Humanity is no different. Change can appear confusing, especially in a snapshot mode, i.e., a present time review that gives little insight to the slow and gradual momentum of a particular item of interest. But, by the accumulation of additional information, i.e., an overview and perspective, we can reinterpret a snapshot as simply a portion of a movement forward that is this thing called life. As we gain a broader perspective, snapshots can be regarded as no more than healthy aspects of long-range change for the better.

As soon as we wake up to our inherent nature, we can get on with the business of bringing heaven to earth.

Only recently have we learned how to look at the stock market in a broader perspective. Where once the appearance of a downturn had investors jumping out of windows, we now see the stock market as little more than a bit of up and a bit of down as it naturally rises and falls, and, by a strange term, "corrects itself." So, too, we realize that life continues to rise and fall and otherwise corrects itself, though sometimes the appearance is a bit overwhelming or confusing. Sometimes in the short overview or present time misinterpretation, or snapshot, we lose sight of the ever-expanding and ongoing nature that is life – and its assured long-range outcomes.

As we learn a little bit more about how we create our realities, we understand a little bit more about how life works in general. As we regard our capacity to create and learn to regard what we leave for the next generation, we have a more useful effect on the whole. As we have less regard for the miscellaneous ups and downs of personal or culturally created reality, we begin the process of smoothing over the negatives and accentuating the positives. Though we are responsible for our individual reality, we, as conscious and unconscious creators, are responsible for our collective reality as well. We make choices; we develop consensus; and it shows up as our reality. Quality perception underlies the quality of our choices. Quality choice begets the quality of our reality, individually and collectively.

To get back to one of our initial thoughts: Do we understand that we each create our realities? Do we realize that we are 100-percent responsible for the realities we each have in our lives? How many of us believe that some outside force causes our realities, or influences our outcomes in some manner, or wholly? How many believe that we get intuition or guidance from outside of ourselves? How many of us accept that guidance is an aspect of ourselves rather than a foreign intervention into our lives? How many of us actually believe our realities are beyond our own control?

If we are not 100-percent responsible for our outcomes, we are on one end of a stick, and we had better hope that whoever is wagging our stick is completely benevolent and has only our best interests in mind. Otherwise, we have serious trouble. Common sense suggests those assurances leave a great deal to be desired based on what we have seen in the typical experience that is life.

We begin to see that the mechanism so insistent with our survival is built-in and fully functional. We begin to see that reliance on outside mechanisms for our survival is inefficient and subject to numerous interpretations. It seems there are those who prefer to interpret for us as "middlemen" or "power brokers" in what is otherwise well within our domain. If it is our belief that our solutions lie outside of ourselves, then there is the distinct possibility that we become reliant on outside information and the possibility of degraded or inaccurate signals or insight. This would be similar to passing a message among a number of intermediaries before the message finally reaches us. Even if the message passed through one intermediary, it would still be degraded before it reached us.

A signal or insight that comes directly is clearly to be interpreted by no one but ourselves. We alone are responsible for the quality of the interpretation and insight made available to us. We alone are the ones who can tell whether something is true for us or not. It is in this final delving within and directly accessing Innate Intelligence that we discover and understand our true nature and our power as human beings and creators. And, handily, this is well within our capacity to learn and understand. This is what is important. Our gut feelings tell us whether we are on track or not. This is where our true education begins.

It is important to realize that it is not in our best interest to be advised by unknown benefactors, "well wishers," powerbrokers or other authority figures who claim to have our best interests in mind. There is no meaning to this type of scenario, though it is ever popular. After all, we continually witness the influence of outside authority inflicted upon others for which we know we can do better, or would like to see it done differently. We are here with the possibility of complete dominion over our affairs. As soon as we wake up to our inherent nature, we can get on with the business of bringing heaven to earth, or at least realizing they are one and the same.

One of the first judgment calls to make as an adventurer on Earth, and possibly attributed to Albert Einstein, is to discern whether the universe, of which we are an integral part, is inherently friendly or unfriendly. If the world in which we live is inherently dangerous and evil, meat-eating dinosaurs aside, and if there really are such equal powers as good and evil, then we must take this important fact into consideration regarding a game plan for our very existence. If, on the other hand, we live in a benign Universe and our souls cannot be latched or liened by evil ones, the playing field becomes significantly different. This difference is important to note.

Einstein and others realized that the universe is void of evil as a basic force. There is no evidence of inherent evil in the universe, on this planet, or in this solar system. There is no graffiti during particularly awesome sunsets; there is no inadvertent banging of planets overhead; and there is no evidence of competition for the incredible beauty and order as it exists within the known universe – or for our souls, for that matter. Other than the human frailties of hate, anger, jealously, shame, pride, etc., which are clearly man-made and the result of choice (maybe uninformed or poor choice), we find ourselves in a universe of vast harmony and order. Ultimately, the Universe bends to our wishes (but more on that later). No matter how we fuel our thoughts, we have free will and we have dominion over our affairs. The existing world is our result thus far. There is no force "out there" that interferes or regulates our affairs.

One of the most expansive programs study of our own nature is the very large telescopes and arrays that dot our planet at the highest mountain elevations for peering into space. Clearly, this scientific look into the heavens is reminiscent of most animals' inability to recognize its features in a mirror. In our sophistication, we look beyond our own features and look for the face of God, or at least evidence of God in outer space. And though, clearly, we have found vast order, beauty and surprise, we have not found evidence to suggest there are forces that influence us beyond our own imaginings. Clearly, we exist and evolve in a very orderly place – the cosmos. Clearly, we live in complete safety, for which no evidence exists to the contrary.

Ultimately, this means that all of our focus can be turned within, for we have little need to watch our backs or guard against the intricacies of evil, as suggested by some. On the other hand, we do need to keep an eye out for the priests, fire keepers and other middlemen who would tell us it is unnecessary to know about our true nature.

Knowledge

Now that we have evolved past our minimalist and purely reactionary existences, we are absorbing insight about ourselves and truly beginning to evolve. When the Beatles began to sing about love, when we first put footprints on the Moon, when fax machines began to appear everywhere and when we became able to catalogue and access information with the help of the personal computer and the Internet, we entered a time that says we are breaking the shackles of our limitations and our past. With information and insight comes an overcoming of fear and doubt. New vistas come to light, and we begin to thrive as a species.

With the advent of the computer, available to almost anyone, we are suddenly able to access and catalogue untold amounts of information and knowledge for our personal use. We are able to verify and research what someone says is so, whether it be medicine, government, science, or the Church. Now everyone has access to information and ultimately the power to communicate and make choices effectively, powerfully, and personally.

One of the benefits of accessing knowledge and communicating among ourselves is an awareness that problems are being solved and solutions are being shared. Problems that we might have once thought of as unique to ourselves, and maybe kept to ourselves or even hidden, are coming into the open because others are discovering and communicating the same or similar issues. Problems that may not to be problems we thought, once we discover others are solving them for themselves. Problems and solutions seeing the light of day is bringing humanity together. Humanity working together helps us see that we are far more the same than we are different.

Knowledge is the great illuminator. Knowledge is the "Light" referenced in the lore and mysticism of our ancient past. And until knowledge becomes available to us all, we live in the dark. Individuals in the dark are isolated, and in isolation is not only the possible danger of meat-eating dinosaurs, evil ones and middlemen, but the wanderings of the mind that include imagined dangers and conspiracies. In the dark, we are unable to compare notes among ourselves to solve problems. And just like in prehistoric times when we gathered together for safety and comfort, so today we gather together under the caption of knowledge and awareness, which comes as shared information and solutions. We move from the dark to the Light; it is our evolution. We move from fear and doubt to knowledge, solutions and experiences shared, as well as commonality and union as a species.

Fear and Doubt

With information and insight comes an overcoming of fear and doubt.

Today, our evolution has a different face. We have spent a number of generations beyond the tribal comforts of safety. Today we group together to share information and compare notes about, among other things, accessing innate power and aligning with Innate Intelligence. As once the bow and arrow or the plow were quite the valuable tool, today the tool of choice is information and the capacity to communicate effectively. Our capacity to overcome adversity, doubt and fear and to share solutions is the beginning of discovering our common bonds. We learn to trust each other, and then we are much better able to move forward as a whole.

As long as we have fear and doubt, we have room for improvement. Today, our fears may be a bit more sophisticated, but, as long as fear drives us, we are out of our connection with each other, as well as our connection with Innate Intelligence. We get garbled insight and confused perceptions at best. Fear and doubt are poor mediums for quality communications, either inwardly or outwardly.

In the speed and sophistication with which we operate our lives today, we bump up against many opportunities to see what we are made of. Our fears and doubts may come from our successes, including how to keep what we have, how to get what we think we must have and how to continue pedaling in the 21st century. And, of course, we still have those fears that we prefer to keep deep inside ourselves. Are we good enough? Are we entitled to be happy, joyful and at peace? Can we make long-range, forward thinking and responsible decisions? Are we ready to know more about ourselves? Are we ready for the power and capacity that conscious connection brings? What if we fail at such an endeavor, or what if we just don't get it? And, on and on.

What about death? What happens upon our death or the death of a loved one? How do we reconcile the teachings of a vengeful God as taught by Christian theology – how do we deal with the ultimate unknowns? Might we really go to hell for certain actions, reactions or thoughts? As our awareness grows, so too does our quest for accurate information.

It is in this quest to better ourselves that we find ourselves beginning to access knowledge that has been accumulating throughout history, often accessed as non-traditional study, ancient knowledge and non-traditional texts. There is still a great deal of knowledge that doesn't seem accessible to the masses, including the secrets of the wealthy or technical information about numerous subjects deemed to be beyond our individual needs. But suffice to say, by sharing what we are learning about ourselves amongst ourselves, we overcome the obstacles of fear and doubt. As we embrace and refine our existences in a more positive and more useful manner, we become more useful to the whole.

Through use of the computer and the Internet, a great equalizer has come into existence. Anyone can now share and access untold amounts of information as peers and equals. Only a few years ago, the gun was considered the great equalizer, though we have come to see those shortcomings. Today, knowledge and information is the great equalizer. We are rapidly coming to the point of sharing the wealth that information and informed thought produces.

Now, and only just recently, and becoming moreso every day, knowledge is for the asking. It is no more complex than a simple computer, a fast modem and a filing system for cataloging (saving) information. And don't forget the well-mannered "Google search." Anyone has the ability to learn to one's heart's desire. Vast realms of information are available, simply by doing searches on the Internet!

Thanks to the Computer Age and information revolution of the late 20th century, mankind is moving into a wealth of new knowledge. Knowledge is what allows individuals to escape the limitations of their birth and to move and grow to heights never imagined 100 years ago. And since fear, doubt and limitation fade in the awareness of knowledge and comparing notes, we find ourselves at the beginning of a long and prosperous ride into the Light.

We are on the brink of truly breaking away from our past, our limited thinking and inadequate survival scenarios. We can see the cracks forming in the egg that represents our birth. We realize we are escaping the limitations of our past birth heritage by the availability of the tools of the 21st century. Truth and knowledge, a bit of personal discipline (self-regulation) and access to Innate Intelligence are taking us in a new and far healthier direction in our lives.

This is important. Never in the history of mankind has there ever existed a large-scale possibility of escaping the bonds of our birth temperament and moving toward our potential under our own steam. Over the years there has been a vast increase in individuals moving toward their potential, but, until just recently, it has still been an infinitesimally small portion of the population. With the advent of leisure time and access to communications and knowledge, individuals are discovering how to lose the blinders that have kept them in fear, doubt and limitation of their potential for so very long.

Sovereignty

As we begin to have the leisure time to delve within, attend universities, study the stars and esoteric knowledge, and review and make personal decisions about God, Church and the role of government, we find ourselves in a new place of choice. As mankind begins to sort through the vast amounts of knowledge and misinformation and make choices about what is truly important, we take charge of our own well-being. As we make more conscious choices, our worlds begin to twirl a bit more to our liking. As we become the directors of our momentum and our learning curve, our realities begin to improve *ad infinitum.*

Ultimately, our goal is to discover that we each generate our own good will, our own direction and our own outcomes and possibilities. Everything leads to the fact that we generate our realities from our own beliefs, and that overcoming fear and doubt represents the largest return on investment for a young species beginning to look out from under its rock. Tools of the past, including fear of the unknown and habitual patterns taught to us by generations before, have had their place. But it is time to hoist our sails and go beyond what we were taught or not taught. It is time to go past what will ultimately prove to be our own self-limiting horizons.

We discover that our minds are our ships, our thoughts are our sails, and our intuition and access to Innate Intelligence our navigation and our rudder. And, it is in the comparing of notes among ourselves, the sharing of what we know and believe we know, that we chart our possibilities with more authenticity and alignment for what is true. It is a good use of our time.

CHAPTER THREE
INDIVIDUALITY

*H*umanity seems to be in a unique position among the inhabitants of planet Earth and likely represents the most potent wellspring of that thing called life. It has grown, learned and clawed its way up the evolutionary ladder to the point that it now has conveniences far beyond its modest needs of survival. By the mechanisms of tools and reason over the landscape of time, mankind finds itself with the capacity to feed the world, destroy the world, travel to the near and far planets and otherwise begin to take a new and different look at its surroundings.

Mankind has reached a point in its evolution where it can stop and observe for a moment, take a look at what it has accomplished thus far, and, with a bit of wisdom under its belt, cast an eye toward its future. Humanity has reached a point in its evolution that it now has the luxury of choice. Having been so hell-bent on getting to this point, we had no idea what this might look like or what to do with ourselves once we got there. We are still unconscious as a species, but moving toward becoming conscious and intentional at an increasingly rapid pace.

This doesn't mean that we have earned huge kudos for the superlative directing of our experiences up to this point. But, for the first time, we can sit back and consciously begin to review our accomplishments and consider our possibilities with an eye toward the future. Some might say we are close to becoming intentional as a species.

We have achieved a world court system and a basic mouthing of the importance of human rights[1] on a planetary scale. Though the actual practice of such lofty goals continues to be unavailable to a significant portion of the world's population, it is clearly something we are striving for as a species. And while there are attempts at "hands off" policies regarding the autonomy of newly emerging or weaker or ideologically different nations, the commandeering of resources by more powerful countries and multinational corporations continues unabated.

Portions of humanity are beginning to acknowledge the importance of individuality, self-reliance and self-determination as we emerge from under the enormous weight of barbarism, authoritarianism and heavy-handed policies that have been a part of our survival mechanism for so very long. What might have been considered acceptable behavior as recently as several decades ago is now considered unacceptable or even criminal behavior against the people of the Earth.

Slowly but surely humanity is beginning to shake its old, narrow-minded survival mentalities and become cognizant of newer and wiser values, including, specifically, the importance of others' values. It is becoming acceptable to allow what might be different to escape the annihilation of our past narrow-mindedness. We are beginning to see attempts by nations and governments to allow aspects of society to become self-governed and self-determined.

There is also the enlarging world view of the rights of animals and endangered species, bringing people together in common cause. During the summer 2001, a whale ran afoul of a fishing net along the northeastern coast of the U.S.A. In danger of starving to death, this incredibly benign and powerful creature was rescued after repeated attempts to remove the net from its jaws. During the same summer, a juvenile killer whale in the Seattle area was nursed back to health and flown to its familial pod in the Artic for a successful reunion.

As we grow in our system of values, we become stewards of our planet by learning to protect the indigenous plants and animals. Of the many endeavors in this regard includes a recent reassessment by the inhabitants of a Pacific atoll group who had been hired for pennies a day to live-vacuum their reef fish for shipment to the Far East restaurant world. Communications and solutions shared are powerful indicators that the human species is beginning to look after itself and upon its dominion with a bit more care.

Slowly but surely humanity is beginning to shake its old, narrow-minded survival mentalities.

Humans or Government?

It is important to note that the makeup of a country, society, tribe or ethnic group is ultimately the individuals of that nation, society or group. What has eluded us for so very long is the recognition of the importance of the individual. After all, individuals were responsible for the discovery of electricity and the invention of the light bulb that now bring invaluable comfort and services to vast portions of the planet.

And it is through the individual and the perseverance of his/her ideals and values, that we have personal transportation that so capably influences us as a species. Consider that just barely beyond "down the street" on a planetary scale, Henry Ford, Thomas Edison and the Wright brothers invented machines (beginning as ideas in their heads) that have helped us in so many ways. Automobiles, electricity, flight, the recording and playback of music and video, light and heat for homes, freeways, autobahns, iron, steel and supersonic flight, to name a few, are ideas that came from the perseverance of individuals and their dreams.

Initiated as a thought, Ray Kroc, a member of Team HomoSapien™ in the 1950s, pioneered not only a worldwide hamburger and fast-food franchise, but took his concepts to vast new levels of expansion. Another individual by the name of Harland Sanders, age 62, began a 12-year sales journey fraught with legendary rejection and franchised 600 Kentucky Fried Chicken restaurants, ultimately growing to 11,000 restaurants in 80 countries. Another individual with an idea in his head created what became Coca-Cola, likely the most widely known corporate logo on the face of the planet.

Because of the ingenuity and inner drive of pioneering individuals and members of Team HomoSapien™, McDonald's, KFC and Coca-Cola have become household words. Individuals with dreams, ideas and fortitude have pioneered every conceivable convenience imaginable – everything from steel and railroads, to airplanes and huge ships, to communications, education, advances in the law and human rights, cures for deadly diseases and even new ways to pop popcorn. All have come into existence by a single common denominator: individuality and focus. Where and how could we look and not see the indelible influence of the individual as we continue the course of our evolution on this planet?

Today, individuals and their inventions, products and services traverse the world in considerably less time. Bill Gates of Microsoft Corporation, Michael Dell of Dell Computers and Fred Smith of FedEx Corporation, engender world recognition based on ideas that began in their heads. These individuals created companies based on values, ideals and perseverance, for which we all benefit and happily ride on their coattails. Individuality is a vast and powerful resource, not to be overlooked as a distinct part of our evolution as a species, and an important aspect of what "Team HomoSapien™" offers the planet and its ongoing evolution.

The newest pioneers from the ranks of Team HomoSapien™ produce goods and services that enhance productivity and generate new levels of efficiency, often lending to individual and collective advancement and empowerment. And while government and religious leaders do not seem to promote or encourage expansion or individuality in this manner, they do provide essential services that we seem unable to provide for ourselves. Authority figures come into existence to keep order and maintain direction as we mill about, unaware of the potential found within our individuality as unconscious and semi-conscious members of Team HomoSapien™. It is assumed that as we continue to expand into our own power, the need for authority figures will continue to diminish.

As the progeny of God, we have circuitry that tells us right from wrong.

It is interesting to note that inventions, goods and services that have propelled humanity throughout the ages do not seem to come off shelves, nor seem to be gifted to us in the appropriate time frame by perceived leadership. It may be true that Columbus was financed by Queen Isabella of Spain, but it was not the queen or her office that had the fervor to find India, or ultimately the Americas. It was pioneering individuals with ideas in their heads.

Inventions and goods and services are the result of individuals expressing themselves in countless ways. It was adventurous individuals who were behind the continued improvement in sailcloth, which eventually allowed for safe long-distance voyaging. And, it was individuals behind the ever-increasing power of personal computers and laptops and the millions of other microchip technologies and software that are becoming commonplace in our everyday lives.

Individuals are behind the push for alternative fuels for automobiles and other "clean" methodologies for transportation and energy efficiency, as well as the voice of concern about toxic waste sites, presently known as Superfund sites. Who invented encryption programs for digital privacy that, at the very least, allowed for secure credit card transactions over the Internet? Humans, or government? Plainly it can be seen that humans power society and bring the advances we enjoy.

Though government appears to be a leader, it is not a leader in any sense of the word, nor was it ever created to be a leader. According to the United States Constitution (and state constitutions), governments are created (as artificial entities) in limited authority to represent the people, umpire over certain issues and protect the fundamental rights of individuals from the usurpation by "others." Governments, as a public servant, are created to protect and serve "We, the People" – the humans. This includes keeping the stripes on the highways painted yellow, the stoplights red, the currency supply intact and the court system fair. Governments are not a leader in any sense of the word.

If the bottom lines and values of humans and corporations are vastly different, should we be looking to the latter for leadership?

For example, individuals with complaints against each other have always needed a fair and impartial venue to sort out their differences. As we have outgrown dueling in its many and varied forms, governments are charged with the maintenance of impartial venues (judicial systems) for the settling of disputes. According to the American system of law, human beings have inalienable rights,[2] for which impartial courts are required for a complaint to be fairly heard and adjudicated.

Though it is one of the government's most important functions as a public servant, it fails to measure up to this task and responsibility. Ultimately, the people are responsible for the failings of artificial entities[3] to perform tasks assigned in specified and exacting manners. (Among other things, the court system would be where humans air their grievances with artificial entities – clearly not an impartial venue.)

Humans have always been the pioneers and inventors and leaders of what's next for society and the planet. Why? Because humans have the intelligence of reason, the capacity for creativity and the access to Innate Intelligence for solutions. They also have the capacity to know the difference between right and wrong. As the progeny of God, we have circuitry that tells us right from wrong. Government and religion as institutions do not have the circuitry to access Innate Intelligence, and thus are incapable of true decision-making and true leadership. Church and State can never be relied upon for more than servant positions held within the restraints of the law or its creed, i.e., contracts as established by the people.

Individuals have always decided what was needed and then set about accomplishing the required result, often at odds with conformity. Johannes Gutenberg is credited with the invention of the printing press, though the actual pioneering/problem solving that made his name famous was ink that did not bleed. This allowed for the beginnings of any semblance of speed for printing on paper. In fact, getting inventions and hardware to the marketplace is a rough and tumble business, taking enormous perseverance and a desire to overcome any and all obstacles.

Artificial entities run out of perseverance once they run out of money, though printing more money seems to be a temporary lifeblood transfusion and solution. (It is interesting to note that the printing of money creates debt that humans have to pay at some future point with something that is real – their labor and their capacity to produce.) Humans, on the other hand, seem to be able to go vast distances, driven by their tenacity, spirit, hope and desires alone. It is in this comparison of the differences between the two that real leadership is defined. This is the source of the term "Team HomoSapien™," as we come to understand the difference between artificial entities and human beings.

The number of human failures are beyond counting. The amount of despair at "Let's try it one more time," or "There's got to be a better way," is represented as numbers incalculable and only available to the capacity that is the human spirit. Humanity's will to survive, pioneer and prosper, linked to life itself and expressed as expansion, growth and determination, is never-ending, and for which we can all be quite grateful.

Thomas Edison, in the harnessing of his own potential, became intentional about napping during the day and waking with solutions to problems. He would program his mind to bring solutions to his business problems as he awoke from naps, an idea that neither the Church nor the State was able to offer him in his bid to produce the electric light bulb or electricity. Thomas Edison's growth and determination were not taught to him by artificial entity leadership or authority figures, but by access to Innate Intelligence, his own inner delvings and spirit, and his own tried and true experiences. This is true leadership for which the rest of Team HomoSapien™ basks, though it is assumed that we will one day each more effectively carry our weight, further our heritage and make a better place for our progeny.

Within the zeal and comfort of everyday living, it is easy for us to lose sight of this most valuable of resource: our own individuality and our own capacity to envision and solve problems. It would be easy to assume that our solutions are being handled for us. It would be easy to sit back on the sweat and perseverance of generations gone before and bask and enjoy. But we are here for much more than that.

Leadership?

Big government, religious organizations and large corporations continue to expand. Is it fair to assume that our best interests are being looked after in all of this expansion? Can we assume that artificial entity expansion is looking out for our best regard? What if the life blood and bottom line of artificial entities is vastly different than the bottom line of humans? What if the bottom line for humanity is family life, joy, peace and love? What if, as humans, our values are our health, enlivening ourselves, teaching our children and evaluating our spirituality? What if the bottom line of corporations is money and profits? What if we are their only source of money and profits?

If the bottom lines and values of humans and corporations are vastly different, should we be looking to the latter for leadership and direction or even advice? After all, powerful corporations produce a great many products and services that do not seem to meet the true aim of human values and true human interests. Corporations, goaded by profits, produce a staggering array of bad foods, chemicals, toxins and pollutants, as well as an astounding output of pharmaceuticals, munitions and products of which humanity becomes the recipient but at what expense? What could be the harm in that?

As readily as we might inadvertently assign the advances of our cultures, or the evolution of our species to the Church or government, General Electric, PepsiCo, Wal-Mart or other gargantuan multinational corporation, we need to recognize that *we* are the building blocks of not only our society, but also our evolution. Only humans are

Our success as a species relies upon the power of the individual.

capable of making important decisions, and our decisions come from what Innate Intelligence is telling us is right as we continue to refine our alignment with natural forces and learn to thrive in our own way.

All of our useful decisions and choices come from individuals striving for more. As individuals, we may have to compete with government and large corporations and their agendas for profits, but who is in the driver's seat here? Who are the humans anyway? Aren't we the top rung of the pecking order here on planet Earth? Didn't we create the artificial entities in the first place? Who are the leaders here? After all, Bill Gates took on the best and most powerful at their own game and brought vast services to the private sector in a whole new way. Within a time frame that we all remember, Bill Gates brought more individuality and personal power to the private sector than anyone in the history of the planet, and his wealth grows correspondingly. Bill Gates is a true leader and pioneer, and clearly a member of Team HomoSapien™.

One individual connected to his essence is more powerful than one million who are not.

Because we have become so busy in our lives, is it possible that we believe life simply runs on its own? Some would comfortably believe that this is all predestined, that we are too small, that corporations are too large, or that government carefully and capably anticipates our needs. This is simply not true. Luckily, Bill Gates didn't believe this, nor Steve Jobs of Apple Computer, Larry Ellision of Oracle Corporation, or Phil Zimmerman of PGP encryption fame, or any of the other producers and shakers of the last 30 years of the 20th century.

Is it possible that, at the speed of our growth, many of us are beginning to lose sight of our individuality – or we have not yet discovered it in the broader sense? The individuals who are responsible for Coca-Cola, Dell Computers, Microsoft, AOL-Time Warner and so on had one very powerful thing in common: They believed in themselves and they believed in their vision and their dreams, above all else. They were so dedicated to their own needs and their own insights that the world around them came to mean much less. Thus the definition of individuality and visionary focus becomes apparent, for which the results speak for themselves.

Individuality is that drawing out of us what is inside "come hell or high water," rather than accepting the status quo or operating our lives in a reactionary or defensive posture. Our individuality is created as insight offered by Innate Intelligence, propelling us into brave new worlds and toward undiscovered horizons. It is this individuality that we draw upon, some sooner than later, that pushes our horizons to newfound levels of existence.

Progeny

There are many who blindly follow what has been laid out for them by either the previous generation, assumed leadership, or simply a lack of interest. This is readily apparent as children grow up. Usually they find their initial independence at an early age, but by the time they enter into the public school system, many begin the process of accepting authority, accepting roles and personas and accepting a pecking order in their lives. By the time most children leave public education, their capacity for creativity has been reduced from a basis of 100 points down to about 5 points, according a study by George Land and sponsored by NASA in 1968.

Unless the environment provides impetus for the individual to grow and stretch and find its own individuality, many stagnate and find themselves increasingly unhappy and disillusioned with the world around them. Never mind the mid-life crisis that has been so thoroughly documented and mapped for the over 40-set. Children and teens who are not allowed to express their individuality may instead express frustration, anger, resentment and a lashing out, well outside of the standards they are expected to fall within. It is likely that the rash of high school traumas are related to the thwarting of the individuality of the student combined with a massive channeling of violence from television. It is also possible that we have begun to drug our young people, the brightest aspect of our society, for which their creativity now comes out in the most unusual and horrific of manners.

The importance of the above is the recognition that our success as a species is not defined by a pecking order or alphabetization, nor our capacity to fit collectively into "norms." Our success as a species relies upon the power of the individual and the recognition of his/her own importance, as well as a recognition of the individuality of others. Attempting to coerce individuals to be the same, or a one-pattern-fits-all role model, is not only dangerous, but may undermine what makes the human species so resilient and capable of vast outpourings of potential in the first place. It is in our differences and our individuality that the power and the strength of the human species is found.

By the use of new tools and new understanding, young individuals can be protected and encouraged to dialogue with their inner nature and the "within" to which we all have ready access. As children, not too many years into the indoctrination of the more traditional spheres of influence, many continue to have ready access to their innate connection. It is by an awareness of the error of our ways that we can begin to reinterpret how we can support children in a most useful manner. We want young people becoming what is best for them, and what is best for them, they brought with them.

Our true nature requires us to express our individuality, which is more important than we know. Our true nature requires us, individually, as well as collectively, to experiment and to even get it wrong until we get it right. This is the nature of wisdom and the nature of reason, something artificial entities are slow to understand. After all, the electric light was not invented on the first try. Our true nature requires us to experiment with life, to experiment with our sexuality, to experiment with choices, to experiment with personal responsibility and to experiment with our outcomes. We refine, refine and refine, for, after all, this is our very nature.

What might be more important than individuality? What might come before our individuality? What might be more important? True individuality is an outpouring of the essence of the individual. The essence of the individual – what could be more important than that? What could be more important than the essence of individuality expressing itself?

What kind of a world might we live in if the most celebrated aspect of humanity was its essence and its individuality? What might our survival scenario look like, if all of our individuality and essence were instead seen as a garden and a resource to be nourished and nurtured and cherished and loved for what it truly was – a gift and outpouring of the Universe from the center of our species? Individuality is humanity's most important resource!

A Natural Resource

One of the most valuable resources on the planet is one of the planet's most renewable. Though deforestation and pollution of the oceans are of the utmost importance, there is one resource that far out weighs the rainforest or any of the other aspects of our seemingly dwindling supply. And, interestingly enough, not only does the survival of our planet depend on it, but we also depend on it. What is this, the greatest of the planet's resources? Humanity itself!

As we become more conscious, more intentional and more powerful, we will begin to shine as a species.

We are the greatest natural resource on the planet, because within our individuality lies the seeds of all of our possibilities and solutions – solutions found in the last place we might look, and for the most part, haven't looked. Our survival is dependent upon our essence, our individuality and our connection with Innate Intelligence. Our connection with Innate Intelligence gives us vast horizons, vast possibilities and vast unknown solutions – all without the limits of authority figures and middlemen. We have a survival mechanism that is built in – our connection to Innate Intelligence! It is the best that can be had, and it is ever renewable.

Our survival mechanism sits on a shelf of sorts gathering dust. Though mostly unused and undiscovered, it remains the gem of gems – the Holy

Grail, the Fountain of Youth, the elixir of life, the alchemical turning of lead into gold, the pot at the end of the rainbow, the gold ring – all wrapped up in one. It is what everybody has searched for, and what we, as a species with leisure time, are discovering for ourselves. Our individuality and access to Innate Intelligence – altogether an inside job, is directly available to all of us.

Humanity can save the rainforests, humanity can save the whales and humanity can save the humans in alignment with its own highest good. Once we begin to understand our individual essence, once we understand our collective essence and our collective focus, anything can be accomplished.

There is an idea that begins with the expression "One individual connected to his essence is more powerful than one million who are not." Imagine an individual tapping into his or her inner nature and intentionally generating focus, choice and truth. Imagine a species tapping into its inner nature and intentionally generating focus, choice and truth. We are doing so but so far, it's not much to write home about. Mostly, we are in silent and unconscious consent to the world around us and the few who claim it is so.

As we take stock in the potential that is our inner nature, we shall have increasing dominion over our affairs and outcomes. Our governance is truly internal and comes from our ability to access Innate Intelligence and make choices accordingly. All we have to do is access our internal guidance system, and we are off and running. In our willingness to seek out strange new worlds, to go where no man has gone before and solve problems where once we thought solutions did not exist, we find our true power. And, in our true power, we find that we are all wired the same way. We find that we are all peers; we find that we are all cut from the same cloth.

We are ready to take this step; we *are* taking this step; and we are becoming conscious. It goes on every day as individuals partner with

Innate Intelligence, expand their individuality and essence and rely upon themselves and each other more and more – and upon outside influence less and less. There are more and more teachings and disciplines that promote a quantifying of the quality of one's outer life as a reflection and awareness of one's inner life. The solutions are becoming more apparent and getting easier. We are finding and becoming ourselves! We are discovering and becoming our true natures!

There is a distinct movement within the last several generations to move inward, to move toward inner trust, inner guidance and an acceptance of our true natures. As we discover the positive influence it has on our outer worlds, we will continue to move inward in ever-increasing numbers. It is in the completion and reintroduction of the connection with our spiritual nature that we find the source of our solutions, individually and collectively. It is in our natural progression to refine our existence, to gain solutions and new growth that we catapult ourselves to our next and more refined levels of existence.

Innate Intelligence has always been there and always been accessible by pioneering individuals. And, it is just beginning to be discovered en masse, as we take the time to compare notes among ourselves. As we have entered the Information Age and the communications revolution, we are beginning to realize our true power, our true source of governance and our true solutions. It turns out it is you and me.

Most of us know individuals who are taking a more active role in accessing Innate Intelligence because they have discovered how to listen to themselves. There are now several generations substantially impacted by meditation and the multitude of self-help courses and doctrines available, as well as individuals who have left marriages or careers in their quest to be more genuine and authentic. A certain dissatisfaction with the status quo (group mentality) and making changes to live more genuine lives are both important milestones in the evolvement of humanity.

A needing and wanting – and perhaps an inner prodding to be more in touch with our inner wisdom, our inner truth and our inner nature – is the beginning of humanity's steady rise as a species. It is a whole new world of individuality beginning to heed its inner promptings and become more actualized. We are becoming more alert and alive as members of Team HomoSapien™.

Choice

Individuality is rapidly spreading as a result of trial and error. Humanity is beginning to recognize the importance of choice. In other words, hearts and minds are beginning to align with Innate Intelligence as the source of our corresponding realities. Slowly fades the day that choice is made the old-fashioned way, i.e., deceit, manipulation, greed, abuse or the simple trampling of others. In alignment with Innate Intelligence and the rhythm of the Universe, we are discovering new choices and more refined methods of accomplishing goals that feel better, individually and collectively.

We are here for more than the simple acquisition of possessions and running our lives on automatic.

Choice is becoming a reflection of newly acquired systems of belief, as well as clarity about Innate Intelligence and what is true for us. And, surprisingly, choice made from the perspective of the whole person is a healthy choice, not only for the individual, but for the many. As we learn to make choice based on inner guidance, we begin to see choices and outcomes, not only as right for us, but aligning perfectly with others as well. As we accept access to Innate Intelligence and honor the same in each other, choice become an empowering experience for one and for all.

Choice made by first ascertaining the "wishes of others" has not proven to be a successful method of establishing one's individuality. In fact, many find the technique so daunting that they make no decision at all, which is a choice in itself. Empowered choice chooses what is right for the individual and assumes others to be making their own right choices in their own highest regard. Empowered choice says that my reality is driven by my intentionality partnered with Innate Intelligence, while your reality is driven by your intentionality and your partnership with Innate Intelligence. Conscious choice says that being true to oneself is primary and carries with it the additional benefit of being an excellent mechanism for aligning with others practicing similar ideals.

Conscious use of our inner connection and inner dialogue is the next step in the evolution of mankind. It is inherent that we finally go "where no man has gone," that final frontier and inner space. It is in the discovery and the bringing of our inner essence, potential and wisdom to the surface that the next step on our evolutionary path becomes clear.

Conscious Choice

As we begin to understand the power of conscious choice, we move to a different level of being –
- we begin to accept the vitality that comes from being conscious and intentional creators;
- conscious choice brings about quality results. Since we are aligned with our inner and higher drives, our outcomes continue to evolve and prosper;
- in our intentional access to our inner nature, we begin to recognize the fact that we are all powerfully similar; and
- we continue to refine our most important inner dialogue and connection, our access to Innate Intelligence – clearly a conscious, intentional and useful choice.

Conscious choice brings about personal respect, and personal respect is the precursor to love and acceptance of ourselves. As we harness one of the most innate aspects of the human being, we find ourselves learning how to love and accept ourselves (and our creations), and we begin to relax. But, best of all, we have access to Innate Intelligence as our indwelling guide and confidant. We begin to become whole.

Conscious creating brings peace to one world at a time, to one individual at a time. The days of powerlessness and frustration are over as we make conscious choice and conscious decisions. We discover that we are no longer a part of the victimhood, nor the unhappy recipients of someone else's decisions or actions. After all, our choices make up our worlds, and our realities are a manifestation of our decisions. In the discovery of our individuality, as we view and review our world, we choose and refine, again and again and again.

We make choices and we fail to make choices, and we live within the momentum of those choices. We reap what we sow. We are each creators, consciously and unconsciously, intentionally and unintentionally, and thus our worlds lay at our feet. We attune, we align, and we refine. This is life. This is how life expands, this is how we expand. It gets better or it gets worse, but at its seat is a driver, i.e., an individual, and an accumulation of choices that makes it so.

As we become more conscious in our choices, decisions and creations, we find increasing comfort in our worlds. This adventure, this discovery of conscious choice, offers us an inner game of ever-expanding improvement and refinement. We find ourselves compelled to refine our access to innate wisdom and intelligence, for which our corresponding outward realities continue to expand inwardly, outwardly, and upwardly, ad infinitum. Ultimately we will come to see that how we feel is a very large part of the game, which is discussed in great detail in a later chapter.

It is in this fine-tuning of living life that our thoughts and creative capacity is catapulted to new and more refined levels, thus making up the real juice of living and life. It is in this refinement that brings a spring to our step, and a capacity to share the vast energy of love and compassion that is within each of us, and brings a still small world a bit closer to its brilliance – something a corporation could never experience. Just because some get there a bit earlier than others, is no reason to hold back, doubt or languish.

Trusting the Process

It is important to recognize that when individuals, young and old, make decisions that others might see as destructive or onerous, that they be respected as the creators they are. As much as one would like to intercede, it seems best to honor and support the choices of these naïve creators, just as if they were responsible for their choices and outcomes – which they are.

Allowing the trial-and-error aspect of the life path to fall where it may is an important aspect in the transition for those learning to trust in a bigger picture and higher order. Besides, it is hard to recommend choices to those hell-bent on their own self-discovery, no matter how painful it may appear. Luckily, individuals disconnected from Source cannot hurt themselves too badly and will tire of the struggle far sooner, without the influence of one attempting to forcefully intervene in their behalf. For, certainly, we should know by now that one in struggle simply includes others as outlets and targets for resistance or frustration, as we inadvertently feed their frustration.

Eventually we begin to discover the power of our connection on a larger scale. As a young species, we are fledglings at the doorway of great promise. We see conscious creators becoming inadvertent leaders simply by their own clarity and ease. After all, individuals (and humanity) will eventually gravitate toward what does work. If nothing else, individuals not quite connected, but aware enough to feel the tuggings of a soon emerging essence, find themselves drawn to meetings, environments and books, or acquiring or adjusting friendships with those who practice the deliberateness of conscious creation and personal responsibility.

Conscious creating leaves invisible tendrils and trails similar to the wake of a slow-moving boat on a quiet lake, or the sense of a slow migration toward better feeding grounds – and to some earlier than others. However, there will always be those who risk the most for something unseen and unproven, but strive they will as their inner nature dictates and drives them accordingly. And there will always be those who bring up the rear, for which they hold a much more important mission than might be suspected on first impression.

There is an innateness and deliberateness to the salmon moving up river to spawn. Ask the salmon why they choose such a difficult journey and they will tell you that it is innately within them to go up river and not even mention that it is for the survival of the species. This innate mechanism, so deeply rooted within their psyches and nervous systems and repeated generation after generation, is ultimately no different than that of the human for which we see similar but slightly different commitments.

Make no mistake about it: Humanity has a similar innate migratory need based on self-preservation and expansion. But as humans, our migration and our continued success is inward toward the conscious accessing of Innate Intelligence that we discover on the road to our individuality. Ultimately, we are not so different from the salmon.

Over the past 40 years, and increasingly moreso in the last 15 or 20, we are seeing evidence of a waking population. Children are born with considerably more capacity and awareness[4] and alertness than those of 30 or 50 years ago. (Could this begin *in utero?*) It is assumed that parenting is becoming more of a conscious choice and thus a conscious reality, not only for the parent but also the child.

Old ways of discipline and reactionary choices fall away as respect for the conscious nature of the young individual becomes recognizable as so close to the surface. As humanity discovers that its most valuable resources are innate and that children come in freshly connected to their innate nature, we will begin to treat children and young adults more like the diamonds that they are – not diamonds in the rough, but flawless diamonds at their brightest, most crystalline clarity.

As we discern our possibilities, we are drawn to the resources that bring us the highest likelihood of success. It is only natural that we eventually discover and learn what is inside of us, as well as the riches represented. After all, there is the story of the most valuable gift ever bestowed upon humanity, for which the most secure hiding place was not the highest mountain, nor the deepest sea, but, ultimately, somewhere where it could never be lost and in time certainly be found – the hiding place, of course, within.

The purpose of our gathering is to bring to us a conscious realization that we are here for more than the simple acquisition of possessions and running our lives on automatic. I don't believe we are here to smell the roses, or otherwise delight in the earth's bounty, as much as to discern and discover our inner and divine nature, our true heritage and our innate capacity for expansion. We are spiritual in our makeup, or as someone once said, "We are spiritual beings having a human experience." It will turn out that discovering our true nature is only the beginning of the expansion available for our time on Earth.

As we are little more than bodies made up of elements from the ground and electrical and energy connections, we would still be not much more than lumps of clay without Innate Intelligence instilled deep within us. That we have come to live on the earth with all of its bounty is only the beginning of our possibilities. We have within us a certain camaraderie and connection with Source that is still mostly unspoken, and, as yet, little explored. There is a spark that lies deeply within each of us for which we are its protector and its partner. It is our migration toward our individuality and our uniqueness that is our real bounty. For not only are we guests of the world in which we live, we have within us a divine Spirit that makes us guests of a whole other magnitude.

CHAPTER FOUR
BELIEFS

*H*umanity, through science and reason, has discovered that we live in a very orderly universe. As we prod and poke and search our surroundings, we find nothing but order and consistency, much moreso than we might ever have imagined. Everywhere we look – outwardly, inwardly, underneath and around – we find order and more order. Through the range of our largest telescopes and our most powerful electron microscopes, to the depths of the oceans and everywhere in between, we find consistency and harmonious order. We find growth and expansion and, always, a refinement of our old understandings.

The question is: What part do humans play in this playground of vast wonderment in which we find ourselves? Are we here to interact in this very large scale order that is the Universe, or are we here to live our lives in quiet ignorance or quiet amazement and just hope for the best? The big question is: Why do we seemingly live our lives in such a state of disarray, in consideration of an overall picture that is otherwise so orderly and inherently consistent?

It is our disorder within a world and universe that is so vastly in order that gives us our first clue. If the entirety of nature, i.e., the ecosystems of the planet and the organization of the human body, as well as the birth and death of stars, are all in order, can't we assume that order is the fundamental nature of our existence as well? If we all have noses in the same place, if we all have the same numbers of toes and fingers, if we all laugh and cry, the nature of order must include us. With just the flip of the mute button while watching an international Olympic competition on television, we can barely differentiate between the international multitude of competitors and spectators. We are actually all very much alike, though there has been huge focus as to our differences.

In the newest sciences of quantum physics is the discovery that the smallest particles of matter contain not only the vastness of order, but consciousness, as well. It has been discovered by the observer of scientific experiments in the quantum realm that the observer has a distinct influence on the experiment being observed. It turns out that consciousness is the bulk of what lies within and among the atom's spinning protons, neutrons and electrons, all having been assumed to be primarily empty space.

Consciousness is everywhere found, and as a part of consciousness, we are everywhere connected.

Imagine that we have discovered the smallest particles of matter. They swim in an ocean of consciousness, and in our observance of these tiny particles, our thoughts and beliefs influence what we are observing. The reality of quantum physics is that the viewer influences what is being observed. Our consciousness connects with and influences the consciousness that is the makeup of the atomic structure of things. There is more to us, and to order, than we thought.

Is it such a tall step to imagine that the distance between the planets and stars is filled with the same common ingredient found within and among the atoms, molecules and inner workings thereof? Perhaps this common ingredient is, in some manner, similar to what the ancients were trying to describe, or what the descriptions about the omnipresence of God may have been attempting to explain for so long?

On the other hand, humanity is still quite naïve, though apparently quite resilient. Coming from our infancy as a species, we have surely come close to extinction a number of times and possibly even been snuffed out a time or two. Suffice to say, we are learning from our mistakes, and we are beginning to understand how very far we have come. We are able to discern through the sciences and the history of religion and mythology much about what we have had to overcome to reach our present status. In a similar manner, we can review the growth of present time cultures and young nations as we see their fledgling movements toward individuality and sovereignty, for which life continues to refine itself and expand.

Approximately 800 years ago (1215 A.D.) the French and English devised the Magna Carta as the first modern-day declaration of human rights on the planet. For more than 800 years, they tried and variously embraced these principles until, in a reaffirmation of these ideals, individuals created what became the Constitution of the United States.

As an interesting aside, the United States of America is a vast 225-year historical documentation of ideals and values, as well as failings and shortcomings in its original charge and intent. Best said, America, as well as the rest of the world, individually and culturally, nationally and collectively, are all works in progress. We have "watched" America's progression from its infancy to its present state of evolvement as it migrates toward becoming a better representation of its people and their values and heads toward a more useful leadership role on the planet.

Slowly, we have crawled from the muck and the mire of our history as a species and donned the accoutrements of modern man. We find the pre-eminent tools of our survival and evolution revolve around our capacity for conscious decision-making, ultimately represented as choice aligned with order. But, to get there, we had to have an accumulation of beliefs and what we knew to be so (from trial and error), as conclusions gained and tossed, as grist for new choices. We had to have a repository of what we "knew to be so" as a backdrop for making new choices and decisions for becoming more.

One of the most important aspects of our early growth includes what we pass as information from generation to generation, a slow and tedious process. No matter that it was packaged as superstition, legend, spiritual or religious knowledge, or came from the hunter-gatherer, medicinal or military perspective, or otherwise the most basic of survival concerns, it was what we knew and passed on, generation upon generation. As we have learned, grown, resolved differences, thrown away inaccurate or misapplied information, we have come to know the makeup of the Moon. For as we might assume, the Moon was for quite some time no more than wonderment or fear, but eventually a question, and eventually an answer.

Humanity in its evolvement is made up of its beliefs, collectively and individually; collectively, because initially a group was the only strength and the only safety. But as humanity evolved, individuals began to speak out and the influence of the individual began to be more powerfully felt. As the same time, individuality was often perceived by those who held power as competitive, or at odds with the good of the whole, and thus individuality was exercised as a lonely and risky endeavor. It was in the reflection of the individual's review of "sacred" beliefs and a newfound capacity for perception that finally allowed an exodus from the safety and limitation of the huddle of the masses.

We view our modern-day world based upon what we have come to accept as wisdom and knowledge that comes from before our time. We are taught based on what has been passed on to us as the status quo. And though we are beginning to outgrow what is blindly assumed to be the truth, many continue to accept our slow-moving growth curves just as they exist. Though there may still be parts of the world that do not know that man has set foot on the Moon, the world is waking from its slumbers and limiting beliefs and doing so quite rapidly. Only recently have the limitations of our beliefs truly begun to break down as individuals begin to think for themselves, share information and refine their knowledge accordingly.

In Utero

Our beliefs and values begin to form well before we are born. We are born into a reality that has been substantially projected by our family and society before us. Furthermore, there is significant documentation suggesting that fetuses are absorbing information from the womb as part of their earliest development. After all, a fetus begins as a nervous system, and nervous systems collect, absorb and convey information. Absorbing information from the mother and her immediate surroundings may be one of our earliest sources for what becomes part of the imprint of our belief systems.

Is it possible that humanity carries imprints of beliefs that we absorbed over centuries or even thousands of years?

There was a study establishing that babies remember music that was played to them *in utero* as much as a year after they are born. According to this study, music was played to fetuses on a regular basis, for which they later showed a distinct recognition for that particular music. A very capable musician friend was, from *in utero* and his earliest infancy, heavily influenced by his parents, both of whom were accomplished musicians. He finds himself (pleasantly) overwhelmed by the influences deposited into his psyche at such an early age, which have clearly influenced the outcomes of his life. His interests are thoroughly wrapped up in tone, resonance and harmonics for which he can readily see its source. He displays this particular imprinting perfectly, as I suspect many of us do in our own way.

Linda, a talented and full time artist, is the daughter of an accomplished artist. The question is: Is Linda copying her mother's capacities and values or is she, in fact, filled with beliefs and values that draw her to become a capable artist herself? How much of her ability is from her outside environment and influence, versus her inside environment and deeply held beliefs and values that may have come to her at a very early age?

Is it possible that our earliest impressions are part of that transition into physicality, that merging into the physical world for which we begin to take hints as soon as we are able? A sort of precursor to one's soon-to-be existence and maybe as much of a warm-up as we get? As babies emerge from non-physical to physical existence, clearly there is a transition that takes place. Maybe the young fetus/nervous system begins to absorb information as soon as possible in preparation for the next stage of its existence? After all, a young soul coming into existence from non-existence is in quite a bit of transition. Why wouldn't a fetus begin absorbing hints about its future as soon as it is physically possible?

There are a number of methods for releasing old belief patterns and replacing them with more refined beliefs. The cochlea of the ear is one of the earliest, fully formed organs of the human body. By day 145, it is completely formed, and, of course the function of the cochlea is to discern vibration. Eyesight would be of little value to the unborn, but feeling and vibration would be early pathways for the baby accumulating information hurtling toward its birth.

Why wouldn't this start as soon as possible? Why wouldn't the fetus begin to absorb information from the glandular secretions of the mother's body as well as the sounds, tones and emotions available from its outside world and, correspondingly the mother's outside world? Why wouldn't the fetus begin to absorb insight into its coming existence, all of which are imprints and precursors of its learned belief systems?

Why wouldn't a baby coming into existence acclimate to its up-and-coming reality through any senses that it had available? What would the comfort or wild gyrations of the mother's heartbeat, hunger pangs or tones of sweet innocence bring to that new nervous system? And, from that initial perspective and insight, wouldn't that baby and young child continue to absorb information and gather knowledge?

Might this also be so on the scale of humanity itself? Is it possible that humanity carries imprints of beliefs that are absorbed over centuries or even thousands of years? Is it possible that we carry unconscious or subconscious beliefs that were concluded or absorbed in a manner that have not seen the light of day in quite some time? Are certain beliefs and systems of beliefs, though they may have served us at one time, becoming obsolete in the 21st century?

Experiences of good and bad, pain and suffering, trials and tribulations and opinions and accomplishments are all part of the fodder that instill and refine the beliefs and values of what is to become the individual. As children, we accumulate information based on our surroundings and preferences, and, last but not least, that vast reserve of unconsciously and subconsciously held societal beliefs.

Belief systems and accordingly, perceptions, are built upon absorbed conclusions and information realized intentionally, unintentionally, consciously, unconsciously and subconsciously. Young children have little capacity to be intentional about what they absorb, thus they are the products of their environments and upbringing. It is my belief that Innate Intelligence initially has the upper hand, but, as children merge into society and its held beliefs and values, the black-and-white illusions of the world become predominant. We become the belief systems of our surroundings, consciously, unconsciously and subconsciously.

Race-consciousness

From the beginning of time, humanity has always tried to improve itself. It is a part of our basic nature and it will continue to be so. As we find more time to work on our personal growth, we realize the importance of understanding what we believe and know to be so. As we come to understand the influences of what we believe, we learn to refine our belief systems in no short order. After all, up until now, we have had little to say about much of what we believe.

As we come to an awareness of our mind/reality connection™, we see that much of what we think and output is a result of our beliefs and values based on our past and reinforced by our present time experiences. We create our occurring and re-occurring realities and circumstances based on our existing perceptual natures, which are based on what we believe to be so, i.e., what we know to be so – accurate or not. As we move into the 21st century, we are becoming aware that our realities are a product of our mental and emotional makeup. As we become increasingly aware, we seek tools and technologies for the evaluation and upgrading of our belief systems, so that we are able to create higher quality and better-balanced realities for ourselves.

Beliefs associated with the human condition, brought along genetically or generationally, may be referenced as race-consciousness. Race-consciousness includes values and beliefs that may go back several thousand years, or as little as several hundred years, or even as little as several generations. Race-consciousness can encompass belief systems that include all of humanity, more localized subdivisions of cultural humanity, i.e., Middle Eastern, Eskimo or Pygmy, or those collectively held by very small segments of tribes or national populations.

Race-consciousness can represent the rich history, heritage and lore of a people, as well as its prejudices and its fears. It identifies how things have been done for quite some time, often colliding with modern day newfound thinking. It also can identify strongly held religious beliefs,

beliefs in a hierarchy or pecking order, entitlements, interpretations of spiritual matters, dogma, its own future, its own past and sometimes its demise.

Race-consciousness as folklore, culture or historical perspective, forwards and instills beliefs within the next generation. Sometimes these concepts are blindly continued for no other reason than it has always been so. Often, folklore is used as a tool for motivation, manipulation or protection. Sometimes what is most effectively transferred between and among generations is a fear-based interpretation of issues and concerns. Fear has been used for centuries to instill values and give lessons substantially more depth and meaning.

Race-consciousness can represent cultural goals, aspirations and healthy conclusions, as well. It can represent what has been successful in the past and an inkling of ideas yet to be born. As a country, America was a melting pot for race-consciousness for which a great deal of the old fell away, and in its place a whole new world view sprang up. A great many habitually held belief systems, ages and generations old, began

Knowledge is often passed as fact from generation to generation, though it had no present time applicability.

to fade as newer habits formed and merged with other and differing race beliefs. What many had in common in young America was hope and possibility for which a whole new affluence and prosperity came to exist. And, of course, America has come to represent a type of thinking that is full of hope and a promoter of freedom and fundamental rights, as will, hopefully, always be the case.

Either way, race-consciousness has a distinct impact on the still young individual and, through them, generations to come.

It is interesting to note that race-consciousness, assumed to be, in partiality, an issue of skin color, is actually far more divisible along lines of belief. After all, there is vast disparity and disagreement within cultures of the same skin color. It is true that distinctions created by skin color may indicate popular divisions of humanity, but an individual's skin color less indicates what one believes than might be expected.

In fact, religious beliefs represent the strongest divisions by and amongst humanity. Much stronger than color or nationality or family ties, political beliefs may run a distant second. Religious zeal based on interpretations of faith and the unknown represent and promote very powerfully held beliefs and divide humanity more effectively that any other issue. There have been more people killed, more wars fought, more disruption and more displacement of people from their homes in the name of religion and its associated beliefs than all other causes combined.

Division comprises less the issues of skin color and much more ranges into held belief systems. Imagine, for example, a room full of sophisticated white people at a cocktail party. Imagine a similarly dressed, similarly principled and well-educated black man walking into the room. By comparison, imagine a white man dressed in army fatigues, with a condescending attitude and a chip on his shoulder, walking into the same room. Who is going to meld and fit into the group? Though the individual with a chip on his shoulder is white, he would find himself at odds with the group because his beliefs and attitudes are at odds with the group. Though possibly an oversimplified example, our values and beliefs tell us far more about ourselves than we might think.

How we imprint our next generation is of paramount importance to our very survival!

Over the centuries and decades, belief systems and survival values have often included hatred, prejudice and anger, as well as the superiority of one's own genetic or religious importance. Much of the existing hate and anger on the planet has no legitimate foundation other than what was taught by one generation to the next, often as a completely unconscious act.

We teach our fears to our progeny. We assume that what hurt us would hurt those for whom we have charge, and we advise them accordingly. And though this may have as its basis ancient concerns for survival, there comes a time when the "locale" no longer needs or requires such old style input.

As we evolve as a species, much of our unconscious, fear-based insight no longer carries value or importance. In other words, the importance of apprising and attuning the young person's psyche and newfound individuality with positive feedback and adoration has much more of a useful impact. What is termed survival these days might be more akin to the issues of self-esteem and personal responsibility, or communication skills and the use of the computer. Knowledge based on fear or protection, or a mistrust of one's neighbors based on religion, culture, or ethnicity, has become useless information as we head into the 21st century.

We are discovering that review of what we "know to be so" may be our most important consideration as we consider the survival of a community, a corporation, and certainly one's own personal growth, because the days of keeping things the same is the slow road to improvement. As we acknowledge what we have learned, we are more willing to use newfound methods for acquiring, advancing and supplanting old levels of what we knew to be so. Survival based on fear and protection mentalities now gives way to survival based on acceptance, allowance and a grasping for what is true. Fear-based survival mentalities become obsolete as we gain better access to the tools of insight and Innate Intelligence and thus a better understanding of what truly works.

It is not unusual to see a parent instructing a child with statements such as "If you do this, that will happen" or "Be careful, that can hurt you" or "Watch out for this" or "Watch out for that." Parents unconsciously teaching "what they know" can permeate their children with limitation and fear-based thinking. Parents later wonder why their children do not carry themselves well or respond questionably later in life. These teachings can create a dependency on outside authority and subvert the intellect and capacity for powerful individuality in the child. Children are like sponges and accept what authority figures tell them is true. Children build their beliefs and value systems based on available input. How we imprint our next generation is of paramount importance to our very survival!

Children grow up in a world where clearly there is a pecking order. This pecking order has a powerful influence on how and when, or even if, they find themselves. One of the earliest influences that they have little capacity to question is information about religion. This may be their first installment in understanding a pecking order. Jesus died for their sins – ouch!

It is not unusual for a child's most significant early training to be completely on faith, especially issues of the (apparent) importance of salvation and the soul. Though this may be thought to have a minimal impact, others think quite differently, including recovering Catholics and other past religious believers. An interpretation of a God we cannot see, who promises to send us to hell for eternity for any number of differing infractions, might very well have an unhealthy influence on the young and the old alike. This is an interpretation of God that little serves them and interferes with their innate connection with Source. This assumed and absorbed belief system has to be sorted out at some point in their lives.

As one becomes a bit older and wiser and these religious teachings are tested and examined, they are often discovered to be quite confusing with applicability to the day-to-day world. After all, religion is a significant and substantially held belief system for which one may become wholly indoctrinated with little regard for choice. On the other hand, a bad system jettisoned does not necessarily infer that we automatically find a better system for navigating life. It is possible that this is the issue many of us face in our search for new and different answers to what had been presented to us as fact.

Even at a young age, I challenged and challenged what I was taught, knowing that Jesus dying for my (and yours, but not everybody's) sins on a cross just didn't make any sense. On the other hand, there are many who have reconciled values as taught by the Church and have a deep and comforting satisfaction in their lives.

It cannot be said that one is right and the other is wrong, but it is becoming increasingly acceptable to remove or replace beliefs that do not serve us or bring personal enrichment to our lives. We may prefer values more aligned with discovering our inner nature for which other values may no longer be compatible. We are entitled to our beliefs, we are entitled to our outcomes, and we are entitled to the time it takes to conclude what is important to us as we begin to rearrange out lives accordingly.

As we become intentional, we become conscious; and as we become conscious, we become intentional.

It is not hard to see that we are all individual and different. It is simply a matter of how we address and codify incoming information that dictates our beliefs, our choices and our outcomes. While many may believe in conscious choice, pre-destiny, karmic obligation, or the influence of past lives, others believe we get our ticket punched for heaven or hell upon our demise. Either way, our belief systems have enormous impact on our lives, our outcomes and our reality creation.

Rhythm of the Universe

On the other hand, Innate Intelligence has always been with us. Some have memories and beliefs from the earliest of times, a time some may remember as past lives or experiences they bring into this lifetime that have no traditional origin. I, for one, was very strongly influenced by experiences of my early childhood; dreamy or hallucinatory or true, it makes no difference. My world was powerfully influenced by experiences I hold as true, for which these beliefs and memories continue to influence me to this very day.

I did not discuss these experiences as I was growing up. Frankly, I probably never mentioned them until I was well into my adulthood, and then in only the most intimate of terms. I still have vivid memories of being a young child, possibly as young as three or years, and being totally in touch with where I came from before I was born. This included a visual representation of a large closed door with a substantial gap under the door, with perhaps a gap of 18 or 24 inches. Beyond this door was an expression of love, Light, camaraderie and support, as well as a sense of communion, that I have always found hard to describe.

As a young child I knew this camaraderie and communion would fade as I grew into boyhood, and so it did. I believe I maintained this sense of connection until I was approximately 8 years old. I was aware that this was a powerful representation of where I had come from before my birth, and where I left my peers as I came into this world. Truly, I was loved and appreciated from the other side, and I knew this. This was, and still represents, a very powerful experience in my life.

My life has been driven by this series of memories that reside as part of my belief system. From this period of time I carry two expressions and ideals. One characterized as the expression "the rhythm of the universe," which I have spent a great deal of my life attempting to discern the subtlety of its meaning, and, the second, a remembrance of something about a grid system for communications, sharing information or nodal or power points, for which I still get occasionally flashes and insights. To this day, though I am little less able to see and describe either of these ideas, they continue to influence me as I attempt to match my memories and my beliefs with my unfolding life.

Though we are all influenced by outside events, many of us carry within us substantial beliefs and experiences that bring enormous influence to our beliefs and the direction of our lives. Undoubtedly, this is an alternative to the more traditional sources of beliefs we've acquired. And, though we rarely speak of them, are no longer aware of them or have effectively buried them, many of us have had these influential experiences that live on as we search for intelligent life on this planet.

I have spent my entire life devoted to an understanding of the expression "rhythm of the universe," and, in this process, I have come to throw off many belief systems that do not serve my quest. I continue to find my life driven by a vision of what seemed so very substantial and influential at the time. It would be safe to say that this set of experiences has had a significant impact on my life and outpourings as an adult.

There comes a time when we begin to examine our instilled belief systems in relation to the realities of our lives. When the mind/reality connection™ begins to dawn on us, we begin to pay more attention. This may come about from different forms of self-improvement or self-discovery, such as jogging, excelling in sports or meditation, but we begin to see the mind/reality connection™ in all of its glory. Or, it may be more of an inner drive, a drive to access something we all know is there, with a little bit of time on our hands.

It is not unusual to see habits of destructive behavior begin to resolve themselves as we discover what makes us tick and begin to take action in a new manner. There are numerous variations of what might cause us to turn within, but within all must go, at some point or another.

Harmony Through Conflict

I was initially introduced to my mind/reality connection™ through an observation I made about myself when I was younger that I called harmony through conflict. As I became conscious of the quality of the life I was striving to produce for myself, I realized that the only way I was able to produce enhanced outcomes seemed to come from generating conflict or disharmony first. This may be no more complex than learning about life through trial and error, but it seemed that as I strived to create more order in my life, I seemed to create difficulty or conflict first. Usually, I arose from that destruction or destructive habit to some final clarity or stated goal or objective.

As I gained clarity about preferred outcomes, I realized I was falling far short of my goals. I seemed to be competing with a powerful aspect of myself, i.e., my existing momentum and unregulated beliefs. To write of the subject reminds me of how far I have come, and how much intentionality I put into my life over the years. Regardless, I coined the term harmony through conflict, and, in my own personal evolution, I was well into my twenties before I finally left that aspect of my learning curve behind.

I was so determined to overcome my shortcomings that I would continuously take mental notes of what didn't work to the point of finally discovering what did work. Apparently, my method was the process of elimination and the proverbial 100 buttons, for which I tried 99 before finding the right one. I came to believe, as I traversed this circuitous route, that I was acquiring a capacity for compassion for "others" attempting to crawl from their particular point in the ooze.

As we become intentional, we become conscious; and as we become conscious, we become intentional. As we learn to refine our thoughts, our corresponding existences begin to flower. And though this may look a bit like trial and error, we are moving along the continuum of becoming conscious in a very healthy way. Though I may have had certain insights and drives from my earliest memories, bringing that insight into focus took a substantial amount of footwork on my part. After all, I had no outside source of reference or help; I was clearly working it out on my own. It wasn't until I became aware of my inner connection and internal teacher that things became a little easier.

Consciousness Simply Defined

Consciousness may simply be defined as the discovery of our own identity in the midst of everybody else's identity. The world is a busy place, and the commotion of groups and individuals asserting themselves, with their many and varied values, may initially overwhelm our own sense of innate individuality. But as we come down the birth canal, we are met with beliefs, values, "shoulds, coulds, and ought tos," as well as certainties of who and what we are suppose to be. Our parentage, extended families and society have quite a bit of intention already established for us.

Sometimes it takes quite a while to wade through the values, beliefs and projections "of others" to find what best fits our own individuality and innate nature. It is finally in the comforts of the modern world that we begin to find the time to discover our own true selves. We are finally able to take the time to stop, look and listen.

We learn as best we can. We begin with beliefs and survival dictums as given to us, until we are old enough to make our own way. We outgrow traditionally generated beliefs and outmoded models of thought as we develop our own sense of self, for which we now have the significant advantage of living much longer lives. Now that computer power doubles every 18 months, it would be assumed that our learning curves are capable of moving much more quickly as well.

Our perceptions of what serves us become more personalized and individualized as we mature. As our lives become our own, experiences and feedback from our choices and beliefs tell us of the quality of what we hold dear. It might be analogous to our minds being hardware and our beliefs being software, for which we continually upgrade as we catch on.

The process of growing toward adulthood and eventual wisdom is a process of evaluating existing beliefs, as well as concocting our own. This is a trial-and-error process that brings greater depth to our own convictions as we discover what is true for ourselves. After all, we are going where no man has gone. We are going past what our parents and theologians have recommended for us and we are going beyond what perceived leadership might recommend for us. We are discovering our identity and making our own way, which nobody could do for us anyway. We are becoming conscious, alert, alive, awake and aware.

Consciousness may further be defined as the acquisition of access to Innate Intelligence, such that one draws more and more insight from themselves/Innate Intelligence and less and less from the outside world. Enlightenment may be defined as the process by which one takes 100-percent of one's insight from inner guidance and connection with Source and lives in reaction to the outside world 0-percent; something about being in the world, but not of it.

Increasing consciousness and awareness is the next step for humanity, embroiled in its own evolution and survival. Turning within is the next step, as revealed by the quality of our reality as a feedback mechanism for the beliefs we hold and value. Sometimes this is brought on by the thought "There has to be more," the need or wish to excel, or sometimes the need to escape circumstances once thought to be beyond our control. Sometimes, it is the pain of being so out of alignment with our own inner nature that we have no choice but to step up to the plate.

CHAPTER FIVE
TOOLS

*A*s we see the wide variety of belief systems we all possess – yours, mine, ours, and theirs – we realize that we live in a world of projections and beliefs and attitudes of our own making. Beliefs are little more than values based on what we "know to be so" – conscious, unconscious, accurate, inaccurate, etc. And since what we "know" is so, and what we know continues to change and refine itself, our realities continue to change and refine themselves, as well.

We realize that our lives are projections and interpretations of reality as seen through the screens and filters of our beliefs and values. We understand that by changing our beliefs, and questioning and refining what we know to be so, we acquire new and empowering influence over our lives. Imagine our lives as a great ship plowing the oceans of life and space and time, and imagine a tiny rudder or a massive steering gear as our beliefs and our values. After all, what we know is so, and what we know charts and creates our lives and our realities.

I remember as a young boy learning to overcome my fear of the dark. My family lived in a home with a basement that contained my dad's shop and tools at one end. At this far end of the basement, I learned how to overcome something that, to that point, had been a powerful part of my beliefs and values.

I was afraid of the dark in that alien basement in the bowels of the house, and I "knew" my comfort was with the light on. I remember many times going down the stairs and, as I approached the light cord, I would swing my arms for maximum contact for grabbing the safety of the pull string. But as I became accustomed to that swift jaunt across the darkness of the basement, I would move to the vicinity of the light cord and stop and wait.

As we learn to perceive in alignment with Innate Intelligence, we can take more charge of our lives.

I slowed down long enough to feel my discomfort in that dark basement. I found myself rationalizing the dark and resourcing my perspective about what might happen, knowing fully well that the light cord was well within my reach. I taught myself to be comfortable in the dark, and, in the end, I "knew" differently about the dark. I remember discovering that I could maintain my wits about me in other darkened and frightening spaces as I continued to expand my knowledge base about what was true for me. I continued to learn and came to know new things. And as my belief system expanded, correspondingly my world and my reality expanded.

The point is, I knew I was afraid of the dark, though I would likely have denied it at any cost. My beliefs, my thoughts, and my experiences – everything I knew told me I was afraid of the dark. But what was the end result? I came to know differently; I came to know that I was no longer afraid of the dark. I became empowered by overcoming a belief that was having a huge influence in my life. I changed a specific value and belief system that was negatively impacting my life, and at a minimum, my self-esteem climbed a notch or two. More importantly, I learned that by changing my mind, I could change my realities.

This analogy may be broadly and capably used to describe how we live our lives, as well as how we expand and mature. Our lives are based on what we know, accurate or inaccurate. And, as what we know shifts and grows, our realities and how we perceive them also shift and grow. In fact, everything that is available to us and that limits us comes through our perceptions and what we know to be so, accurate or not. Sometimes distinct events change our knowing – a family death, crisis or other powerful event – and our knowledge base and values change instantly. And very often we have ongoing experiences that change our beliefs in a useful way so that as our perspectives shift, we come to see and know the world in a more refined and relaxed manner.

One of the premises of this book is to introduce the idea that what we "know to be so" may be based on misinformation, assumptions that are off-track, partially accurate information, correct information or hunches and intuitions that have more foundation than we understand. Typically, what we know is based on what we have been taught and information that we have gleaned through our experiences in life thus far. What we know is a repository of our beliefs and habitual patterns of thought, again, accurate or not. And handily, we continue to review and refine our beliefs and values and what is important to us throughout our life. As we learn to interpret and perceive in alignment with Innate Intelligence, we discover that we can take more charge of our lives and our outcomes. As we become more effective at what we know, we become more effective at understanding what is available to us.

Our beliefs are installed in our minds similar to computer software, which is, of course, upgradeable. And as we see our beliefs shift, as we have new insights, our worlds correspondingly shift. Why not begin to examine what we believe and learn to put what we believe to better and more intentional use for ourselves?

If our thinking and our beliefs create our realities, then by the intentional refinement and adjustment of our beliefs, shouldn't our outer circumstances begin to refine themselves? Otherwise, don't we simply drift and bounce among life's unknown intricacies and complexities? We are unaware of what is coming next, and we are innately unable to chart our own course. We are the victims of "reality."

Ultimately, it will be clearly shown that our realities are a product of our output, and ours alone. Others' realities are a product of each their own output, and the combination of individual realities and multiplicities of output and consensus give us what is perceived as our reality in general. Relationships revolve around shared perceptions for which common and similar realities are the common denominator. This could be business relationships, the focus of couples, organizations, cultures, ethnicities, nationalities, religious groups, the purpose of corporations, etc.

We each have our own unique upbringing. We each have our own unique combination of circumstances and events that mold our beliefs and what we know to be so. Is it no wonder that we are all so vastly different? We are all the same, but we are not the same. We are each unique and individual, even from the same family growing up in the same environment.

We have already touched on the idea that we are born and raised in cultures that are no more than consensus of accumulated belief systems in momentum, for which we are immediately impacted with "certainties" upon our birth. What if, beside basic survival skills, we were introduced to the idea that our beliefs power and steer our individuality through time and space?

What if we discover that our beliefs hold us off-course and on-course, decide our outcomes, dictate our health and our death and otherwise allow our nose to be held to the grindstone, or give us vast freedom and individuality? What if we discover that unconscious output of what we "know to be so" continues to bring us more of the same? What if we were to become conscious of our beliefs and intentionally began to review our corresponding realities as feedback? Wouldn't this bring new insights, new opportunities and new possibilities into the reality creation process? Wouldn't this be worth looking into?

Breaking Up Patterns

Ever notice the comfort, joy and serendipity that occur when we travel for pleasure, or make a choice to do something that is truly desired, or in some manner, shake up our daily patterns? Clearly our realities are held together by our habitual patterns and as we shift our habitual

Why not learn to put our habitual thinking patterns to more intentional use for ourselves?

patterns, our worlds open up right in front of us. As we move out of our traditional patterns of thinking, our realities and outcomes begin to shift immediately! It is not so different from walking from one world right into another.

Once we leave our habitual patterns behind, we experience present time with a present time mindset. Imagine we have left our habitual patterns behind for just a moment. Depending upon our awareness and receptivity, the Universe kicks right in with great ideas, synchronicities and quite a bit of enthusiasm for infusing "life" into our lives. As we release our stranglehold, life can happen in surprising and "life-inspiring" ways.

A young woman friend has just reported back after a birthday trip to Chicago to see family and friends and kick up her heels a bit. She found herself in a number of exciting adventures, including meeting new and engaging people. Seemingly synchronistically, she had invitations to museums, restaurants and a menagerie of new sights, sounds and insights available to her. By a simple shifting of her circumstances, she found herself having far more excitement and adventure than her daily regimen seemed to offer.

A number of people taking this same trip would have had their own variation of the excitement that my friend experienced, while others might have found no one to talk to – a ho-hum trip – and be ready to get back to work and the comfort of their daily patterns. But the point is, when we remove ourselves from our habitual patterns, our world suddenly opens up right in front of us. As we step away from our day-to-day habitual patters that create the monotone of our realities, we often find a bright and shiny new world to play in – a world just beyond our existing horizon and only a matter of an attitude or perceptual adjustment away.

I remember making the decision to move to Florida about a year after my divorce. I was the owner of a one-man business, which I was slowly rebuilding when a recession hit Texas in 1982. As I remember, Braniff Airlines had just declared bankruptcy, and domestic oil production had just become deregulated. As a young man already in a struggle to get my business back "over the top" after a divorce, becoming part of a recession was not my first choice. It might be said that I had my hands full when the recession hit a part of America that some considered recession-proof.

> *When we remove ourselves from our habitual patterns, our worlds suddenly open right up.*

I decided to disband my business and do what I really wanted to do, which was to take advantage and make full use of my 39-foot sailboat lying in Key Largo, Florida. Even in the middle of a deeply felt recession, I began to feel better. After all, I had made a decision that was in line with what I wanted to do more than to have a successful business in troubling times. What I really wanted was to be on my boat in some of the prettiest sailing waters of the world.

I distinctly remember my moving sale, as well as the preparation and results. New and friendly people came from out of the woodwork. Everything was exciting; everything was exhilarating; everything was vibrant; and everything was alive. I am not saying my life was boring, or that I had a poor regard for myself, but I had been doing what I (almost) wanted to be doing and I was happily plodding along. But when I made the decision to do what I really wanted to do, reality took on a whole new meaning as the Universe bent over backward to bring me new and exciting experiences and outcomes! The quality of what I "knew" had jumped a hundredfold, and my newfound outer circumstances really begin to click!

I wondered where these people had been all of the years I had lived in Texas. When I made the decision to move to Key Largo, it was as if the Universe couldn't move the old stuff out of the way fast enough to shower me with surprises, experiences, new acquaintances, new adventures and one serendipitous event after another. I honestly began to wonder if I wanted to leave everything that was now coming to me – new and interesting neighbors, new women friends that didn't want me to leave, exciting new opportunities, etc. – a whole world (that must have been right there) that I just couldn't see from my habitually patterned existence.

I am sure many can relate to the picture I am trying to paint about making new decisions, stepping out of old patterns and finding new and exciting experiences waiting just beyond. Part of the intent of this book is to understand this phenomenon. It becomes obvious that as our patterns of thinking settle in, our realities settle in. As our patterns of thinking become disturbed, upgraded or rearranged, our realities shift right in front of our noses! This is known as a paradigm shift. At some point we learn how to maximize these adjustments by recognizing that breaking away from our old patterns brings us new and more refined results and spins our growth curves into something all together more useful. Ultimately, we can learn how to dictate our outcomes and create open-ended realities and adventures by harnessing what nature has in store for us just beyond our presently existing horizons!

What we want to explore is the importance of our beliefs, the habitual thinking patterns we hold dear, the resultant output and the end result that is the creation of our realities. By learning how to review and adjust what we believe and how we perceive, we can generate differing outputs and differing resultant realities. Accordingly, we have stumbled upon a major secret to life! It is my belief that this is what was taught and discussed as ancient knowledge in the Mystery Schools of old. I believe this is the essence of what Jesus taught and knew for himself.

Our prayer is a 24-hour broadcast from the center of our being.

This is not a matter of positive thinking, or a simple reinterpretation of the way we speak or act, but an evaluation and re-investment in our belief systems and what we know to be so. If, in fact, what we know is the nexus between who we are and what we have in our lives, we now have a tool for our success that far surpasses anything that we have ever been handed in our traditional upbringing. What we know is what we get. What we believe is what we experience, and, as our habitual patterns of thinking stream out in front of us, we create our realities, similar to a movie projector.

We need to know what we hold deeply inside of us. We need to know what makes us tick and creates our realities. And, until we have sufficient management over what we think and focus on, and an understanding of our underlying core beliefs, we can be thankful our survival mechanism includes a buffer such that our daily over-imaginative chatter does not generate our realities. On the other hand, patterns are patterns, and what we sow is what we reap.

Core Beliefs

In 1980, I wrote a statement of my own beliefs titled "Abundance, Cause and Effect, and The Ultimate Goals," in which I reported that our realities are a matter of what we broadcast from the core of our being. I suggested that we radiate what we know to be so and that our realities are our corresponding result. I conceptualized this by introducing the concept of "Core Belief Systems" (CBS), indicating that as we broadcast our beliefs, our realities flow out in front of us.

I have since come to understand that what we broadcast is our prayer. Though most assume prayer to be what we ask of God or wish upon ourselves, our prayer is, in fact, a 24-hour broadcast from the center of our being. And, conversely, our realities provide us with a great deal of insight as to what we are broadcasting from the core of our belief systems. It is in the correlation of our thinking and our reality creation that the great adventure, the mystery and discovery of our own nature, individually and as a species, is found and begins.

Our realities tell us everything about what is lodged within our core beliefs just as our core beliefs tell us everything about our realities. As we shift our inner circumstances, our outer circumstances revise themselves. And, as our outward circumstances change (new environment, new insight, etc.), our beliefs revise themselves accordingly.

It is the intent of this book to help individuals discern that –
- we, and only we, are responsible for the realities we each have in our lives;
- our realities are directed from deep within us, i.e., our core beliefs; and
- as we root around; as we shift and revise our beliefs, we create new realities for ourselves.

Luckily, much of the momentum we already have, i.e., our habitual patterns of thinking, can be harnessed and realigned for our new momentum. This is simply a matter of a bit of conscious intent, a bit of nudging and a bit of listening, as we shall soon come to see.

I would also suggest that this process is far safer than we might imagine, far safer than updating the operating system on a computer. With

Innate Intelligence as our technical support, we are in alignment with nature's growth, so haphazard reformatting and unknown results and outcomes are not possible. Because we are fundamentally spiritual beings, we have spiritual machinery for our motherboards, processors and hard drives. Our jobs become to "log in" and line up with Innate Intelligence. We live our lives within far more order than we know.

Self-improvement that does not embrace and include our spiritual nature cannot and will not have deep or lasting influence. Once we find the key to delving within, not only will our connection improve, but it will become self-perpetuating. For once we have found the key that makes us tick, Innate Intelligence becomes more available and our momentum naturally picks up. This is our inheritance and the promise of sages, mystics and poets from the beginning of time. As we come to discover our underlying nature and inherent connection with Innate Intelligence, we will more effectively contribute to humanity. We become more successful, individually and as a species.

As we discover our individuality and connection to Source, our success as a species becomes assured.

Initially, the ego will resist. But once the ego is understood as no more than an off-track survival mechanism and once the ego recognizes the sanity of the new course of action, it will happily fall in line. It will accept its new role with relish.

The ego might simply be characterized as an aspect of the hardware that connects us to Source. Imagine the ego as a small receiving antenna dish. When we are born, this small antenna is pointed at our highest survival source and connection with Innate Intelligence. As we grow into childhood and begin to absorb the mind-numbing, black-and-white thinking patterns made available to us, the ego mechanism begins to lose its connection with Source. As the ego mechanism finds itself losing its connection, it begins to develop its own survival story and theory based on available information. But the survival-sensing organization that is the ego will readily accept its reconnection as we make the effort to realign to Source.

All we have to do is start monkeying around with the mechanisms that are our belief systems. As we learn how to shift and upgrade our beliefs, we upgrade our realities. As we shift our beliefs, for which we have corresponding feelings such as joy and satisfaction as our first insight, our new realities come into focus, which is our second insight. We are capable of becoming awash in new and useful information as we set our sights a bit higher.

It is of the greatest importance to know and understand that this mechanism exists within us and represents the red carpet and stairway to heaven, so to speak. To understand that our minds hold our beliefs and our beliefs create our realities is fundamental. And, as we get feedback from our reality creation, we continue to refine what we know to be so. As our realities and beliefs begin to mirror our higher aspirations (compassion, joy, peace, ecstasy and love), we raise the quality of our output and our realities continue to refine themselves. It is simply a matter of changing our mind, which is well within our capabilities, and, as usual, an inside job.

Initially the process may seem difficult. After all, one who is unconscious to the source of one's realities is sleeping, and one who is sleeping may be a bit drowsy upon awaking. For those who have been consciously attempting to improve their lot in life, a few pointers might be in order. And for those who can readily identify the inner prodding to expand and become more intentional in the creation of their realities, they are in the right place at the right time.

The place to start is to understand that we are the source of 100-percent of our realities and that no part of our realities comes from outside of ourselves. It is possible to defer to someone such that their beliefs and their knowing become our knowing and our influence, and this is a regular occurrence. This scenario is the source of the expression of "taking one's power back." This is nothing new, because, as infants and children, we begin reality creation within the guidance of someone who says "it is so" in their particular and caring way. And, of course, we eventually come to be on our own anyway.

There is also the case for the idea that God knows what is best for us, and it is simply for us to defer to Him (or Her as the case may be). But other than a biblical interpretation of who and what God may or may not be, there is little evidence for the existence of a God who strategizes in our own best interests such that we can sit back, relax, and let God do the driving. There is nothing in modern science or modern theology that identifies anything new with regard to the God phenomenon as identified by the Bible or other ancient texts.

On the other hand, there is a mechanism that clearly can be understood when someone defers to "God's will," or to the power of traditional prayer. For, as we will come to see, newfound focus, i.e., our capacity to move beyond resistance, and our willingness to expand can readily be seen as the underlying mechanism that has been the success many enjoy in their traditional beliefs in God.

As we become empty, as we allow God to shoulder the problems (or successes) we face, we can see that we have clearly shifted our focus from the problem toward the solution – and often an open-ended solution at that. Ultimately, powerful traditional prayer and powerful beliefs in a traditional God can be seen as a mechanism that gives our belief systems a rest, deferring to one more powerful for potent outcomes. It is simply a matter of clarity of one's focus by one means or another. It is also the success of releasing what we do not want as our focus, to what we believe is a solution that comes from "one" more powerful than ourselves, though there are limits to this applicability as we come to discover our own true power.

While this particular format for reality creation may have some merit, it becomes apparent that, as we instead accept responsibility for the quality of our creations, we enter a powerful period of intentionality and personal power in our lives. What we have in our lives becomes under our dominion and as feedback, tells us of the quality of our beliefs on our way toward true abundance and wholeness. And, of course, the only real adjustment we are making is to move God within – as an aspect of ourselves – for which we take full responsibility for the quality of that connection.

Self-Help

It is in the discovery of our samenesses that we find our solutions and our successes as a species.

Mankind began to crack the egg of personal naiveté with the beginning of the self-help movement in the 1940s, and what came to be known as Alcoholics Anonymous and its many variations. Initially, AA sprang up as an alternative to other treatments for alcoholism that weren't working. It was discovered that by a certain amount of personal self-discovery and acceptance of one's powerlessness with this disease (dis-ease), that one began to find relief. As these individuals stopped fighting the problem[1] and instead began to realign with their inherent connection with Source, many were able to again lead fruitful lives.

Self-help programs were the beginnings of individuals making the effort to revise their unconscious habitual patterns. With insight, they were able to overcome what they inadvertently knew to be so. By giving up resistance and old patterns of thinking and focus, as well as finding new intentionalities, the reinvention of one's beliefs began in earnest, for which mankind has taken a huge leap.

The age of powerlessness has begun to fade. It took fortitude and courage, as well as a meshing of spirit and Innate Intelligence, for this to come to fruition. In fact, the road to meshing with one's spirituality has always taken a bit of courage and commitment, though it is no more than a matter of infusing one's beliefs with newfound clarity and order.

There has been an incredible explosion in self-help and self-improvement over the last 50 years, all of which is preparation and guidance to our willingness to know more about ourselves. Everything, from modern psychology, group counseling, bio-feedback and hypnosis to inner dialogue and relationship communication courses, has become the norm. Discovery and awareness of our inner resources is common ground many of us share in this day in time. Sales courses teach more about satisfying customer's needs and corporations use holistic counseling to discover and engender leadership in individuals while new companies spring up identifying principles and values that support win-win growth and success in the world of commerce and personal reality.

As our values expand, as we delve within individually and collectively, as we turn to self-help curriculums and personal development courses, we bring newly refined vision to ourselves and each other. There is no doubt about it: We are in the middle of an explosion of personal knowledge, and, accordingly, personal transformation.

Everywhere we look, we find gatherings, groups, meetings and discussions about self-improvement. Bookstores now have whole areas dedicated to the substantial growth of self-improvement, and Web sites continue to churn out their messages to a growing audience. Multitudes of companies and individuals have sprung up offering empowerment in the formats of consulting, seminars and coaching, while mentoring crisscrosses the globe. Life coaches and seminar leaders find themselves in boardrooms instructing CEOs during the week and introducing concepts of self-esteem and personal power to the hungry masses on weekends.

There has come to be a full-time, mainline awakening of the mind/thought movement and its sacred connection to Innate Intelligence, with ongoing seminars by numerous leaders of our time. All are saying the same thing. We are prodding and poking and awakening to our innate calling and knowing. We are learning to uncover and dig deeper into our unconscious beliefs that allow our innate knowing to shine forth. The promises of the ancient sages are no more than a matter of discovering what is inside of us and learning how to let it out. We find that beyond our limited perceptions is a whole new world. Our solutions have been lurking in the last place we have looked.

Self-improvement has always been an individual endeavor, and, for a great many years was referenced as not much more than "pulling one's self up by one's bootstraps." Imagine, if you will, the incredible courage and resolve it took for Christopher Columbus or any of the early navigators, to sail beyond the horizon, overcoming the fears and legends about the edges of a flat world. There was the likelihood of dangers and fates worse than death just beyond the edges of the known world, clearly the consensus of the vast majority of the population of Europe at the time.

Of course, greed may have played a part; adventuresome natures and the whisperings of ancient maps, and stories of travelers before them may have played a part. But it took an individual with a great deal of intent and courage to accomplish the selling of a voyage to the banks and queen, as well as enormous fortitude to make eventual landfall far beyond the edge of what was known to be true at the time. All of this can be perceived as the power of individuality and a listening to that inner prodding saying there has to be more.

Large segments of the population are finding that self-improvement is becoming a way of life. We are moving from the unconscious doing of what we had to do to survive to conscious intention of exploring our mind/reality connection™ in alignment with our ever-expanding need to create improvement in our lives. And, luckily, our passages are not anywhere near as frightful as what Columbus and so many others had to endure.

To break away from habitual thought forms and old patterns of thinking, as well as fears and intimidation, takes courage and plenty of it. When one is attempting to break away from commonly held thought, there is always a great deal of momentum and opinion that says "It can't be done," or "This it is simply wrong," or "It is easier to stay conservative and keep your heads low." And so it will be with you in your early passages, until your newfound beliefs and perceptions begin to support you, as you venture beyond your own self-limiting horizons.

Consciousness is a matter of self-discovery, self-reliance, self-determinism and alignment with Innate Intelligence, all handily inside jobs. Consciousness begins with the statement that says "There must be more." It is in the discovery of the self and personal responsibility, that we find the treasure. And, as a bonus, in addition to the satisfaction of dominion over our affairs, we have a very rich access to insight from Innate Intelligence, which becomes ever expansive.

Self-discovery carries distinct advantages as we grow into responsible and capable adults and citizens. This also translates into a species beginning to stand tall as it learns to share in the secrets of the stars and the Universe, of which we are all a part. Birthing ourselves becomes our most important priority and part of a vast hierarchical order, for which we are just beginning to glimpse our potential.

Though courage is the invaluable first step, it would be nice to understand a bit more about how all of this works. To simply head out unaware, one risks whirlpools and eddies, storms and blackened seas, and the likelihood of losing one's soul, similar to the sailors of old. And, as this was not their result, neither is it your own.

For nowhere is there evidence for anything other than a most completely benevolent Universe and infinite order. It is only man, through the disruption of his connection to Source, who suggests reality exists in a manner that is at odds with the order and nature of the Universe. Getting back to our connection, getting back "from whence we came," will not prove as difficult as it may seem.

CHAPTER SIX
THE LAW OF ATTRACTION

*T*here comes a time when enough inquiry generates a response. There comes a time when, at the behest of the student, the teacher appears. There comes a time when, as we become open to new interpretations of life, the Universe in all of its knowing and capacity responds.

As a result of my own quest, I was introduced to Transcendental Meditation in 1973 and I have been meditating ever since. Interestingly, I find the daily discipline of meditation a match and an equal to the process of meditation itself. The mind is initially quite unruly and meditation is a great antidote. After all, if we are going where no man has gone, a bit of order for our minds is not a bad idea. For those wishing to become more intentional in their lives, meditation brings a great return on investment. The discipline and regularity of the practice alone is a very powerful tool.

There is the concept of right-handed and left-handed crutches. A left-handed crutch is similar to alcohol or drugs or other "helpers" to get us through the day, though with a strong potential for debilitating side effects. A right-handed crutch successfully aids in our daily affairs and enhances the quality of our life for the long term. Meditation brings a comfort and certainty to our lives as we become accustomed to becoming quiet and "listening" with our nervous system. As we make choices to include habitually healthy routines to enhance our being, we begin a process of ready expansion and growth.

For those wishing to become more intentional in their lives, meditation brings a great return on investment.

Meditation is a process by which we attune our nervous system to the thrivings of the Universe. Meditation is about sensitivity and refining our existence. It would be fair to state that learning to align with the cosmos is the purpose of meditation. For example, think of the nervous system as an extensive antenna system,[1] for which meditation attunes and aligns us to a bigger picture. Refinement of our nature is the result.

There is ample evidence that a majority of people go through their lives without this introduction due to a fear of the unknown, or a fear of what might be their underlying nature. We all know we are full of wreckage, so why go to the trouble to look? Certainly there are many who go through life with the least introspection possible, much less as their primary objective. For many, ignorance equates with bliss.

When I first began to meditate, I had never spent 20 minutes alone with myself. In fact, I had never been introduced to myself. I did not know myself, and somehow, I thought that what was inside of me was going to be far more sobering than I cared to experience.

Besides, who was "me"? One of the few things I knew growing up was that I didn't want to be like my father. But I didn't know how not to. I had no idea how not to. The idea of venturing within seemed like no-man's land, and certainly I was afraid of what I might find out about myself. Besides, what would I do with what I found? I wasn't sure I wanted to know. It wasn't much different than being afraid of the dark and dealing with the unknown, except this was "me." But my life was not flowing effortlessly along, and the question "Is this all there is?" was clanging around in my head, telling me I needed to be doing something different.

Slowly but surely, I decided there had to be more to life. In combination with the memory of my earliest years and wanting to put the expression "rhythm of the universe" into some perspective, I decided to move forward. It was during a particularly trying time that I heard a radio commercial extolling the virtues of Maharishi Mahesh Yogi and Transcendental Meditation that caused me to act. The next thing I knew, I had shown up with a piece of fruit as a gift, and I was off on a lifelong adventure that had a deep felt influence on my immediate life, and, ultimately, a vast influence on the direction and outcome of my entire life.

Within the safe structure of Transcendental Meditation, I ventured into myself. Initially, I noticed, besides the introduction of myself to myself at the ripe old age of 23, my day was calming down. My day was becoming a bit easier to manage, a bit less frazzled on the edges, and for that matter, at its core. I meditated for 20 minutes twice a day, every day, and, over a period of years, customized and refined the process quite a bit. After all, this was in the privacy of my own mind and my own free time. Adulthood was complex and confusing, and I needed all the help I could get. Meditation was a great deal of help.

Meditation brought a type of peace to the fray that made a difference. During hectic periods in the early days, I took advantage of sitting in bathroom stalls (as was taught) or out in my car and meditated for a quick five minutes, which seemed to bring me back to that state of comfort and peace. I then went back to my day renewed and refreshed. Over a period of years, and now after 30 years, I relish the time spent alone and have come to rely on meditation as an important part of my daily routine. It has never occurred to me to quit. It was actually 10 years before I even took my first major break during the America's Cup Trials in Newport, Rhode Island, in the summer of 1983.

That summer, Australia's entry, "Australia II," skippered by John Bertrand and their secret winged keel, won the America's Cup from the New York Yacht Club and Dennis Conners for the first time in 132 years. Obviously, America and the New York Yacht Club had dominated yacht racing for quite some time, and this was a huge upset. This particular summer was the setting for vast intrigue and extensive rule book review, not to mention extensive partying and celebrating by the spectators. Newport's America's Cup competition and reverie became so predominant that meditation took a back seat for the one and only time in my life. Of course, when my life settled down, meditation came back like an old friend.

Other than that one significant time frame, I meditated every day because, as I often expressed it, "Meditation glued my day together." Meditation gave me an edge that I could not get anywhere else.

I remember making a decision sitting on a bar stool at the young age of somewhat less than 30, that I could either continue to generate substantial bar bills and ego-generated gratuities or take my life a bit more seriously. After all, I finally decided that running up hefty bar tabs and getting out of the bar without knocking anything over and backing my car out without hitting anything was little more than a big ego trip. I remember choosing intentionality and the commitment to self-improvement over the easy road of drinking myself into a fun type of stupor with the limitations of that sort of adventuring.

I discovered that meditation, self-hypnosis and goal-setting worked very well together. Somehow, meditation and clarity about goals and subconscious programming was bringing me everything I wanted. I was married to a beautiful woman who was also a flight attendant. We traveled extensively, and I sold sailboats for a living. With the help of meditation and goal-setting, I traded up through five boats in five years, and by the age of 27, I was at the wheel of my new 39-foot sailboat, moving it down the intercoastal waterway[2] to its new home port of Key Largo, Florida. By my divorce at age 30, my wife and I had plenty to split, and we were ready to go our separate ways. Though I'd had a few bumps along the way, life was beginning to make some sort of sense.

I discovered an aspect of my inner life in meditation and the focus of my outer life in goals and goal-setting. I became an observer of my realities and began to look to see how I could influence and improve them. As any commission sales person knows, how we prepare for the day has a great deal of influence on how our day turns out. And, as any commission salesperson knows, we understand a great deal about how to "season" the mind and how to accept setbacks as we move toward our goals.

I learned that every "no" was one more no toward getting the yes that I required for a sale. Selling became much easier as I learned to look for buyers instead of attempting to sell boats to potential customers. Luckily for me, selling sailboats was an easy and comfortable lifestyle. I still remember eating lunch by myself most days to regroup after the first half of my business day and many, many days sitting in my car meditating, and otherwise doing what I could to encourage the quality of my outcomes. I was absolutely driven to improve the quality of my life, which, in my earlier years, was more predisposed toward the quality and quantity of my paychecks and building my asset base. At the same time, meditation was a very pleasurable experience.

The Busy and the Quiet

My meditation shifted over the years. At some point, the mantra fell away, and meditation became second nature to me. I discovered the teachings of Bhagwan Shree Rajneesh (Osho) around 1979 and, among other things, I was introduced to "Dynamic Meditation," from which I added a bit here and a piece there to my own meditation. In "Dynamic Meditation," one dances wildly in place in a darkened room to wildly beating drum music going through four phases of instruction and catharsis until suddenly the voice on the tape authoratively commands, "Stop!" When we come suddenly and perfectly to a complete stop after wild gyrating, mindless dancing and perspiration running down our face, we discover that God or Source or Infinite Intelligence is "right there," and, of course, the realization that God or Source has always been "right there."

The point of the meditation, the dancing and crying and hooting and yelling and catharsis, was to throw the mind (habitual belief systems) so far off-center, that when we came to a stop, we suddenly found ourselves for several minutes faced with a perfectly quiet and still mind. A quiet mind has a direct link to God, or, Source. This is the purpose of meditation. What I now incorporate into my meditation and do so every day is a quiet aspect, a somewhat dynamic aspect, and then a quiet aspect for an even deeper meditation experience.

For a number of years, I used a yoga asana called "Salute to the Sun," which settled my brain into a disciplined pattern of activity (throwing the brain off its regular noise) for which I would do 12 sets (144 repetitions) and then immediately settle into meditation. After a period of time, I began to include affirmations. During the "in" breaths I would state a short affirmation, similar to "I am open to receive" or eventually "I am open." On the exhalations I always used "I release the past" and eventually "I release." I would then immediately go into my meditation. I found this to be a very powerful experience as I continued to refine my attempts at fusing my conscious and subconscious belief systems with intention and interaction with Source.

Today, I meditate for approximately 20 minutes, do some yoga stretching (without disturbing the meditation state) for 5 to 10 minutes, and then I go back to meditation for another 10 minutes or so. The last 10 minutes is typically much deeper. Typically, I then journal for another 15 minutes on the computer as I attempt to maintain the state I have just come from.

Somewhere I learned that by keeping one eye closed when disrupted in meditation I was able to maintain my connection. As I moved from meditation to journaling, for example, I would take advantage of one eye closed, allowing me to bring the state of meditation to my computer and my journaling experience, which eventually surfaced as this book. Typically, before I write, I meditate. I then bring my meditation experience to my writing, having full appreciation for the quiet that is available to me as I attempt to transpose what is in my mind onto paper.

The less the mind runs unconsciously, the cleaner our realities begin to show up.

I find journaling to be a very valuable and insightful discipline. Initially, I used journaling as a catharsis to relieve and release whatever was floating and bumping around at the surface of my mind, and then as a tool for moving deeper toward contact with my inner nature. I then discovered the technique of pretending that I was writing from a third-party perspective. The third-party perspective allowed me latitude and freedom of expression. It also removed me from the constraints of my day-to-day beliefs. I used to begin: "Good morning, Jim. We are pleased to speak with you," and then I would begin to write.

What I learned is that meditation takes me from my busy mind to my connection with Source. My natural state is my connection with Source, Infinite Intelligence, God, etc., while my noisy mind drowns out this subtle insight and connection that is otherwise so readily available to me. The more we are connected with Source, the less our mind runs endlessly. The less our mind runs endlessly, the less our mind runs unconsciously. The less our mind runs unconsciously, the more capacity we have to listen, and the cleaner and clearer our realities begin to show up.

I invite you to experience this. It is apparent that what we output, we create as our reality. As we output cleaner and clearer thinking and less extraneous thinking, what has been producing our reality begins to settle down. Our outside world begins to show more order, more symmetry and more harmony. Our days are held together by a new type of glue, of which I will speak more a bit later.

The Abraham Teachings

I was introduced to the Abraham teachings in about 1994. Abraham is the name of a non-physical group of teachers who take the name Abraham, which to them means teacher. Abraham, as a group of entities and corresponding wisdom, is channeled by Esther Hicks. She and her husband Jerry have amassed a substantial library of tapes and techniques to improve one's life and generate alignment with one's inner nature. Abraham seminars occur most weekends of every month around the country and comprise a relatively simple, introductory 20-minute statement and theme, with the entire balance of the seminar as a question and answer session from the audience.

Abraham picks audience members in an order that allows for an expansion of ideas, culminating in what is always described by the audience as a powerful and heartfelt experience. There is a purity, love and compassion for the attendees that attest to the character and wisdom that is Abraham's much broader view and overview. There is also vast compassion for the inquiring minds that show up for these seminars. Similar questions are often asked again and again, for which the Abraham perspective continues to offer answers, perspectives and tools for the inquiring mind without fault.

What we broadcast matches up with Universal Forces and our realities come to exist.

Time and time again, vast wisdom is displayed before audiences, for which one's gut and internal mechanisms clearly indicate that they are hearing information that is useful to their journey within. Abraham explains that individuals may be picked for questions because they have better formed their questions, or their questions lead off in a direction such that the most "bang for the buck" is assured for the audience. There is also the issue of clarity of desire, because those with more intent and clarity are more likely to air their questions and insights. Abraham also reminds the audience not to worry about how all of this is done, for no matter, they will "wedge their message into the cracks."

Abraham-Hicks Publications of San Antonio, Texas,[3] and many other teachers, physical and non-physical, exist because of the desires of an increasing portion of the population wanting to know more about the truth of their natures, their spirituality and their connection with Source. These teachers' messages are in direct response to an increased wanting to know more about the truth of their being. People want assurances that their inner journey, oftentimes fraught with the rediscovery of the pain and angst of old hurts, or the seeming miscarriages of justice in the outer world, are OK and a necessary part of the process of discovering ourselves.

Abraham and others like them, embodied or not, are in response to us wanting to know more about our inner nature, and the teachers are showing up. Our history and ancient lore is replete with stories of access to wisdom, insight and information from beyond our traditional interpretations of reality. Such are the ramifications of questioning, focus, a wanting to know more, and the corresponding delving within, individually and collectively. This is an age-old adventuring for which there have always been questions and there have always been answers.

As I have traveled these many paths over the years, I have seen that my ultimate teaching apparatus is found within for which the Abraham teachings and many others successfully engender and support an introduction to our own inner values, inner guidance and inner teacher. This is where life truly begins. I invite you to "Knock, and the door shall be opened to you."

The Abraham teachings promote the idea that there are three fundamental concepts or laws to be known or understood. These concepts are referenced as laws because, to Abraham, laws are principles that work anywhere, anytime and any place. These laws are immutable and certainly not issued, withdrawn or made available to some and not to others (as in the manner of man-made law). These laws are so consistent that their principles work on or off this planet, inside or outside of our solar system, and anywhere mind and thought can be found.

To Abraham, something so fundamental that it is true in any time or any place is true law. As we discover the importance of the realms of mind and thought, we come to realize the importance of these immutable laws and principles that connect us to our realities, as well as to Source. As has been recently discerned in quantum physics, science is discovering that thought (as a representation of consciousness) may be as fundamental as we get. We are discovering that focus (qualified by intent) connects us to a web or latticework of consciousness that is timeless and without distance. One day we shall come to know our true playground and the rules of its use.

Unconditional Love

There is a variation of an EKG machine, in combination with a piece of equipment called a Fast Fourier Transformer, that can measure the frequency of the human heart. This piece of equipment can measure and differentiate between an angry heart, a heavy heart or a heart filled with love. It has been discovered that an individual whose heart is filled with love can radiate and send love to another individual, and the hearts will begin to resonate with each other. This is true, whether in controlled experiments across the hallway or across town, and seemingly, without limits to distance.

In an unforgettable workshop titled "Love Force" with G. Patrick Flanagan, M.D., Ph.D.,[4] Dr. Flanagan recounts the story of querying an audience to ascertain which audience member was having the biggest health challenge. An individual was selected and asked to come to the stage. Though she and the audience assumed the intent was for her to be the recipient of love from the audience, the opposite was true. She was instructed to become comfortable and begin sending love to the audience. As she and the audience became attuned to each other and completed the process, she discovered that her aches, pains and discomforts disappeared – an important variation on a simple idea.

The point of the Abraham material is that there are three fundamental principles or truths: the Law of Attraction, the Law of Deliberate Creation and the Law of Allowing, for which everything is a subset of these laws. Ultimately, we want to thoroughly explore the Law of Allowing, but first we must build on fundamentals. The benefits of allowing (unconditional love) become readily available to us once we understand how the Universe and all of its connectedness works. Once we understand the mechanics of how reality comes to exist (or is manufactured), our capacity to find comfort and acceptance in the world around us grows substantially, and allowing becomes second nature.

If we can access that quiet place in our mind, we can vastly increase our lot in life.

One of the intents of this book is to introduce a grounded interpretation of unconditional love. As we come to have a bit of technical understanding of how life works, we become substantially more capable of accepting "the world around us" and everyone's part in it. Practicing and understanding unconditional love and acceptance generates huge benefits, not only to the perceiver and the perceived, but also to the world at large. After all, we have got to start somewhere, and, as proverbial as it sounds, the answer is going to be the last place we expect to find it. The answer is clearly contained within the resonance of our very natures.

The Law of Attraction

The Law of Attraction says that what we focus on expands, because what we focus on becomes an aspect of our attention. As a portion of our attention, our focus becomes a part of our broadcast and our output, i.e., our prayer. We do this intentionally or inadvertently and in the simplest of terms; this is how we create our realities.

Another way to explain the Law of Attraction: As we have an initial thought about something that is important, another similar and more powerful thought joins the first thought. This is the beginning of the creation process for which the Law of Attraction is the foundation, the Universe is the intermediary and we are the initiator. Two thoughts, held with attention, create and draw a third and more powerful thought for which the original idea continues to grow exponentially. As we continue to review and revise our focus, we eventually have an outpouring of reality.

It is in the listening to Innate Intelligence, that we begin to flourish in a more useful manner.

This law does not say that opposites attract, or that positive and negative attract or become equal. It says, "Like attracts like." The extension of this would be that broadcasting our beliefs and habitual patterns of thinking draw to us more of the same. In this way, our realities are fortified and maintained by our continued outgoing broadcasts in sync with the Law of Attraction. What we broadcast – our attitudes, belief, focus and what we know to be so – matches up with Universal Forces and our realities come (or continue) to exist. As we take on new focus, as our attention and beliefs shift and expand, our realities shift and expand.

If we were to return to the concept of core belief systems and a recognition that we broadcast our realities from our deeply held beliefs and "what we know to be so," we would discover in our confusing or orderly amalgamation of our outpourings that we create our realities quite precisely. This is the source of our realities and endless-loop existences, as well as the potential for open-ended possibilities and vast refinement in our lives. To take this idea a bit further, if we would choose our focus with a bit more intent, we could more capably dictate our output and thus begin to create realities of a more positive and useful impact in our lives.

What we need to discover for ourselves is whether this is truly an immutable principle, whether this is truly Universal Law, and whether this is something that we can use in our lives on a consistent basis. There seems to be ample evidence that our held beliefs and daily output are strategic aspects of the worlds in which we live. There seems to be evidence that our output in the form of attitudes, beliefs, what we were taught (rightly or wrongly) and our zeal to improve or perform at the top, is a matter of our own stream of consciousness, and thus our own harnessing of Universal principles.

We need to know whether this is true, because if it is, we have discovered the basis for understanding how we have what we have in our lives – good, bad, inconsistent, indifferent, etc. If our thinking and focus draw what we have, if our lack of focus and lack of commitment bring those realities as well, we now have a formula for putting our lives together. If our daily focus generates a portion of our vibration and output, then it behooves us to understand what we output. We then learn to choose our focus with more intention and purpose.

What We Resist Persists

What we fight or resist or detest is a strong and powerful focus as well. Many manage their lives from a perspective of resistance or retaliation to what they believe their circumstances to be. Many blame "others" for their experiences in life. And, many believe that what they have or do not have is a matter of a higher authority for which they have little to say, while others feel they cannot get ahead, or are racked with guilt, anger, fear or doubt. All of these are sources of focus and bring results.

Many wonder why "What they resist persists." If we don't want what we have in our lives, it would seem that we should be able to push it away. Though we sometimes go through elaborate and forceful means of pushing or resisting what we don't want, or are quite clear about what we don't want, it's possible we are using principles that we just don't understand. If what we don't want continues to be in our lives, it behooves us to look at how we think and what we focus upon.

Eventually, we come to see that the Law of Attraction simply says that – based on our focus, whether it is conscious, unconscious or subconscious, consistent or inconsistent, healthy or unhealthy - we attract our realities. As creators, it is beginning to look like "pushing against" is not an effective way to create reality.

Imagine the amount of focus from beginning to end, in the creation of a new and modern baseball stadium. Imagine the focus and drive behind the wishes of the developers, or those wishing to promote the stature and symbolism of such a facility dedicated to the enjoyment of the sport of baseball. Imagine all of the workers bringing their focus every day, dedicated to applying their specific knowledge, wisdom and experience to the building of such a facility. Imagine the players themselves, with their focus and talent, many of whom have dedicated much of their lives to the sport of baseball. Now add the desire and focus of the spectators and their excitement, wishes and desires for numerous pennants and awards won over the years. This is how baseball stadiums come into being – with vast focus, intention and commitment. Humanity is capable of awesome creative outpourings!

If we can apply this rationale to everything that is man-made, we begin to realize that humans are creators. Humans create in a vast array of differing worlds, including career, family, lifestyle, science, enterprise, art, etc. As we discover the common denominators that underlie reality creation, it becomes apparent that everyone has access to the same capacity and in equal amounts. Our beliefs and capacity for focus are our only limiting factors.

Ultimately, the cleaner and clearer our focus, the more we are able to generate desired results. One whose focus is haphazard creates haphazard results, which is precisely what the Law of Attraction says.

Imagine a number of neighboring cities vying for the contract for a new baseball stadium within a large metroplex area. Imagine some of the smaller cities without the experience that leads to a successful proposition and ultimate contract and stadium. Imagine communities without the resources (focus) to put a proper proposal together in the first place. Imagine cities or communities with the experience of having successfully mounted similar campaigns, knowing how to get the voters motivated, the city councils galvanized toward their objectives, and the end results of a stadium.

Imagine even years before, some forward thinking individual putting aside a large tract of land that could become available for such a project at a later date. Imagine how one group might have more focus than another and thus achieve the prize. Ultimately, as individuals, as a group, or as a species, we all have this capacity to focus. The Law of Attraction is precisely aligned with this.

To live our lives in alignment with our innate nature brings a much grander way to explore the world.

The mechanism that is our thinking and capacity for focus is identical among us. As we are clear about what we want and have little extraneous focus, our results appear more readily. As our thought processes are random, the results may be unrecognizable or minimal at best. The Law of Attraction is very powerful and used either artfully or without understanding generates results. Luckily, the results we receive are a matter of the quality of our focus, well within our capacity.

The Great Equalizer

There remains one other matter with regard to focus, and it can make anyone the equal of any experienced city council or experienced and savvy promoter/developer. As we learn to become quieter in our minds, we discover that we have access to Innate Intelligence and corresponding insights. These insights come in the form of feelings and, as we have thought or focus, we always have an associated corresponding feeling.

Based on the quality of the feeling associated with our focus, or even the initial first thought, we always know the appropriateness of that thought or focus as an eventual reality. The higher the quality of feeling associated with our thought, the closer we are to our optimal capacity to create. If our focus is off-track and we disregard the "warnings" associated with our corresponding thoughts, we might find ourselves – in several days, several months or several years or a whole lifetime – with a train wreck at our feet, for which we had ample warning.

Thought, combined with feeling, tells us everything we need to know about creating our realities. Through the power of the underlying nature of reality, the power that keeps the planets from bumping into each other, the sun coming up every day, and tomatoes consistently coming from tomato seeds, our capacity for alignment with higher purpose is readily available to us. It is in the listening to our inner nature that our success has always shone. It is in our capacity for thought combined with compelling information from Source that we, as Team HomoSapien™, continue our evolution and learn to create in alignment within an order that is much larger than we readily understand.

A visionary is one who has come to peace (allowance) with the world.

It is through listening and feeling that we create our realities with quality and intention. If we can access that quiet place in our mind, if we can have insight into the quality of what we think, we can vastly increase our lot in life. It is important to note that humanity, the only species on the planet with free will, is finally beginning to discover its innate inheritance – en masse. It is also true that humanity has been listening to its inner nature since the beginning of time. As we evolve into the comforts that come from just beyond basic survival, making use of the tools available to us, we begin to approach our potential.

It is important to note that any sort of reality, be it a stadium with lights blazing into the night sky, a grocery list, or a first date leading to marriage and children, begins with a first thought and a first feeling. According to the Abraham teachings, a thought purely held engenders and draws to it another thought, similar and more powerful, for which a corresponding feeling accompanies it. Those two thoughts held purely will attract an exponentially more powerful thought, for which there is always corresponding insight as feeling.

We are creators and we have insight available to us at every step of the way. Thought is generated; Innate Intelligence responds; and reality comes to exist. And, it is in the care and feeding of our thoughts, as well as listening to the insight made available by Innate Intelligence, that our realities grow and flourish in a more useful manner.

On the other hand, it is obvious that a painful or a ho-hum feeling is a warning about a thought or focus out of alignment with our highest good. And often, we will go to great effort to dismiss the lack of resonance (dissonance), or feelings of pain and disharmony, which become increasingly louder as we continue to attempt to force outcomes or generate realities at odds with Innate Intelligence and our inner nature. Eventually, we learn about alignment and the ease with which we can live our lives.

If we were surprised at the size of the train wreck at the end of the ordeal, we would find the corresponding dissonance from Innate Intelligence to be a match. If we were to heed the still, small voice telling us of the quality of our thoughts and focus early on, we could revise our thoughts and choose our focus (and outcomes) with more clarity. We could learn to refine our focus and intention, and thus our commitment to what is important to us.

To live our lives in alignment with our innate nature will not only bring a more useful and harmonious lifestyle, but a much grander way to explore the world around us. And, we will feel a great deal better! This is a much more fitting legacy to leave those who follow in our footsteps.

As we come to understand the insight that feeling associated with thought brings to our reality creation, we become more powerful and more useful to ourselves, as well as the world around us. As we get in touch with our feelings, we learn to abandon focus that is not in alignment with our higher insight and higher motives. If we do not heed our inner voice, our creations are for naught, other than as expensive, though valuable, lessons, and rightly so.

As we come to understand that creation and reality begin as a thought and an initial feeling, we listen with more intent and subtlety to ourselves and our inner nature. And, if the feeling is too subtle for our capacity to listen, as we continue in this same line of thinking and focus, the messaging and feeling becomes correspondingly louder until we eventually do hear it. Consciousness is, in part, a matter of listening and hearing subtle insight from Innate Intelligence. The sooner we catch on, the sooner we know whether we are on track or not. The sooner we know we are on track, the sooner the world becomes a more powerful and peaceful place, one person at a time. This is the purpose of meditation. We learn how to listen.

As we refine access to our inner nature, our worlds and realities improve dramatically. As we, individually and collectively, wake up to our inner connection, we see a vast improvement in the human condition. As we become more capable of listening, we find inner tuggings telling us, "There is far more available," and we become better able to follow our innate messaging. We begin to shine with a brilliance that is the full power and authority that is available to us on planet Earth.

Three Types of Focus

Resistance is focus and, correspondingly, brings warning signals of pain, though often these signals are completely disregarded. According to the Law of Attraction, pushing against what we do not want attracts more of the same, for which the signaling from Innate Intelligence is capable of screaming into our lives. This is the source of mental pain, anguish, anger or jealously as we fail to heed our momentum and focus. Individuals whose intent is wrapped up in resistance do not realize what is going on in their nervous systems. Resistance brings nothing but more of the same. There is no such thing as pushing away what we do not want. What we focus on expands. How to break this circuitous existence is thoroughly covered in Chapter 8.

Another type of focus is when our thoughts and focus are a representation of what we want but actually fueled by what we don't want. Though focus might be claimed to be on what we want, the underlying intent is to escape what we don't want.

On the whole, the variations of this type of focus are much healthier than resistance but still contain messages of what we do not want, thus creating less than ideal and often confusing results. It is within this range of focus that most live their lives. It would not be unusual to find some motivations based on pure resistance, and the balance of one's motivations a combination of what one does and does not want. Output is confused and therefore produces less than optimum reality/ circumstances.

At the same time, our feelings tell us that we are not producing realities to the best of our ability, which may be identified as mediocrity, listlessness or resignation. Ultimately, it is out of this contrast that we learn to grow and refine our nature.

Another variation on the above is focus aligned with what already exists. It does not take too much review to understand that the status quo and mass-mind mentality, though healthy in many regards, is made of vast limitation and conflicting beliefs. Focus made up of acceptance and adherence to the broad consensus, as practiced by the masses, is not the stuff of visionaries.

There is a third type of focus, which is characteristic of a truly successful creator. Visionary focus is clear focus. It is centered on about what one wants, with clarity such that one's intent is not impaired by outside activities (the status quo), or negative inner dialogue, and certainly does not include what one is trying to escape. A visionary is one who has come to peace (allowance) with the world and takes only "insider" cues and insights as he or she builds output and focus and momentum. One with this kind of clarity achieves results, measures the results in relation to the associated feelings, refocuses and refines their vision and continues on again and again – the creation process at its best.

This is the nature of the visionary, successful scientist and teacher and ultimately a successful species. This type of creating and focus draws the most alignment from Innate Intelligence, for which joy, peace, ecstasy, and contentment are some of the associated feelings. This is the mechanism by which the light bulb came to exist and humanity's advancement moves forward. Visionary focus aligned with Innate Intelligence creates what are often perceived as miraculous outcomes.

It is obvious that we have options as it regards our capacity for thought and focus. It does not take too much awareness to realize that we create our realities with our everyday thought and focus in concert with what we hold as our beliefs, unconsciously and subconsciously. All of us use a combination of the three above scenarios by which we manifest everything in our lives. It comes from nowhere else. As we move beyond survival mode, we are motivated by higher aspirations and ideals. And, it will be discovered, we are humanitarians at the core of our being.

Faster Than the Speed of Life

In the last several years it has become apparent that life is moving much faster. Though many would decry it, the benefits far outweigh any discomforts. We make decisions, reap results, make new decisions, reap new results, and literally define and refine reality as we go. Reality comes and goes much more quickly, because, as feedback, it gives us new fodder for new focus, new decisions and new outcomes.

As we become aware of our God-given talents, we see new intent and new quality outcomes rapidly overcoming past decision-making and old momentum, and establishing new values in their place. The faster reality creation moves, the faster we are able to revise old potential outcomes and momentums and steer humanity to a more successful habitation with its surroundings.

As we understand our capacity to make decisions, generate results and then create new decisions and refined choices, our capacity to solve humanity's problems grows exponentially. Conscious evolution becomes available to us. That we create our realities is becoming common knowledge and palatable to many. And, just as the lab rat tries all of the options before it finds the food, so, too, the human refines its capacity for gratification and comfort. Always moving toward higher awareness, humanity compares what works with what doesn't work. No matter how it looks to the untrained observer, life has the upper hand, and, ultimately, humanity follows in its footsteps. We, as an evolving species, are moving ever faster toward understanding how life works.

We find that as we achieve a certain plateau of mastery and comfort in our lives, we continue to look for a truer interpretation of success. As is our very nature, we continue to attune, to align and to refine who and what we are. We continue to discover ourselves and we become more. Though we have achieved a certain level of comfort and success, the reverberation of "Is this all there is?" continues to echo deep within our souls. We find that Innate Intelligence beckons us to continue to move inward, upward and onward.

CHAPTER SEVEN
DELIBERATE CREATION

*T*he second immutable law, according to the Abraham teachings, is the Law of Deliberate Creation. Deliberate Creation is no more than a deliberate and intentional use of the Law of Attraction. As we come to understand the capacities of our mind, our thoughts and our feelings, we discover we have access to chosen results, as well as the insight which Source lends to this process. Depending upon the quality and the intentional use of the above, we generate the results we achieve in our lives – muddled and/or chaotic, highly refined order, creation and reality, or somewhere in between.

Successful bank robbers have access to deliberate creation, as do corporate marauders and others who do not seem to have what might be considered healthy values. Results, expected or chosen, but not in alignment with their inner nature, may come but at the expense of great difficulty, hard work and high maintenance. They do not have the benefit of the far-reaching power and capacity of the Universe's innate support and beneficence. In a similar manner, individuals in poor alignment with Source will also have to extend considerable effort to gain and maintain their goals.

Someone in focus and alignment with their inner nature has a much easier path. Results come as adventurous, exciting and harmonious journeys aligned with pleasurable steps and synchronicities, rather than the movement of heaven and earth and the expenditure of enormous amounts of energy toward chosen goals. The difference is we have the support of all of creation aligned with us, or we are forcing our way and winging it on our own. Abraham mentions that one individual connected to Source (thoughts and feelings aligned with inner clarity and insight) is more powerful than one million who are not. Those are big numbers and may behoove us to rethink our creation techniques and how we achieve results in our lives!

As we have thought and develop focus, we have accompanying inner guidance from Innate Intelligence telling us of our alignment with Source. As we focus, inner guidance sends its own communication in the form of feeling, giving us a sense of potential and alignment to our thought processes. As our thoughts are aligned with higher purpose, Innate Intelligence generates signals of joy, peace, comfort, etc. Also available is the scintillating zest that comes from having a series of thoughts that our body and innate wisdom clearly tells us is correct.

As we grow individually, we grow collectively.

These feelings, similar to gut feelings, are capable of bringing the exhilaration of energy pouring through our body, oftentimes to the point of unusual and healthy emotions and outpourings. These powerful feelings of right and wrong running through our nervous system are powerful interpretations of road maps and inner guidance as we learn how to intentionally create our way through life.

As we compare notes among ourselves, not initially understanding some of the feelings we are experiencing, we realize we are the recipients of vast senses of order that sometimes can only be felt as powerful outpourings of love and often expressed as tears. For many, this feeling is often brought on by the witnessing of newfound awarenesses about ourselves, or the connection and "samenesses" we discover by and for and about each other. Often these types of insights are capably displayed in films for which these feelings arise within the audience.

As a male, I am quite familiar with resistance to these inner feelings, or at the very least, the confusion they have generated as a part of my past. I now understand that my nervous system is capable of carrying vast amperages of love, joy, peace and other similar states, as well as octaves of higher vibration and knowing. As I open to the love pouring through me and allow instead of resist, I become the recipient and "throughput"[1] of vast cosmic energy and joy, as well as an ever-increasing clarity and connectedness with the world around me.

It is interesting to have access to this higher order of expression and feeling. Our nervous systems are capable of carrying amperage far in excess of what we may typically find in a sexual encounter. To have the energy of creation coursing through our nervous systems, the stuff of which creation is made, as we walk the sidewalks or converse with friends or experience life on this planet, is to discover the possibilities of humanity. To discover that we have a connection with Source that extends itself as "amped up" feelings of joy and exuberance, as well as feelings of wisdom and peace, is a gratifying and grounding experience indeed!

Of all places, to discover that our connection with God/Source is found within our own body and nervous system – obviously our true temple. As we refine our own nature, i.e., the nature of the cosmos and our connection with Source, we find our lives becoming more exciting, with numerous payoffs.

In the psychological makeup of male and female, males are generally known for the fight and resistance reflex. While at one time, physical strength, protection and defense were their domain, as we shift and grow as a culture, it becomes clear that humanity's needs are shifting. Males who resist their newfound innate messaging system may be stuffing the true Boy Scout aspect of themselves.

As we settle into the newfound comforts that survival brings to us, it behooves the male to consider this journey within. For, without this journey, many may find themselves falling behind in this next step that is our evolution as a species. Women seem to have benefited from the cultural acceptance of intuition and choice based on feeling, and often have a more refined perspective available. Though women seen to have the initial benefit of this access to their feeling natures, there is still a great deal more to be done to refine our understanding of the signaling and messaging system that is available to us all.

I wrote the first draft of this chapter during the week of the 9/11 tragedy and destruction. I was living in a cocoon of my own feelings, as was everybody else in their own manner. But in my particular case, I was deluged with a huge response of love in response to an e-mail I broadcast to more than 500 people on the morning of September 13, 2001. I had seen the nightly news when it resumed on the evening of September 12 and, in a reporting of the celebrating of a few of the Palestinian citizenry, in the background I saw a poster board hanging from a chain-link fence that simply read: "Imagine all the people."

This, as you may know, is a lyric from a song by John Lennon titled "Imagine," and not only was I overwhelmed[2] with the love for my fellow man far across the planet and the commonality we all share, but I felt[3] the need to display this message as capably as I could, to as many as I could. I spent the rest of that evening and the next morning putting the e-mail broadcast together and sent it out as quickly as I could. During the next 10 or more days, while most were caught up in the continuous repeats of horror-filled news reporting and constant chatter, I was basking in responses of love and deep introspection from as far away as Australia.

In 500 e-mails, I only got one back that was angry, not understanding the point of the message. I coped with that tragedy in the highest possible state of grace, peace, acceptance and loving support imaginable. (It is also true that I turned my television off, which is now off permanently.) This is an example of deliberate creation, for which my inner nature and the love that is found within guided me through a very difficult and confusing period of time. I was simply compelled to communicate with my fellow man, for which I received a sharing and camaraderie that exceeded much of the noise and confusion that was prevalent at the time.

Humanity embroiled in its own survival is one of the most beautiful activities we can support.

Relief

Many experience lives of quiet desperation, outright anger or other forms of unhappy emotion. They may live with the perception of some sort of conspiracy or anger vented against them by someone or something "out there." Their goal may be aligned with escaping what they perceive as their realities, or what they perceive as what someone is doing to them.

In their attempt to escape or retaliate against their perceived threats, their thoughts and focus bring corresponding insights of disharmony and distress, as well as the subsequent feelings of pain, fear, anger, angst, etc. Because they are not aware of the source of their issues, their inner signaling continues to tell them they are thinking and heading in the wrong direction. This type of messaging is characterized as any sort of downward spiral of emotional pain or distraught feelings of individuals caught up in too much reality.

The Law of Attraction works both ways. Many of us go through situations where we just can't see our way out of a downward spiral and fail to recognize the Law of Attraction at work. There is no such thing as turning off the Law of Attraction. Often, though, we reach a point of getting used to the pain, living our lives in a state of quiet desperation or numbness, or otherwise holed up in some sort of tenuous stability. But the point of the jangling and distress is that we finally become so weary of the pain of being at odds with our true nature that we finally say "There must be another way," for which a new focus and desire immediately begins to form. As soon as we come to this conclusion, the pain and heaviness begin to let up and we cast our eye and attention to newfound and healthier solutions.

As we come to better understand and align with our inner nature, we discover how to feel better, and accordingly, how to create higher quality realities and outcomes. Many have already concluded that a garage full of Cadillacs and a multitude of stocks and bonds do not generate joy. Once we begin to work toward and achieve that certain sense of calm and peace and serenity that is available to us, we begin to truly thrive. And, of course, calm and peace puts us into a receptive state of being able to discern what our inner nature may be attempting to tell us.

"Observers thrive in good times And suffer in bad; Visionaries thrive in all times."

The vast majority balance anger and pain with joy and comfort, and variations thereof. Although many find themselves continuing to refine this balance in their lives, there is little information on the streets about how to successfully align with our inner nature. Because there are no manuals and few traditional insights available to escape what doesn't work, we continue to go round and round, though ever so slowly upward. As we individually and collectively come to understand the Law of Attraction and Deliberate Creation and how we are meant to function as conscious and sentient beings, we find we are better able to affect what we sow and reap.

As we grow individually, we grow collectively. As we grow collectively aligned with our true nature, the quality of life improves for us as a species, and individually we become better leaders. As we become better leaders, we continue to generate better influence and better outcomes, and true expansion becomes available to us – all of us.

Contrast

So, if Deliberate Creation is –
- the intentional use of the Law of Attraction;
- increased receptivity to our inner nature;
- the discovery that how we feel is a benchmark for our alignment with Innate Intelligence; and
- visioning and intentionality creates our outcomes

– what else is involved? After all, there is an enormous amount of poor quality creating out there. And make no mistake about it. Everything that exists, does so as a matter of focus and focused thought first, with the corresponding feelings of joy, alarm, etc. What are we to do, and how are we to proceed, if fighting what is wrong is not the solution? How do we climb out of this monkey barrel of naïve human creating that we find ourselves in?

It is essential to understand that the Law of Attraction is no different than cause and effect or, "As we sow, so shall we reap." As we discover deliberate use of the Law of Attraction and come to understand insight from Innate Intelligence, we become more intentional in our focus and more capable in our outcomes. And, it is out of the contrast of our creations that we come to refine our focus. Contrast is that awareness that helps us know what we want next, based on what we presently have, or wish we had, or don't have. As we review and understand what we have, or what we have created thus far, out of this awareness comes new strivings and new clarity about our next step.

Ideally, this can be seen as no more than a refinement of the results we have already achieved by projecting new clarifying focus. Contrast is the comparison between what we presently have and our next step. It is by the use of contrast that we are able to find our way out of the ooze that nurtures us in such an unusual manner.

The trick is to let go of what we don't want by not including it as part of our new focus. As we have discovered, we create our focus in one of three powerful ways:

- *Resistance to what we don't want* – creating a very powerful focus in another direction (fight or flight type focus), which can still be handy in some cases, i.e., touching a hot stove, etc.
- *Clarity about what we do want, but including a smattering of what we don't want* – focus that includes what we are attempting to push away as well as what we do want (mixed signals).
- *Pure clarity and vision about what we want* – this type of focus has left behind all limitation of what we do not want in our experience.

Contrast is the clarity that allows for the refinement of our focus and the quality of our desires a step at a time, until we reach true clarity. "Out of contrast comes new clarity" is the stepping-stone out of unintentional reality creation. Initially we may have been motivated purely by what we don't want (resistance as focus), which becomes a huge amount of fodder for new decision-making. As we become aware of the differences between what we have and what we want, we begin to reach out for new goals and experiences. While our focus may still be muddled, we continue to refine and reflect and output accordingly. As we become more conscious, we are able to use what we have in our lives for new clarity about our next step. This is the nature of our solutions, and, interestingly enough, again an inside job.

Eventually, we come from pure vision. Focus based on pure vision comes about as we harness the mechanics of creation, as we choose focus and desire aligned with our inner nature and innate signaling processes only. Pure vision is chosen and maintained such that we are in the highest alignment possible for the creation of our realities, and for which enormous insight flows to us from Innate Intelligence.

When we are in alignment with our inner nature, we have access to that pure sense of order that brings clarity to our focus and vision, and our world revolves and evolves a little more to our liking. When our focus and desire is aligned with love and acceptance and neutrality, our realities come to pass much more quickly, and, of course, in a much higher state. We are also much more accepting of others in their capacity to sort this process out for themselves. Alignment with our highest intuitive nature allows us to trust the process we must pass through in our own learning curve and personal healing.

Humanity embroiled in its own survival is one of the most beautiful and adventurous activities we can embrace and support as we come to understand and expand our own nature. Understanding the importance of contrast, combined with an awareness that all must find their own way to their own inner nature, and each in their own time frame, allows a peace and comfort that only the few can know.

What we focus on expands.

Observers Versus Visionaries

Before we move into Allowing and the importance and value of this immutable law, I would like to introduce another concept, an idea so simple that it is easy to overlook. Consider the expression –
    Observers thrive in good times
    And suffer in bad;
    Visionaries thrive in all times.[4]

This is an important and valuable principle. Observers are focusers. Visionaries are focusers. Observers take in and focus on what is happening around them, rightly or wrongly, with an assumption that this simply is the way things are. This is an entirely unconscious approach to focus. They take in what is occurring around them, assume the importance of that reality, (maybe assuming it to be the only reality) and include the information as part of their consciousness, often in support of beliefs that don't really serve them, and rebroadcast it right back out.

From the perspective of assuming an interpretation of reality that is very subject to review, observer focus inadvertently becomes a part of one's makeup and thus one's prayer and output, and detrimentally so. As one assumes the validity of this particular version of "reality," one's focus and output now include this most unfortunate and unconscious outpouring (and re-creation) of creative energy, and hence the merry-go-round continues.

It turns out that we are all producers, we are all creators and we are all visionaries.

The news media focuses on and broadcasts the bulk of its "news" from as unhealthy and sensationalized a perspective imaginable. It is amazing that a population and culture, as sophisticated as we might think we are, would ever allow the most painful and banal of information, largely in the name of advertisers and ratings, straight into the core of our homes, the center of our lives, deeply penetrating our nervous systems. The news services report, time and time again, the most sensational and unhappy trials and tribulations of humanity as if it is entertainment, as if it must be reported, or is worth reporting, or as if it has any redeeming characteristics or useful social implications. What is unconsciously perceived as entertainment by a naïve public, instead wreaks of tragedy, death, destruction, anger vented, and otherwise a whole host of human atrocities and mistreatments of each other.

Though it is true that humanity has a vast preoccupation with death, dying and apparently all forms of destruction, this stream of information focusing on some of the worst atrocities we can perpetrate against each other is of little use for improving one's lot in life. Rarely does the news media report of the successes and sharing and caring found in vastly larger proportions of the human experience. The media will even go to the trouble to import disheartening news from faraway places to fill up their hour or half hour for the purpose of the maintenance of ratings, sensationalism, pain, dislocation of values, etc.

(On the other hand, one can see the slow rise and refinement of life as the human species wrestles with choice, though at a horrendously slow pace. The worst of the lowest common denominator of mankind is broadcast into one's home in the name of entertainment. This is worth a bit of our review and reconsideration.)

This is not about putting our heads in the sand. This is about being selective about what we choose to accept into our nervous systems. This is about choice. We could as easily spend the same time with a book, meditation, hobbies, political activism, gardening, or otherwise becoming intentionally selective with our focus. To assume that the continual broadcast of the worst common denominator of human tragedy is fit for the aspiring nervous system would describe the unconscious observer and the sad state of affairs for many in this day in time.

An observer is not a selective reviewer of life. An observer is one who does not understand the Law of Attraction. An observer does not have intentionality within his/her focus, and certainly no idea why the sights and sounds of the merry-go-round never change, and most certainly, an observer does not have dominion over one's affairs. In an interesting use of an analogy, one might simply switch one's channel – switch one's focus.

A visionary is one who, in becoming selective about focus and input, has learned the importance of choice. A visionary is one who realizes that focus has an enormous impact on the stability and entrainment of our beliefs. As we choose our input, we choose our output. As creators, we cannot afford to build our realities with faulty or poor quality circuitry or vision or input/output, if we expect quality and orderly results.

The programming of the human consciousness/nervous system with a constant bombardment of the frailties of humanity serves only two purposes. First, it reinforces the hopelessness of the worst states of human nature by continually broadcasting pain, death and destruction, for which many still align – keeping us ripe for marketing solutions to what ails us. Two, it provides a stimulation of feeling brought about by the broadcast, such that feelings are generated within our nervous system for which we have little more to do than sit.

This allows the proverbial couch potato to sit in a darkened room with a constant input of sensory information such that the recipient clearly has feelings coursing through his or her nervous system, and of course, no responsibility for what they feel beyond the capacity of the TV remote. This seems to be a type of self-medication that allows us to know that we are alive with the least amount of responsibility and effort possible. Furthermore, this type of artificial focus and poor quality sensory input running through our nervous system disguises and keeps us from the awareness of the subtle voice of our innate messaging system, which is otherwise constantly available to us. It seems that we cannot have both.

We have feelings coursing through our system, reminding us of the inequities of life (shared common ground among observers?), as well as the fact that we have a pulse and that life is going through us, albeit at a very poor level of existence. The quality isn't high, but we are getting feedback that we are alive. It might be concluded that broadcasters (as huge corporations) see humanity as little more than a resource for the purpose of purchasing products beamed to them via bizarre and intellectually barren television and advertisements. It is a very sad state of affairs. Ultimately, we exist for the possibilities and capacities our feelings can bring to us, and, while the size of the possibilities are enormous, a limp heartbeat, a dazed look, and an empty wallet are its opposite extreme.

This brings to mind a song written by Carly Simon in the 1970s titled "Haven't Got Time For The Pain," recounting how, if not for the feelings of pain, she wouldn't even know she was alive "...to survive." But, finally out of contrast, she decided that "...she hadn't the time for the pain." She hadn't the need for the pain, etc. (Suffering was the only thing that made her feel alive.)[5]

Imagine a very powerful and potent visitor from some far and distant world arriving on Earth. Imagine this visitor with no wisdom or sense of truth of its own. Instead, imagine that it no more than a naïve entity with little to go on beyond its capacity to observe. With vast power but no understanding, wisdom, sense of truth or access to Innate Intelligence as a visitor on Earth, how do you think this scenario might turn out?

September 11, 2001, was humanity's biggest cause for introspection ever.

Someone with this sort of enormous power and capacity for observation would soon find themselves powerfully embroiled within the status quo and eventually wondering what is the sense of all of this. Or they might keep absorbing information until they just topple over. That is what happens when Innate Intelligence and the success that is nature is barred from the process that is living and life.

If, on the other hand, a powerful and affluent visitor from another world were to step foot on this planet with all of his or her wisdom intact, how might this turn out differently? Is it possible that this wise one would avoid the travails and confusions of the world he/she alighted onto? Wouldn't the wisdom that had served this individual in his/her advanced culture, serve him/her here?

Wouldn't they know to side-step the typical smorgasbord of confusion and wild array of mass-mind thinking, stay aligned with higher principles and attempt to align with others with corresponding and similar values? How would this entity know what to avoid and what to embrace? Could it be that innate wisdom would be the indicator here? What if the feelings associated with our thoughts gave us all of the information we need to make decisions? What if Innate Intelligence was our always-available partner?

Visionaries create their realities by going forward.

Can we see how by putting our attention in errant focus, this information becomes a part of us, and, accordingly, a part and parcel of our output, and thus our confusing reality? What we focus on expands. We take it in; we carry it around; and, when we let it out, it expands. This is our very nature. We are creators. This is creation and how creation expands. But what actually causes it to expand?

Creation expands because of the interaction of thought with consciousness, intentionally or unintentionally. We think thoughts; thoughts attract more thoughts; and, in the quality of our thought processes, we expand thought and thus creation. And consensus reality is no more than it sounds. What we have in common in our thoughts and realities among us is consensus reality – not as big, or as important, or as powerful as we might think, and, in fact, more poorly held together than we might imagine. But God being a neutral principle, lets us have our own way, with no judgment. Since the bulk of consensus reality is presently held together by unconscious creators, we are in store for vast possibilities as we grow into our wisdom and conscious connection with Source, thoroughly touched on in Chapter 9. There's no doubt about it: Humans create reality, consciously and unconsciously.

Luckily, we are no more dangerous to ourselves than our capacity to think and focus. If our capacity to think is not much more sophisticated than locating the TV remote on the first try, we are in little danger of tipping the world over. On the other hand, as we become more conscious and more accepting of our role in the creation process, our capacity to be effective becomes substantially greater. Again, something about one connected to Source is more powerful than one million who are not.

A Course In Miracles suggests that we are all like windows. As we give up our erroneous beliefs, our windows become clear, and God extends him/herself though us, and thus God and creation (and we) expand. Abraham would say that the non-physical Universe (the realm of God) expands by our capacity to think and to expand thought. As we generate thought, we create reality and Source extends itself and expands. And since Source does not judge, we continue to grow and expand and revise accordingly. Ours becomes only to learn to create responsibly and aligned with what truly works – something we will come to see sooner or later. This is called wisdom; this is called free will; and this is called life and living. This is also our heritage, and somewhere deep within our subconscious, our DNA or elsewhere, this was promised to us.

We, in all of our creative capacity – handicapped by our unconscious awareness of how this works, or enhanced by our connection with Source and higher purpose – spew our focus, and reality is generated and enlarged over and over and over again. Even though observers continue to make up the majority of individuals, observers are generally a naive and irresponsible lot, as they are disconnected from Source to some degree or another. Their "reach" and capacity to create is limited and thus ultimately without solid foundation. Perhaps this is the source of illusion spoken of by mystics and poets past.

Observing what works and focusing on what works brings more of the same. Once we understand this distinction, we will find observation to be the maintenance of what is good in our lives, and vision to be what carries us forward – toward wisdom, our new goals and capacities for higher quality reality. We will also discover the satisfaction of a feeling nature truly in alignment with the cosmos.

Visionaries

Visionaries represent the leading edge of alignment within the human species. All of the producers in society, all of the inventors, scientists and masters at production, as well as the arts and the promoters of human rights, were and are visionaries. Though some may have come from the contrast of what they didn't want, or what they saw as problems or solutions, their focus was on what they did want and what they could do and become. Ultimately, they came to understand the difference. They became <u>un</u>informed as to the daily realities, preferring to listen to themselves aligned with higher purpose, fueling their visions and producing their realities accordingly.

It turns out that we are all producers, we are all creators and we are all visionaries. It is just that some of us produce little of value, being disconnected from Source, while others produce great things and support and generate numerous refinements in society. Of course, the vast lot of us fall somewhere in between, but how do we become more intentional? How do we escape the problems and unhappy reoccurrences of our everyday lives?

What is most interesting about this information is that anybody can become a visionary. Everybody has the same stuff inside, the same circuitry and connection. It is simply a matter of the courage to choose to dig within, to put the garbage aside and become receptive to Innate Intelligence. We all have it within us to hear our subtle inner voice, and as we begin to heed our true nature, we discover our true power and our true calling.

It turns out that visionaries, even though they may use contrast as a springboard for their clarity, create their realities by going forward. Visionaries always have the lead-dog position, happily embracing the horizon and the potential the horizon represents. As it turns out, there is enough Universe, God, time, space and horizon for everyone to be a lead dog. And, it is becoming a well-known fact that an endless loop of mediocrity, though safe, is boring. According to our wiring and the amperage available to us, we are made for much more.

Out of Contrast Comes Clarity

Visionaries have access to unlimited potential and ideas and solutions for a number of reasons. One reason is they have an inexhaustible connection to Source, the repository of unlimited resource and design. For humanity to accept its capacities and potentials, it has to plug in correctly. And plugging in is a matter of accepting our divine heritage and aligning with the sleeping giant (our connection) within. It is the next step in our evolution as a species. Clearly some are discovering their divinity a bit sooner than others, though, at the cusp of the 21st century, we seem to be well on our way.

Conscious connection to Source is the next step in the evolution of the human species.

Visionaries are far more powerful than observers. Not only are visionaries connected to Source, but they are also putting more of their God-given capacities and talents to use. Visionaries understand that contrast (which will always exist in abundance) is no more than insight for springing to another insight, another solution, another exciting and delicious feeling coursing through their inner nature, for which they will always continue to grow and expand.

This is our nature. Contrast will always be with us, and, as we began to get a handle on conscious living, the size of our contrasts become much easier to live with and, ultimately, much more subtle. Always new lessons and new opportunities, but eventually the contrast becomes no more than the distinction between chocolate and vanilla, or the subtleties of the variations of chocolate. At some point, life becomes simply a matter of choice in a very pleasurable and intentional manner – again for which there is no end in sight and increasing joy and satisfaction are the rewards and outpourings.

Conscious connection to Source is the next step in the evolution of the human species. Conscious connection to Source, the new watchword and our most powerful desire and focus, is what makes us intentional as a species. After all, the cars, houses, boats and the airplanes, as well as the multiple and varied extracurricular activities, have their limits in satisfaction and joy. Eventually by trial and error (read: contrast and clarity, and "There's got to be more"), we are, more and more, beginning to refine our thoughts and head toward more important aspects of our lives.

As we began to realize our potential, new goals become the focus of our attention. As we come to discover our connection to Source, our lot in life improves and "others" begin to discover their connection, and even more expansion occurs. This is the very nature of creation and an interesting variation of the Law of Attraction. As new momentum begins individually, momentum begins collectively. Expansion is an ongoing part of life, and we are clearly a part of it.

As we become more conscious, and given a few generations of insight, it will not be long before our motivations begin to take the form of "There's got to be more" in even more subtle and healthier ways. As we continue to refine our alignment with our inner nature, our lives and the planet begin to expand in useful ways we could never imagine!

If the self-medication (including television), the over-reliance on materialism and the misconceptions about success do not bring the desired and corresponding healthy sense of self, then there are only so many variations before we find what truly works. Contrast creates clarity. Trial and error creates clarity. Subtleties of differences create clarity. Eventually, clarity, as focus aligned with inner support, generates a reality that becomes open-ended and our survival moves to the next rung.

The tragedy that is the World Trade Center was the biggest contrast of them all. People are increasingly reviewing their thinking or not thinking, reviewing their focus or their unwillingness to focus, and testing the idea of how much responsibility they each may have contributed to this tragedy. September 11, 2001, was humanity's biggest cause for introspection and its biggest wake-up call ever.

Out of contrast comes clarity. Humanity is, more than ever, clamoring for peace, choosing love, expressing newfound connection and revaluing old connection at new and unprecedented levels. Out of contrast comes clarity. We become more. It is assured.

Humanity is becoming clear about what it wants. Humanity is slowly choosing once again. And this time, at a very important time in the evolution of the species, humanity is beginning to voice "There must be another way" and "There's got to be more." Humanity is beginning to clamor for peace; humanity is beginning to see that force and pushing against, or resistance, is the old way and that according to the Law of Attraction, what we focus on expands. There comes a time when not only individuals, but nations, must move up the evolutionarily ladder and through the doorway that is labeled "courage." And it begins and grows one individual at a time.

When a large enough group becomes aware that something is radically wrong, out of that contrast will come a new clarity, a new vision and a new focus. That new clarity and new focus, aligned with Innate Intelligence, will see humanity learning to solve problems in a new way. Based on the experiences of 9/11 (and more recently Iraq), humanity, in the deepest state of mass introspection ever witnessed on the face of the planet, will learn and decide to make new choices. Humanity is taking one step closer to becoming wise.

CHAPTER EIGHT
ALLOWING

*T*he third immutable and most far-reaching principle is the Law of Allowing. The Law of Allowing becomes available to us upon an understanding of the Law of Attraction and the Law of Deliberate Creation. Allowing is the window and awareness through which all things become possible. Allowing, also known as unconditional love, is the highest condition we can experience. As a motivator and partner to our outpourings, it offers the highest insights, successes and outcomes. Allowing is a principle through which the whole Universe adheres and is the source of order within all worlds. Allowing and acceptance of "what is" glues everything together. All of nature and all of creation move forward based on "what is."

Allowing says that we are able to trust in the order and innate wisdom that is within each and every soul on the planet and within each and every experience or happenstance with which we come in contact. Allowing is predicated upon the awareness that Innate Intelligence and order is everywhere and that it is found within everything. Innate Intelligence can be described as omniscient, omnipresent and omnipotent, a concept often attributed to God and the gods of our lore. Allowing is in alignment with the fact that, ultimately, all is in a very high state of order.

Allowing is the principle that dissolves all obstacles to visionary focus. Allowing is available to anyone choosing alignment, clarity and intentionality as a part of their life and outpouring. As we attract what we have in our lives, allowing becomes the tool that allows us to be receptive to our greater good as we continue to refine who we are and align with innate potential.

Allowing acknowledges a vast order that everyone and everything adheres to whether they are aware of it or not. Allowing includes a recognition that even those who do not know their own best interests live in a world of divine and vast order. Their outcomes are ultimately assured because basic immutable principles are at play. Allowing recognizes free will and that, over a period of time,[1] individuals will gravitate toward what ultimately works best for them. "Allowers" know this.

꘎

Visionaries live within vibratory islands of their ongoing chosen focus.

Trial and error is free will; painful experience is free will; and learning to go with what works is free will. Free will says that we are entitled to as much experimentation and choice as is required for the expansion into our highest feelings of love, peace and joy. In alignment with our inner mechanism, we unfold and expand into our truest success and potential. Our happiness is found and thus becomes assured.

Allowing recognizes that what we have, or are achieving within our own experience, is no better and no worse than what "others" are experiencing or achieving within their own trial-and-error experience. Allowing acknowledges that we see the frailty of being at odds with order. Allowing is the pathway by which we find this order for ourselves.

Allowing does not say that life should look a certain way, that growth should look a certain way, or that anybody will arrive on point, on time or in step based on someone else's time construct or expectation. Allowing knows that each, in partnership with his/her own reality (and contrast), learns to recognize his/her own internal mechanism and eventually takes that final journey toward alignment with true order. Allowing knows this. Acceptance knows this. Visionaries know this.

Visionaries understand the basic principles by which the Universe unfolds. Visionaries selectively include the order, success, strengths and beauty that make up the world around them and make it their own. This is how intentional creators enhance their realities – living within vibratory islands of alignment of their ongoing chosen focus. As we cast our view uphill toward solutions and refine our reliance on Innate Intelligence as we go, we dictate our focus and thus our output, and accordingly, our reality.

Visionaries live within vast order and choose goals aligned with what is true, what can always be relied upon, and a knowledge that all (others) are in their own state of aligning with Source at their own rate of comfort – or discomfort. All is in order, whether we can see it or not. As we find more order in outward appearance, which feeds and strengthens our inner belief system (and vice versa), we find that the Law of Attraction brings more refined order and more refined success to our lives. As we align with Innate Intelligence, one individual becomes more useful to the whole than one million who are not.[2] It is fair to say that the visionary is doing a fine job of supporting those still making their way toward intentionality.

The visionary assumes no responsibility for individuals having difficulty or misfortune as their ally, other than from a sense of the highest order for that individual. As one focuses on the disability of another, one's focus shifts to the problem, which does no more than support the perceived powerlessness of that individual. Visionaries know the wholeness and order that abounds within every individual, every circumstance and every opportunity. Visionaries anchor and bring order to the world.

Trial and error has served us for so very long. As we begin to wonder, as we become ready for more, as we search for more and as we begin to become specific about wanting alignment in our lives, the teacher shows up. The Universe always extends a hand when the student is ready. And, as we are all students, it is for the teacher (Innate Intelligence), not the student, to decide the lesson plan.

It is interesting to note that as we discover the usefulness of alignment with higher order, our vibratory capacity to create begins to shift. In our newfound capacity for reality creation, much of the old begins to slip away. As we learn to unfold our potential, the road that rises up to meet us contains less and less of the misfortunes of the world, for we are no longer a vibrational match. The world becomes more of our making and allowing becomes much easier.

We must judge for ourselves whether we are more effective in following our inner bidding toward higher alignment with Source, or by turning our attention to the less fortunate, who are actually creators learning the ropes for themselves at their own pace.

Namasté

A visionary holding a vision of vast order and living his/her life accordingly provides a far better solution than one bending over to look at another's stubbed toe or bruised ego, or competing with one arguing for what is right or wrong. The importance of only acknowledging what is true about another is a fundamental lesson taught by numerous ancient masters. Acknowledgment of only the divine, the true and the "still, small voice" aspect of the individual continues to be the only true service we can offer another.

And, as we learn to see the truth of our surroundings, we continue to refine our own vibrational nature. What we focus on expands. Discordant energies and experiences tend to be fewer and subtler in distinction, until they no longer exist as a part of our reality.

Namasté is an ancient Hindu expression and greeting that says it all. Namasté says, "The divinity in me salutes the divinity in you," or "The God-part of me acknowledges the God-part of you." This is the highest order of service one can offer another – to have purity of thought and highest acknowledgment about another. A visionary only knows and sees the highest and the best in each direction he or she looks. This is true service to mankind. This is true allowing, this is true trust and this is true knowing. This is unconditional love.

This is acceptance of the order that exists within everything. Being clear and staying clear, being true and staying true is the process; and knowing that everyone else is doing the same to the best of their ability is the solution. This is the highest vision we can offer to each other. True strength

All is in order, whether we can see it or not.

and clear vision become powerful resources of the visionary and the world becomes a better place.

Chaos is Order

Consider the concept of chaos. Chaos is loosely defined as "a lack of order," or "no discernable pattern" to an event. But what has been discovered in the study of chaos is that as we refine our perspective, as we have access to more information and more of an overview, we find order that we were once unable to perceive. As our perception enlarges, we find order where once it did not exist. This is because order abounds at all levels of existence once we have the eyes to see.

Imagine looking at a large painting covered by a piece of cardboard with a one-inch square opening. The cardboard can be slid over the painting, but only one-inch of the color and texture of the painting is available at a time. By observation, the information available would produce little clue as to the overall intent of the artist or medium, or possibly even that it was a painting. This would fit the definition of chaos: something little understood with no discernable pattern.

But, by the removal of the cardboard covering, we can view the entire painting, from which suddenly appear clearly organized patterns of thought, perhaps beauty, and certainly a complete message. What appears to be chaotic by one method of perception becomes order by another. There is a similar analogy about a number of blind men each experiencing a different part of an elephant and reporting back from their limited perspectives. Such is life for many.

Acknowledgment of the divine is the only true service we can offer another.

Perspective that does not recognize the true order of things sees individuals and a world view described as chaotic. To the untrained eye, the world can seem to be made up of undesirable, indefinable and painful patterns, such that no overall assumption or comfort can be established – and no assurances that life is in order, or can be assumed to be in order. Until we look at the painting as a whole, until we see the world in a larger perspective, chaos seems to reign. As we become aware of a larger context, we begin to see patterns and order where they once did not exist.

The visionary sees inherent order in all things. By a reoccurring substantiation of order, the visionary continues to build a vibratory output and vision that refines reality creation, ad infinitum. Allowers do the same thing. By recognition of the fundamental order of things, allowers begin the powerful experience of allowing their realities as they envision more refined interpretations of what they wish for their lives. Allowers trust their outcomes knowing that, ultimately, their vision and the Law of Attraction will carry them through. Visionaries and allowers both know that, as their perception becomes more refined, the order of the cosmos becomes more apparent in their lives.

Receptivity comes from trust, and trust comes from knowing. Trust becomes available as we discover the innateness that is everything. As we come to rely upon a conscious awareness of deliberate creation in concert with allowing, our lives expand in a progressive manner. By an awareness of the size of the order of things, we bask in harmony, peace and abundance.

The earliest photos of Earth had a huge impact on the population of our planet. One of the most published photos of all time is one taken by the Apollo 17 astronauts en route to the Moon in December 1972.[3] The photo identified the incredible beauty and order that our planet truly represents and brought new definition and clarity to the fledgling holistic and environmental communities. Clearly, this first view of ourselves brought new awareness to us as a species. We were reminded that we are each part of a very beautiful, seemingly fragile (but actually very tenacious) and awesome larger whole. We began to understand a bit more about ourselves.

As our capacity for perception shifts and grows, we become better able to glimpse new awareness about ourselves and each other. As our perceptions about ourselves becomes more whole, we become better caretakers of each other and the planet. It is our very nature to grow and expand, and in our envisioning and discovery, we fulfill our potential to become more.

As we learn to shift our gaze, we discover that vast order and allowing are the underlying principles of all of life's expansion. As creators, we become a bridge, spewing newfound order and comfort and ease for ourselves and our brothers. This allows us the comfort of further nestling into immutable principles, further setting us free to pursue our own individuality without the constraints of an unhealthy concern for our fellowman. This is part of our evolution. We know all is in order. We know who we are.

We find that our capacity for acceptance and allowing extends to our neighbor and our neighbor's neighbor. Allowing breaks the focus of absorbing less than useful information about each other. It does this and so much more. By embracing what is true and what is real without regard to appearance, we find ourselves truly of value to others as humanity slowly pulls itself out of its primordial ooze. Allowing becomes a part of our own vibration, offering us a propellant for our own individuality and adventurous nature as visionaries and intentional creators.

Once we begin to grasp the order that life represents, we better understand choice. We could tend to the less fortunate, which we all do in some manner, or we can make our way out of the ooze of the beliefs and culture that our predecessors so unceremoniously dumped at our feet. Though this all has been a culmination of the eventuality of humanity spying the gold ring, it still takes a shedding of our past conditioning and failed belief systems to successfully reach out to "where no man has gone" – to what is true. To identify our true nature and live truly is the most important support we can offer each other. The only way we can do it, though, is to do it for ourselves first. Allowing is the key and the gateway to having more, individually and collectively.

Though it is initially perceived as selfish to look first to one's own good, alignment with innate principles is the most effective method of supporting the still-slumbering crowd, the semi-conscious population and especially those individuals making their way toward alignment. It is important that individuals migrate toward consciousness and dominion over their own affairs. They are then able to be of more help to those who follow.

It will be discovered that the best support for those who follow is for visionaries to complete their alignment first. As the ranks of the informed grow, it becomes easier for those embroiled in struggle and defeat to find relief and eventual direction. For, as the visionary takes in order and spews order, this is felt by the still small voice and the still-slumbering mass. As news of the inward journey begins to stir and is perceived as safe, more will join the experience. If one wanted to change the world, it would be found to be an inside job, first individually, and then collectively.

Allowing in combination with the never-failing Law of Attraction has a multitude of uses, and, among others, represents the manner by which we –

As our perception becomes more whole, we become better caretakers of the planet.

- escape our (karmic) creations based on unconscious observation – representing a mindset of humanity possibly over multiples of lifetimes;
- escape our unconscious or habitually held belief spewing – often sourced many generations old; and
- escape our resistance to Innate Intelligence and our fear of becoming personally powerful and responsible.

Resistance

We are creators whether we know it or not, and immutable principle is always turned on, whether we know it or not. As we come to understand the Law of Attraction and its deliberate use, we suddenly have a vast tool for understanding how our individual realities are created and thus powered. We discover that what we have in our lives is a matter of what we broadcast, inadvertently or intentionally, unconsciously or consciously. We continuously generate and reap the results of our realities.

Allowing includes the discovery that we have been resisting information that is constantly being introduced to us from Source. In our opposition to acceptance and allowance, we wall ourselves off from the very thing that is our most important ally.

For the sake of a simple experiment, make a fist and hold it in front of you. Slowly make your fist tighter, and imagine it similar to your resistance to unsatisfactory realities, fear of the unknown or the attempt to push away what you don't want in your life. Imagine your fist as a representation of yourself walled up and hardened against what you don't know about life, its intricacies and its sublime order. Now imagine that good prevails, imagine that order prevails – the same order that can be found amongst the stars, as well as within the finest particles of matter. Imagine the only thing that keeps you from enjoying all that Innate Intelligence has for you is your focus as resistance. Now, imagine relaxing your fist and feeling the experience of allowing.

We have a vast tool for understanding how our individual realities are created and thus powered.

Imagine realizing that the Universe, the order and the good that is all-pervasive, has always had slight pressure against your skin. Imagine that by releasing resistance, order begins to flow into your body, albeit consciously. Imagine understanding that the Universe has always been there with insight and direction, and that by your choice of alignment with Source and your new insight, the healing process and the journey within can finally begin.

Imagine that God or Source or Infinite Intelligence has always been pressing against you in the subtlest manner, attempting to feed you life-giving information about yourself and your capacity for creation. Realize that in your resistance to what you didn't understand, you were also missing information and insight available from Source. Now adjust the picture and instead imagine this information coming from inside of you, and, suddenly, you have the whole picture.

Yet again, this is the proverbial last place we look. Our bodies are our temples. Our bodies are our connection with the Infinite. We have to look no further than our own innate natures for our solutions!

Understand that resistance is powerful focus and that resistance as focus brings the same results time and time again. It is in the breaking of this endless loop of unsatisfactory outcomes that we escape our poorly formed focus and our karma. Imagine the awareness of what doesn't work being turned toward what does work. Imagine relaxing. Feel the warmth and comfort and relief with the added realization that Innate Intelligence is always with you and has always been with you.

Realize that in resisting our own unconscious creations, we are also resisting the signaling and messaging Innate Intelligence has for us. Imagine realizing there is no evil – only our own "miscreating," doubt and fear. Imagine learning how to relax and let go. Imagine feeling free. Imagine the deeply felt joy and the peace of the Universe flowing through your nervous system. Now, imagine becoming receptive to the orderliness and infinite insight that is available to you.

Loving Our "Miscreations"

As we begin to understand that we are the source of all of our possibilities, we begin to understand the power, authority and capacity that is available to us. Typically, we are all in resistance to a number of things, not the least of which is our power and potential for power, our capacity for creation and potential for "miscreation."[4] And remember, our capacity for miscreating is insignificant compared to our capacity for creating once we become aligned to Innate Intelligence and Source. Our capacity for miscreating is without the exponential multiplier of the power of the Universe at our side. Miscreating is certainly nothing to fear. With just the barest of subtleties for listening, we can access a flawless messaging system telling us of the quality of our alignment with nature – for which our power to create grows exponentially.

It is by an understanding that we, and no other, are the source of our realities that first gives us the insight that it is safe to give up resistance and instead allow our miscreations as we begin to turn our lives around. It is in our capacity for acceptance that we learn to allow our errant thought processes and beliefs as we move toward higher ground. This is how we escape the merry-go-round effect. The solution is the opposite of resistance and fear and doubt. It is the process of accepting our reality creation as the best we have been able to do thus far. It is the process of aligning with Innate Intelligence that propels us to the positive side of the equation, which we have been attempting for so very long without a manual.

It is the most powerful experience any of us can have – to learn to love what we once hated, feared or loathed. As we begin to understand the creation process – to love, to trust and allow our creations and miscreations – we begin to find ourselves in a capacity to allow others their own idiosyncratic capacities to create and miscreate. It turns out we are all in the same boat. We all learn by trial and error. Once we begin to understand this, allowing becomes a very powerful and useful tool.

For some, allowing appears as forgiveness; for others, it is unconditional love; and for even others, simple acceptance will do. Any way we look at it, allowing is the method by which we escape the monkey barrel of naiveté we are all a part of as neophyte creators on planet Earth. Love, forgiveness and acceptance are our most valuable tools as we look at the objects of our attention with an awareness that everything really is in order.

Initially this can be a bumpy ride, but one well worth the results. There is a great deal of momentum and habitual belief behind unconscious creating that we can harness for better use in our lives. As we apply allowing and acceptance to our existing experiences, we begin to escape the merry-go-round effect. It is within this small application of acceptance that we begin to turn our lives around, and the world becomes a better place.

Unconscious creating provides us with valuable contrasts (hints) to help us to clarify our focus toward new clarity and newfound awareness. Conscious visioning begins by first revaluing what we resist, thereby bringing us closer to what we prefer in our lives. Initially with baby steps, and with allowing and acceptance at our side, we begin the migration toward greener pastures. Our poorly created and ill-conceived realities fade as we put our time and attention to allowing what we are presently experiencing, while at the same time, visioning toward what we wish for ourselves. By listening to Innate Intelligence, we are guided to refine our vision, creations and outcomes. Out of unconscious creating comes conscious creating. Out of mistaken assumptions come new perceptions, and out of trial and error and contrast we become more intentional, individually and as a species.

It turns out that "tech support" has been with us all along.

Loving Ourselves

According to the mystics, prophets and poets of our past, love is an inside job. The key to unconditional love is to learn to love our creations and to love ourselves and "others" just as they are. But, before we can love "others," we must learn to love ourselves, i.e., we must learn to respect ourselves. We must also learn to love and trust the process. As lower-octave creators miscreating and missing the mark[5] in sometimes startling fashion, it is hard to have respect for ourselves as we review the emotional carnage, disappointment and confusion we may have left in our trial-and-error experiences. It is enough to make one angry or frustrated!

It is hard to love ourselves when we don't respect ourselves. It is hard to love the world when we see it as dysfunctional, angry and hateful. And, if we can't love our creations and we can't respect who we are, we lose sight of our capacity to love others. As we learn from our struggles, we learn to love others. After all, we are all beginners at this.

Love is a matter of respect for ourselves and each other. As we review our past, we learn that we are all getting our acts together at our own speed and clarity. We are entitled to as many mistakes as it takes to get it right. It is not acceptable to judge others while we are still judging ourselves. When we no longer judge ourselves and instead allow, we develop the capacity to trust each other. This, then, becomes a substantial feather in our cap – and, silently, a feather in their cap.

Interestingly, love is all there is, and love (acceptance) is something we must first apply to ourselves and our creations. Why? Because it is the easiest way to learn to accept the world we live in. As we learn how to turn our lives around and as we learn the mechanics of reality creation, we gain perspective about the world around us. We are all very much the same – though it seems we learn at different speeds. Everything is an act of creation; everything is an act of expansion; everything is an act of brotherhood; and everything is an act of love and understanding. Our creations are little and insignificant and do little real damage. Or we are powered by the forces of God, and nature and Innate Intelligence, and thus, we are more useful to the whole.

When we are aligned with the full favor and force of Universal Forces, we have a major tiger by the tail.

We are creators, and we are spewers of life, sometimes better and sometimes not so good – but this is what we do! Only in acceptance of our past do we gain the freedom to choose again and move toward that visionary mode of creating with intentionality and alignment to what is true and what is right. With the simple act of allowing, we begin the pathway of becoming true lovers of life and true lovers of "others." Otherwise, we are in resistance, and we push against what we perceive as wrong or dangerous. To know the difference is very powerful indeed.

As we learn to become broadcasters aligned with true focus and true vision, our worlds take on new and heightened meaning. Love is acceptance; love is knowing that all is in its rightful place; and love is knowing that we are on the track of refinement in our lives. Love is seeing that our creations are good (even the ones that need work) and that all of our creations are in alignment with nature's bigger picture. Love is realizing that everyone else's creations are good, no matter where they find themselves on the evolutionary scale of practice. Love is seeing the synchronicity and harmony that unfolds as our creations expand and meet with other like-minded creations and qualities of intent. Such is the way of the Universe as we become aligned with unconditional love. This is how we create new worlds.

Amperage

One of the more interesting aspects of allowing is our capacity to allow Innate Intelligence to flow through our nervous systems. When we are aligned with the full favor and force of Universal Forces, we have a major tiger by the tail. The potential for unspeakable joy, aliveness and love becomes a true portal for discovering the power of our connection with Source. It is in the creation process, brought to its highest and finest order, that we find our niche that is the connection of the Cosmos and the inhabitants of Earth.

As we experience the exhilaration life has to offer, we discover what it is like to be the descendents of God/Source. This is the true importance of allowing – allowing ourselves to open up to the love, generosity and definition of life flowing through our bodies and our lives. There are quiet rumors that we, as spiritual beings, have come to Earth for precisely this experience, one for which the outcome can only can be speculated.

As we come to understand the higher-octaves of life, we realize that we are the most sophisticated vessel ever created for the throughput experience of creation flowing into existence. Being the intermediary in this process pales against the perceived hardships of escaping our primordial ooze. There is nothing more joyous, for which our feelings and nervous system are the avenue, than being in alignment with Source and synonymous with creation – no "ifs, ands or buts."

Allowing and acceptance is the way out of the human dilemma. As humanity discovers alignment with Innate Intelligence, our capacity to evolve toward more order continues to be assured. It is our very nature to evolve toward more order; after all, order is everywhere. We see that, in addition to turning around our own internal mechanism to a more useful good, allowing begins the process of breaking down the separation that holds us one against each other in interpretations of grudges, fears, doubts, anger and resentment.

By the revitalization of our own misguided use of immutable principle, we learn how to view others in a similar light. Visionaries know this, and the soon-to-be-conscious beings glimpse this. We are all one. We all have the same mechanisms and search for truth packed away within us – all of us. The bigger the issues – the larger the trial and error and pain and anguish, and the larger the turnaround.

Humanity will soon realize the importance of allowing, not only for ourselves and our outcomes, but also for those we presume not to understand. Our world will, sooner than we think, move toward a trust of each other's lesson-learning processes, knowing that all is in complete order and that all will come full circle. Humanity will discover its humaneness, and, in this discovery, see life as a very powerful and fulfilling experience. Do not underestimate a small percentage of humanity connected to Source. One thousand connected to Source is more powerful than one billion who are not.

As an "allower," as an acceptor and as a visionary, one is doing far more for the advancement of life on this planet than can be readily explained. It is important to hold our vision and alignment with Innate Intelligence on behalf of those who do not yet understand. To align with Innate Intelligence and continue to refine our lives, to see the connection and true part of the other individual – this is more powerful than we know.

As intentional, powerful, purposeful spewers of good, truth and knowingness walking about on planet Earth – not fixing anyone, not saving anyone and just being true to one's alignment with Source – it is a good use of our time.

CHAPTER NINE
INTENT

NOTE: We have (somewhere) discerned the differences between feelings and emotions. Emotions are personal and generated based on one's beliefs, perceptions or sense of outward appearance. Feelings are communications from Innate Intelligence.

*A*s we become aware of our capacity to create, we discover the importance of our underlying intent as a portion of our output. As we understand what generates and motivates reality creation, we realize that the quality of intent underlying our thoughts gives us clues as to our capacity to create more capably and effectively. We discover that, by knowing the quality of our underlying intent, we are able to create more in sync with the Universe, more in sync with order, more in sync with harmony and more in sync with others.

As we become more conscious (discovering what works), we see that focus and thought engendered by higher quality intent seems to gain us a more sophisticated response from Universal Forces and Source. For just as individuals motivated by anger, revenge, shame or pride, create from their focus and underlying intent, visionaries create from their underlying intent, as well. Luckily, while the individual motivated by the lower range of emotions has minimal support, the visionary has untold access to the authority and success that is the Universe and its pathways, i.e., through the characteristics of his or her underlying intent. There is a distinct correlation between the quality of our focus, the quality of our intent and the results we achieve in our lives.

Conveniently, not being aligned with higher purpose, i.e., the continuum that is the evolution and success and expansion of consciousness on this planet and elsewhere, minimizes our capacity to create effectively and thus truly distort our growth as a species. For if we are at odds with the nature and direction of Universal Forces and Source, our wings are clipped, so to speak. Creation of this sort comes only at the expense of great energy and high maintenance, not to mention wear and tear on the human circuitry and psyche. Though one's capacity for creation contains the Law of Attraction, it lacks the exponential progression and magnification made available to individuals moving in alignment with a bigger picture. Without true alignment to Universal Forces, we evolve and revolve upward very slowly. The Universe is but minimally at our side.

The quality of our reality creation is a matter of the quality of our underlying intent.

This is why the concept of evil as a power and authority does not exist and cannot exist other than as man-made shortcomings and outpourings. Evil is at odds with the fundamental nature of how the Universe grows and expands. This is why we don't see graffiti chiseled into our most beautiful mountain ranges, trees growing in grotesque manners of perversion or angry symbolism in nature. If good and evil were equally powered by Universal Forces in the world as we know it, we would be very well aware of it indeed. We would see there is no rhyme or reason to existence and that all is but a massive and endless struggle. We would find the Universe's sophistication to be no more than a mirror image of our own present time-limited capacity for outcomes, and this is simply not the case. The Universe is incapable of supporting principles at odds with success, expansion and the order of life, other than in the most minimal of terms.

Focus aligned with higher quality intent engenders a great deal of support and feedback from Universal Forces. As the motivation behind focus improves, objectives have more alignment with the Universe's expansion. As we become more of a match and partner with the Universe, we find ourselves very well-plugged in, indeed. Whatever promotes the true expansion and expression that is life and order is supported by the Universe and supported by it proportional to its quality. Anchored and motivated by the values of unconditional love, acceptance and trust, we operate with significantly greater support than one motivated by pride, anxiety, martyrdom or fear. Ultimately, this is the key to our freedom and the freedom of the species.

Universal Formula

Thought generated by higher-octaves of intent has a much more refined capacity to travel the Universal neural networks, pathways and byways that make up Universal Mind. The higher and more refined the frequency of our intention, the deeper into the Universe our thoughts are propelled as our focus gains considerably more Universal "audience". The better carried our thoughts into the realms of Source, the more capably the Universe responds and matches our output in a cohesive, congruent and altogether beyond our own imaginings manner.

Imagine the Universe as the body of God (or the mind of God), or as a scientific principle or formula. Imagine it as a series of concentric circles of vibration, with the most powerful at the center. According to the Law of Attraction, what we output is what we get back; the Universe matches us. Therefore, someone aligned with anger or resentment has weak propulsion for alignment with a minimal portion, or the outwardmost circles, of the formula that is Universal Law. One would achieve a limited amount of useful correspondency and effect. As we more thoroughly align with the principles by which the Universe extends and expands, we have considerably more "audience," and thus substantially more depth, correspondence and insight from Universal Forces.

In its own conscious, crystalline clarity and underlying capacity for intent, the tomato seed aligns with Innate Intelligence and produces precise and far-reaching results. The apple tree, with its flawless built-in intent, aligns with Universal Forces and consistently produces apples. The Universe feeds them each at their own clarity, capacity and intent. So, too, with humans, we have the innate capacity within us to align and thus interact with Universal Forces at a very sophisticated level of existence.

Can we see that this Universal formula, this pattern of orderliness and success, this principle of life (referenced as a disgruntled God for so many hundreds of years) is about growth and our capacity for free will and what we can make of ourselves? Can we see this Universal formula is about expansion – expansion that is God, the Universe and life in all of its clarity and ongoingness? Can we see that, as human beings, we, are the most far-flung interpretation of life's expansion and that we are endowed with free will, the capacity for trial and error and, ultimately, the success of intentional access to Innate Intelligence as our compass and our partner? Can we see that we are the most refined vehicles of life's expansion and that all we have to do is accept our capacities, potentials and support, and adventure out? It is simply a matter of alignment with Universal Forces, for which intent plays an inestimable part.

Ultimately, humanity will prove to be more than from which it springs. Nature is our springboard, our loam, our nutrient-rich good earth, from which we ultimately expand and become and join with the star-makers. More than likely, it will turn out that we are members of a family and part of a brotherhood who are, in fact, the star-makers and the creators of galaxies and more. It is likely we will find we have peers once we grow up. As an up-and-coming species, we will discover that we are little more than the difference between two varieties of apples, or the difference between apples and oranges, but far more similar than we might expect. After all, the Universe is a very ancient place, and, at our young age, we simply don't yet have the eyes to see. There is far more to life than we know.

As the most sophisticated (local) recipients of the formula that is expansion, we come to understand our role in creation, with our creations mirroring and mimicking our growth. Albeit, initially by trial and error and more capably as we learn, acquire and sense the order of things, we continue to refine our intent and our outpourings. Thus, the Universe expands as we continue to refine ourselves over and over again.

The higher and more refined our intention, the deeper into the Universe our thoughts are propelled.

All is in order, and it is by our free will that we return home, having expanded order in our own way, individually and as a species. And only through trial and error do we return home after having successfully magnified ours and the Universe's existence as well.

We are surrounded by life. Everything is life, and everything is in a state of creation and "ongoingness." Even decay is creation because it comes from fundamental order that is expanding and cycling back to where it came from and expanding yet again. For humans to assume they are any less is a lack of perception and awareness of the fundamental order of things, large and small. This is the nature of our nature. We are interpretations of life becoming more life, becoming conscious and adding to the whole. We are a part of the order of things.

Can we imagine a formula that truly gives to each, according to his/her wishes, capabilities and intent, and no more and no less? Can we imagine giving a baby a sharp knife? It will never happen. Nobody gets more than they can handle, according to the fundamentals of the Law of Attraction. We are limited in our experiences by the capacities and qualities of our output and perspective or lack thereof. Our lessons, created by what we resist, are safely put in front of us by us. As we slowly advance, more consciously, and then faster and faster, we come to understand the Law of Allowing, the Law of Attraction, the Law of Deliberate Creation and conscious intent.

We learn to align the quality of our wishes with the principles of Innate Intelligence and find ourselves creators in a world of vast order, empowered by expansion and wisdom, and carrying on the work of Universal Forces. As we rise to the occasion and become partners with Source, we come into our power – our true and vast power – something that is innate. This is the promise of our heritage and of the mystics, prophets and poets of ages past. We have a divine aspect that is only limited by our unconscious awareness and lack of use of what is available to us.

Make no mistake about it: We live in a dynamic, ever expanding and ever increasing rhythm that is life's expression. We are an inestimably important and unique cog in Creation's expansion. And, in the nature of free will and trial and error, and in alignment with intent, wisdom and an awareness of fundamental principles, we learn to take our rightful place as spewers of creation without limitation. We come to experience the true power that our systems are capable of delivering, and we become more. For, after all, at some point it only becomes a matter of choice between refinement and more refinement, joy and more joy, and adventure and more adventure.

The quality of our output is clearly the source of our circumstances.

Synchronicities

The higher the quality of intent, the more sophisticated the response from nature and nature's system of success. The Universe's capacity to respond to higher-octave intent fills in the details and "leapfrogs" our creations into still greater creations and synchronicities. Ultimately, this can be seen as a geometric progression and harmonious outpouring that has to be experienced to be believed. Similar to a pebble thrown into a quiet pond with the exponential and concentric ripple effect capable of continuing on and on, much of the subtleness of the Universe's response and insight remains unseen. And, of course, the appearance of synchronicities and coincidences are vivid indicators of the Universe in action – echoes of an interactive Universe.

Dr. Hawkins' Map of Consciousness

As we refine our capacity to create and align with nature and the rhythm that is the Universe, we discover how very much we are capable of being on track. Accessing synchronicities, coincidences, happenstances and serendipitous outflowings to light our way is only the beginning. As our thoughts and desires generate higher and finer feelings, we find ourselves living within heightened experiences and senses of well-being.

Dr. David R. Hawkins, M.D., Ph.D., and author of one of the more exciting and compelling books on consciousness titled *Power vs. Force*, has clearly identified the Universe's capacity to respond to higher quality intent.

Undoubtedly there is a pecking order to thought and quality of intent, and thus reality creation! Dr. Hawkins, a psychiatrist, researcher, director of the Institute for Advanced Theoretical Research and past co-author with Linus Pauling, has used kinesiology (muscle testing) for more than 20 years to research and extensively delve into the inner-workings of Universal Forces and their obvious hierarchy. Much of this research is published as *Power vs Force* (1995), *The Eye of The I* (2001), and most recently, *I: Reality and Subjectivity* (2002). One of the many things he has discovered and carefully documented is that consciousness can be mapped and gradated on a scale between 0 and 1,000, with guilt and shame at one end and the states of joy and enlightenment at the other.

According to Dr. Hawkins, man's drives and desires, based on the low end of his "Map of Consciousness," engender "attractor fields" that have weak continuity and connection with Source (similar to the earlier concentric circle example). As we climb the Map of Consciousness, we find Innate Intelligence much more able to align with our capacity to create (attract) and bring about harmonious outpourings and expansion into our lives. As we select our thoughts, our focus and our prayer, we find the underlying quality of intent (attractor fields) playing a tremendous part in the quality, stability and far-reaching characteristics of that which unfolds in our lives.

(Dr. Hawkins' Map of Consciousness is unavailable for reprinting. A quick review would indicate the lower states of humanity are rated between 0 and 175 and include the underlying qualities of intent of shame, guilt, apathy, grief, fear, anger, guilt, pride, etc. The break-even point at 200 [labeled courage] allows access to the mid states of neutrality, willingness, acceptance, reason, love, joy, peace, etc., falling between 200 and 700. And the states of enlightenment range between 700 and 1,000.[1] The map is available in his books and through his Web site at www.veritaspub.com.)

As we create with higher-quality intent, we align with Source in a geometrically progressive manner, for which our creations are significantly more powerful, fast approaching, far-reaching and stable. This higher quality alignment with Source also brings considerable awareness of nature jockeying "reality" about to best suit our needs, for which we have devised terms such as coincidences, serendipitous events, synchronicities, etc.

It is the author's intent to introduce principles by which deeply felt order, synchronicities and harmonious outpourings become a major attestation to the quality of our lives. Needless to say, synchronicities are reflections of nature putting our best interests in the right place at the right time, for which our allowing perceptual lenses play an ever-increasing role.

We find intention and desire powered by the lesser quality attractors (below 200) orchestrating minimal, if not painful though necessary results; hence the term "unconscious" versus "conscious." The quality of our output is clearly the source of our circumstances. On the other hand, reality as we know it is much more delicate than we might expect because we have poured it forth based on the minimum standards for producing reality.

Nothing outside of us matters in comparison to our alignment with the mechanism within.

Reality built with weak intent (attractor fields of fear, anger or pride, i.e., below 200), is minimally effective, minimally purposeful and minimally life-sustaining. Furthermore, this sort of reality is minimally held together as compared to nature's standard for gluing reality together. If it weren't for the observational aspect and endless loop scenario common to our everyday existence, these poor quality realities would readily fade back to dust as they meet only the barest minimums of life and existence. In other words, Source supports these weak attractor fields and corresponding results at the barest levels as we maintain and "support" these realities by our inadvertent "observer" status as fledgling creators. We create the vast bulk of our realities with unconscious intent, unconscious consent and poor quality habitually held beliefs and attitudes.

As we learn to refine our existence aligned with Source, our foundations become strong, our realities cohesive, and our successful growth assured. It is to be expected that our capacity to create would be initially a bit wobbly in our trial-and-error approach to existence, but this is how everything begins. As we learn to refine the creation process, we rise above belief systems that no longer serve us. As we learn "to get it right," our creations become stronger and more useful to us and the whole. This would be similar to the earliest building blocks of bricks of mud, which evolved to bricks of straw and mud, and then stone and mortar, and eventually concrete and steel. In a similar manner, we continue to refine our processes. Finally, in our expansion and alignment with Universal Forces, our realities and building blocks begin to be built with a truly high quality adhesive and binder – Innate Intelligence and Source.

To heal the planet, we have to have the courage to look at things in a new way.

As humanity achieves the state of courage (an attractor field rating of 200 and where much of the world is barely poised)[2] and neutrality (rating of 250) and head toward allowing and acceptance (rated at 350), humanity begins to source Innate Intelligence as the "active" ingredient in its creations. Cosmic glue becomes an indispensable part of our reality creation. As we climb the scale of Dr. Hawkins' attractor fields, the Universe is much more capable of responding to the progression of our own individual and collective capacities to create. And, as our capacity for creation far exceeds our present capacity for perception, we have a great deal in store for us. As we build our focus with devotion to higher ideals and alignment with Source, we create a better and richer world for ourselves and, of course, our progeny. Such is the way of the individual and, ultimately, the masses, during the cusp of the 21st century.

Allowing

As we come to understand the importance of the quality of intent we infuse into our focus and capacity to create, we discover that allowing becomes more available to us. As we climb the continuum that is conscious intentionality, we draw realities and outcomes that are more comfortable and easier "to live with." Allowing becomes a more easily used, readily available and better understood tool as we take charge of our reality creation. Allowing becomes something we are better able to ease into as we become more intentional in our affairs.

On the other hand, one without the benefit of conscious intent and its growing influence may initially find allowing similar to attempting to withstand the impact of the proverbial "Mack truck," for which the results are relatively assured. Unaccustomed to creating with useful intentionality, sudden attempts at allowing are not an easy task. The old momentum must be tamed; the old momentum must be allowed; and the old momentum must be realigned, for which quality of intent is the key. As we learn of the characteristics of intentionality combined with allowing and unconditional love, we find ourselves on a pathway leading toward a partnership with Universal Forces, as well as a resultant harmony and order for which we will never turn back.

As we become aware of how to create better-quality realities by harnessing the quality of our intent, we create realities that are much easier to get along with and much easier to allow. Hence, our comfort as reality creators begins to grow. This is the beginning of real and lasting change, visionary focus and the capacity for which we are most helpful to others, as we leave seemingly invisible tendrils of leadership in what were once murky waters. For, as we learn to create from a higher perspective, our capacity to allow grows dramatically. As we learn to "plug in," we are far more useful to ourselves and the whole than we might ever have guessed. Life gets easier, and life gets better.

As we acquire higher qualities of intent, we are able to further align with Universal Forces. In partnership with Innate Intelligence and our messaging system as feedback, we refine our capacity to create reality. We thrive, and unconditional love becomes easier to acquire, maintain and foster. As we learn to refine our nature with quality intent, train wrecks and "Mack truck" scenarios become a thing of the past.

Many of us live in worlds of painful reality, because we have not yet discovered how to listen to and partner with Innate Intelligence. We don't realize that we hold ourselves in our own diminishment, or that to escape mediocrity is to accept that we are always creating and that we simply need to review our existing realities with a bit more love, care and intentionality. Lift-off is little more than loving what we presently have, allowing us the intellectual freedom to escape resistance and move toward our visionary mode. It is from this visionary mode that all useful creating begins and that allowing becomes truly available, and we gain new momentum for ourselves and those we intentionally or inadvertently touch.

We have to accept the fact that our "best until now" creating has only brought us to the point of clarity that there has to be more and that digging around and continually rearranging our present experiences offers but the least of solutions. We have come to realize that this process of contrast and newfound clarity is a part of the mix of becoming more intentional and more conscious. We make great strides as intentional creators in alignment with Universal Forces, for which we leave subtle trails of leadership[3] for those who follow.

Nobody ever told us how powerful we are, and nobody ever told us to be careful with our capacity to create. Nobody ever told us how powerfully we can "miscreate," or that recognition of the source of the problem (ourselves) is the beginning of the solution. And the true beginning of getting a handle on intentional creating is to recognize and welcome the significance and the authority of our miscreating. We now know where our realities come from, and we now know how we hold them together. We also know how to let them go.

Welcoming our miscreations and embracing them as brothers, teachers and feedback while accepting that we are doing the best we can, is the beginning of intention, power and success in our lives. It turns out that love is the answer – just as has always been suggested – and few have taken to heart or intellect thus far. Allowing and loving our creations, allowing and loving others their creations and miscreations, is the solution to having more in our lives. By giving others (and ourselves) the benefit of the doubt as we move along our compendium of growing experience, we discover opportunities and applicability for the experiences of unconditional love. We discover a means of participating in the experience that is the potential quality of life available on Earth, for which we are all a part.

Eventually, we see our creations as outpourings of our own true nature, and we discover why we are here. We discover that we are here to become more, to find out what we are made of, and to let it out. To align with love, to align with acceptance, to align with our highest resonance and to align with truth is our merest beginning point. In alignment with life's expansion, there can be no fear, only glorious outpourings that at one time appeared to be huge undertakings. Realities built with glue acknowledged by the Universe's "stamp of approval" is essential to our success. As we continue to expand upon a solid footing, we align with the order that is found everywhere. And sooner than we think, humanity begins to gravitate toward the sun and the stars and we begin our true adventures to and beyond our existing and multiples of horizons.

Are one million visionaries connected to Source such a large number in this day in time?

Can we imagine that all of the order found within the Universe can also be found within us? Can we imagine what it would be like to allow what is inside of us to expand into full order and love and expression? To bloom in the full alignment of Innate Intelligence with a conscious endorsement from ourselves? To become more? To see the possibilities for expansion that is the Universe's next step in our existence? Can we see that we have the potential for far more than patience in grocery store lines, or quietly absorbing the latest round of gasoline hikes, or otherwise, a powerless species on planet Earth?

What would happen if today's naïve consent for popular reality creation instead came from millions of intentional visionary individuals aligned with Innate Intelligence and creating at vast new levels of alertness, aliveness and awareness? Or a million minds and intents connected to each other by an order, harmony and prosperity, and held together by true cosmic glue? What would it be like? One million visionaries, creating their realities, expanding their potentials and becoming more of what comes from inside of them, cued by their partnership with Innate Intelligence and Source? If one connected to Source is more powerful than one million who are not, and one thousand are more powerful than one billion who are not, what would one million visionaries and intentional souls connected to Source be like? Are one million visionaries connected to Source such a large number in this day in time?

At some point, individually and collectively, we find ourselves free of the wheel of karma, that endless loop of a certain type of focus and observation that brings us more of the same, even lifetime after lifetime.[4] The promise of our heritage and a discovery that might have taken lifetimes to absorb can have significant turnaround in two years, by abiding certain principles and coming into alignment with that still, small voice within each of us.

No one creates in our realities but us.

No one can change our realities but us.

As we become aware of the results we achieve, for which we find contrast and new decision-making opportunities ever-present, we learn to refine our output. We realize that we can step out of this endless loop scenario of a certain type of observation and focus that has been with us for so very long – a type of focus known as resistance, fear and doubt, and carried as unconscious habitual patterns and unrefined qualities of intent, a certain type of focus that creates for us less than comfortable, though absolutely perfect and appropriate results, and for which allowing is the key and stepping-stone to more refined experiences.

We come to see that focus, intentionality and alignment with Innate Intelligence brings to us what is important. We discover we are the masters of our ships, that we are responsible for our visions and that our horizons are of our own making. We come to see within us, and not outside of us, that the solutions are found. Nothing outside of us matters in comparison to our alignment with the mechanism within. It is our feelings, our vision, and our connection to Innate Intelligence that defines our successes, our goals and our satisfactions with the world around us. We learn how to become more. It is a very satisfying experience.

The Law of Attraction and the Law of Deliberate Creation, together with Dr. David Hawkins' perspective on intent, brings understanding to the mechanisms that underlie the creation of reality – all reality – our reality. One says that what we focus on expands while Innate Intelligence offers signaling for the quality of our choices, thoughts and intents. Dr. Hawkins' research says that the higher the quality our underlying intent aligned with our focus, the more "stickability" our creations, the more depth and resonance we have with Universal Forces and the more refined our outcomes. As we come into alignment with nature's system of success and expansion, our creations carry an approval rating far exceeding anything that can be manufactured by pride, anger, fear or force. We find that we become better able to influence and affect the world of which we are truly a part.

Fairly simple stuff. The higher the quality our focus, prayer and output, catalyzed by the quality of our underlying intent, the more support we have from Universal Forces and Innate Intelligence. The more resonance, communication and synchronicity we engender with Innate Intelligence, the better we are able to refine the process of creating our realities and outcomes. The higher the quality and clarity of our desires, the more bountiful and wholesome the product and the better the quality of glue we have at our disposal. And then, it just keeps getting better and better (and better).

We have now established useful momentum that we can build on for exploring the world around us. By refining access to our true inner nature and by listening and learning, we have achieved a means by which we become truly useful to ourselves. All we have to do is allow the old stuff as we establish the new stuff.

Courage

As reasoning and conscious intelligence comes to the human mind, we make choices more succinctly and better aligned to innate wisdom and inner guidance. As we generate realities aligned to wisdom and Innate Intelligence, we see our worlds transforming both individually and collectively. And it turns out, all it takes is learning to make a few new choices and building upon our new choices. New choices are as natural and easy as stepping into a mud puddle one day and stepping around it the next day.

For in re-enacting the same old responses, we get more of the same. And more of the same, already in plentiful supply, is not what we are here for. We are becoming too aware for the limited thinking and corresponding scenarios to continue to predominate. Introspection is not only a connecting and a delving within but also a catalyst for the healing of the planet. And for the healing of the planet and ourselves, we are going to have to have the courage to look at things in a new way.

Learning to see what is useful in the contrast of the choices we have made thus far and learning to trust the creation process as we make new and more refined choices is our way out of our present difficulties. We are so very much closer than we know. Courage is a ready and available resource (as a quality of intent) underlying our focus. Luckily, our past realities are built with the minimalist of expression that nature's system of success allows. With a just bit of attention and refinement on our part, we can transform our world into one that is much more successful than its past, much more quickly than we might expect.

In the process of recreating our individual realities more in alignment with nature's system of success, we would be surprised to discover our ability to influence the whole. As we put our individual worlds in order, the order of the world at large begins to align with our newfound intent, for we are very powerful creators in alignment with Universal Forces. Do not trust the headlines and the ones who tell you it is not so. If you were a betting creator, you would bet on the side of the one with the upper hand. And clearly, nature, Universal Forces, Innate Intelligence and what has existed for eons, have the upper hand.

We would be surprised to discover how available and readily accessible Innate Intelligence is as we raise the stakes in this game called life. As this process moves along, we add courage to our tool belt, all the while refining reality creation for ourselves and for the whole. As we move toward higher ground, we discover that Innate Intelligence now has fertile ground on which to expand.

CHAPTER TEN
THE JOURNEY

*A*llowing combined with a measure of courage equals a journey of vast proportion and opportunity. We live in an interactive and alive Universe of order and expansion, and more order and more expansion. We live in a Universe of staggering possibilities, endless capacities and endless resources. And through the use of the tools of the 21st century, our minds, thoughts and intentions, we guide ourselves into a merging with nature's system of success in a conscious and intentional manner.

Make no mistake about it: It takes courage and plenty of it. To leave what we are familiar with – our pain, our sorrow, our story, our comforts and our present relationships and friendships in their functionality and disfunctionality – to move forward does indeed take courage. For what we have created in our lives, though we may not function at anywhere near our possibilities, is what we have and typically all that we know to this point.

On the other hand, the horizon beckons. Our horizon, the horizon, beckons to each of us. We realize that we are made for more than what our merry-go-round, habitually patterned outpourings are bringing us, and, with just the mildest of review, we know we are capable of so much more.

The purpose of our gathering is to expose and catalyze the idea that there is more to our lives than what we had supposed. There is more than those who brought us into the world had supposed, though it has always underlied our existence as lore and innate tuggings. Just looking around identifies a vast order and consistency, a vast system of resources and successes of which we are a substantial part. As we make our way toward a truer system of living and outpouring of potential, a great many problems that humanity has created for itself will cease to exist. In other words, as we begin to align with life, our surroundings will echo our aliveness.

Imagine living with all of our senses intact, living life as a connected aspect and outpouring of Universal Forces.

Imagine giving up the old way of doing things. Instead, imagine our lives as a merging of the "naturality"[1] and divine expansiveness that is nature all around us. Imagine living with all of our senses intact, living life as a connected aspect and outpouring of the Universe. Our mind becomes an entirely new vehicle, one of receptivity, awareness and choice. Our capacity for growth becomes aligned with listening and the subtleties of intent. We tune into our receptivity and connection with Innate Intelligence, and our world begins to unfold in all new ways.

We believe we are in charge of our lives, the planet, the stars and each other. Our knowledge and science has always been about overcoming, or getting a handle on, or having dominion over, our surroundings – except this hasn't worked as well as we might have thought. Maybe our motivations and underlying intent are down in the "twos" and certainly less than 200 on Dr. Hawkins' calibrated Map of Consciousness. Maybe we are not using our circuitry and what is available to us to our best advantage. Maybe we don't yet know how to connect to the world of which we are a part. Maybe our past interpretation of survival says that overcoming nature and the elements is not the answer.

I know a woman who has flung away her Los Angeles finery. Married and partnered with a successful architect and a rapidly growing client base, she made a major decision for a truer sense of happiness above all else. Though her life in Los Angeles brought her much happiness and glamour, deep inside she knew there was more and decided to take a leap fueled by courage and a bit of daring. She divorced her husband, dissolved her half of the partnership and began a journey toward listening to her inner guidance at the expense of seemingly everything else.

The last time I saw Sheri, she had effortlessly landed into a beautiful home in the mountains of northern Arizona. She is now surrounded by all new friends and acquaintances, who seem to have come out of the woodwork as she found her new and more natural (and authentic) persona. She began to pay attention, and she began to listen. She began to take hints, and she began to receive. She accepted insights and took action in a new way. This took courage, and she now has new results. She is a happier woman and a far better representative of our species.

No doubt about it: Courage was her by-word, and over a three-year period Sheri experienced incredible growth and positive results in her life. It is also true that she did not always know what she wanted, or how to get what she wanted, but took on the expression of receptivity, gratitude and appreciation for each moment of her day. Instead of attempting to conquer the world around her, she learned how to merge with it. She paved her way into a new life with the tools of alignment, insight and vision.

In her newfound authenticity, Sheri accepted that there was more order to life than she had been able to put together on her own. She also discerned patterns of order that were more powerful than she had been able to put together on her own. With allowing, acceptance, and a newfound vision of wholeness as her predominant focus, her existence began to improve immensely. I have witnessed in Sheri a marvelous capacity to create incredible outcomes by simply taking cues from Innate Intelligence and nature's system of success combined with allowing.

We live in a world of vast order. And by our use of the proper tools, we operate in this world practically "sitting at the right hand of God," so to speak. This order that creates the incredible diversity of flowers and plants and animals and eco-systems is available to us. The multitudes of systems of life and nature interspersed, intermingled and co-existing in a vast array of allowing and wholeness are available to us but for a choice and a bit of courage – a world that is far beyond our own capacity to create, but available simply for the asking and available as a matter of choice and the courage to make that choice.

Merging with Nature

Our existence is best served by our capacity to merge with a bigger picture of reality. Though we have assumed ourselves to be the smartest outpouring of evolution to date, this has not quite proven to be the case. What if, instead, the smartest outpouring of evolution is nature itself? What if, instead, it is for us to learn to accept cues for our next decision and our next capacity to be responsible? What if it turns out it is in our best interest to create outcomes in alignment with a system that is vastly more successful than what we are able to put together on our own?

What if, we are little more than a very sophisticated apple hanging from a branch of the Universe? What if that branch and connection is a substantial part of our existence and the source of our nourishment and support? What if, in our own naïve individuality, we are missing a bigger picture, assuming we are complete and independent on our own?

Imagine that even though we suppose ourselves to be the top rung of the evolutionary ladder, our primary function is as an expression and outpouring of nature and the Universe's expansion – not too much different from the fruit of the vine, the blossom of a flower, or the expression of a bountiful Universe and living system. After all, nature was here long before we were. What if we are little more than vehicles for nature to expand itself, to extend itself and become more? What if our nervous system and all of our mechanisms, including free will, are little more than outlets for nature to express itself? What if we are slated for a free ride of sorts as we become conscious of the possibilities? What if we learn how to use what is available to us in a new manner?

> *The solution is as simple as learning to listen to what our authenticity is telling us, and then moving forward in a new way.*

What if, in partnering with the success and clear superiority that is nature/Universal Mind/Innate Intelligence/Source, etc., we find our next level of wholeness and completeness? What if we are not as independent as we think? What if all we need to do is to become the perfect apple, i.e., the perfect throughput for Universal Forces? What if all we need to do is accept our connection and partnership with nature, as we find our rightful place in the scheme of things? What if this leads to true happiness and fulfillment? What if this is easier than we think?

Lauren L. Holmes – anthropologist/futurist and trainer and coach to world-class leaders – suggests that nature has a capacity for creating outcomes and handling issues that humanity has never been close to emulating. Lauren, author of *Peak Evolution* (2001),[2] suggests that nature has indisputably superior skills for problem solving and generating outcomes that are well beyond the capacity of the thinking mind. Just stopping to take a look invites and inspires awe and gratitude for the world of which we are truly a part.

If we were to attempt to maintain any of the myriad systems found within the human body, we would find ourselves woefully inadequate for such a function. If we were to become responsible for any of the vast multitudes of eco-systems of the earth, or the weather, or the billions and likely trillions of microscopic worlds included in the order that is nature, we would again discover ourselves woefully inadequate. As humanity attempts to take over the management of certain eco-systems, we see how incapable we are of even the smallest responsibilities overseen by nature in an effortless manner. Could it be that we can't even manage ourselves, or at least we could use a little help?

As we become more sophisticated (in other words, as we become better able to review, take notes, communicate and share information among ourselves), we discover that we are making a vast mess of our planet. We have almost no regard for the continuity and order and cycles that keep the earth spinning, the air clean, or any of the innate balances in order. We seemingly have a blind disregard for the true order of things, along with a consumption mentality that some see as ending in assured wreckage. We appear to be destroying life on this planet at an unprecedented rate.

Why have we excluded ourselves from the intrinsic prosperity, success and order that is all around us?

It is time to learn to exist more successfully and in more alignment with nature and its success. Luckily, we have the benefit of observation, note-taking and a bit of history to see whether we can judge ourselves as successfully making our way or whether we could use a bit of help. Out of such contrast, we begin to reaffirm what is important to us. With regard to my friend Sheri, she gave up being in charge of her life in the traditional manner, and her world began to show new signs of health. As she became more in alignment with her inner drives, Innate Intelligence and a bigger picture, her world began to thrive. And, as some would say, she was successful anyway.

176

There is a better way to live our lives than what we see emblazoned as our newspaper and magazine headlines, or as the continual clatter and chatter of television broadcasting the injustices we inflict on each other in the name of the Church or the State, or "your best interests" or "the State's compelling interests," etc. The solution is as simple as slipping into our "naturality mode,"[3] learning to listen to what our authenticity is telling us, and then moving forward in a new way. As mentioned, it turns out we are connected to a vast stream of order that keeps everything above and below and upon Earth in steady supply, regeneration and abundance. All we have to do is to learn how to tune into this. All we have to do is become a part of this. All we have to do is learn how to "plug in" and relax a bit.

A Good Question

The question might be: Why are we, or why have we, excluded ourselves from this natural and intrinsic prosperity and success and order that is all around us? The beginning of the answer is that we have not because, if we truly were unplugged from nature's system of success, we would immediately cease to exist. We do not and cannot exist separate from this system of success.

Our charge is to become cognizant of our relationship with this vast order and intentionally partner with it for more ambitious outcomes. Ours is to redirect our focus from the raucous and primitive techniques of our naïve interpretations of overcoming the world, and, more subtly, include ourselves in a system of success that is greater than our imagination and beliefs are presently able to grasp. As our perceptions begin to shift and grow, we find answers that we were once unable to discern. Our horizons shift for the better, and visionary focus becomes our reality. We move forward in step with Universal Forces.

Our Ancient Heritage

We are far older than modern science assumes and argues (against). Judaism and Christianity teach that mankind was uncivilized and had little awareness of its existence prior to the time of Abraham and Moses. According to the Christian *Ryrie Study Bible,* a well-known Bible study guide, humanity did not even exist before approximately 4000 B.C. As taught by Christian theology, ancient humanity was little more than ingrates worshipping rocks and trees, and little more than heathens until Judaism and Christianity came along. But as we sift our ancient past with the advancing sciences of archaeology, astronomy, mathematics and even cosmology, our perceptions based on race-consciousness and held beliefs begin to shift radically.

It seems that mankind has existed in a civilized manner for many thousands of years and may readily stretch back 50,000 years,[4] and possibly a great deal further. Recent research is suggesting that our history may be far older than we presently understand.

There are ancient Egyptian references noting 26,000-year cycles and identifying periods of time well into antiquity. Herodotus, an illustrious Greek historian visiting Egypt in the 5th century B.C., reports in *History*, Book II, that Egyptian priests talked of times when the sun twice rose where it normally sets. With an understanding of the Spring Equinox as mapped by the Procession (thoroughly discussed later in this chapter), it takes approximately 13,000 years for the Sun to rise to its opposite backdrop constellation, which is one-half cycle. Herodotus reports Egyptian priests referenced dates "one and one-half cycles" ago or 39,000 years in the past.[5] It is also reported by Plato in the 4th century B.C., that the Egyptians were observers of the skies (stars) for 10,000 years. This is 16,000 years ago in present time

It has been recorded that the Egyptian moon god Thoth, rumored to have ruled Egypt for more than 3,226 years,[6] is associated with introducing geometry, celestial mathematics, astrology, land-surveying, medicine, botany, magic, the alphabet and reading and writing, to name a few sciences, to the ancient Egyptians. Thoth, known as the wisdom god and much later as (Trismegistus) Hermes (Thrice-Great) by the ancient Greeks,[7] is reportedly the earlier source of phrases normally ascribed to God in the Old Testament. The teachings of Thoth are said to be contained within 42 volumes handed down through time. This knowledge may be the source of ancient wisdom eventually recognized as the underground Mystery Schools of our ancient past.

It is possible that the Egyptian culture initially flourished somewhere else. As we uncover our past, we discover the remnants of three ancient civilizations laced with surprising commonalities: Egypt, with the Great Pyramid as the center of the ancient world; South America, characterized by the "recent" Incan culture; and Central America, characterized by the "recent" Aztec and Mayan cultures.[8] These three cultural centers arose somewhat simultaneously and contain substantial similarities, which are revealed by a modern study of their ruins and mythologies.

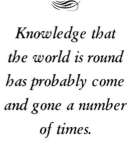

Knowledge that the world is round has probably come and gone a number of times.

Is it possible that what was perceived as the lore of Atlantis, in its demise (overcome by the melting of the ice caps and Noah's flood as reported in the Old Testament and elsewhere?) spawned the colonies of Egypt and Central and South America on higher ground? Modern research suggests this may not be as far-fetched as it sounds.[9]

Clearly, Egypt, the most studied of the three ancient civilizations, was powered by a vast wealth of knowledge and insight and operated in far more resonance with its surroundings than we are able to imagine today. After all, the sophistication of the Great Pyramid and its secrets are no accident, though irrevocably complex. Simply the size of the Great Pyramid and its perfect alignment to true north long before the invention of the compass, or its perfectly laid, white limestone outer covering, gives one pause. Among many unexplained features, the Great Pyramid contains several "sighting" shafts, each capped at both ends by solid rock, unknown to the seeing eye, but suggestively pointing to star systems representative of the Egyptians' ancient beliefs in the cosmos. There are numerous ancient Egyptian sites that modern logic fails to comprehend in size and scope, while others lie undiscovered awaiting our refined perceptual gaze.

Perhaps we have come and gone a number of times. Possibly we have been unable to maintain our connection with Innate Intelligence in step with our advancing technology and eventually lost sight of our connection. Or maybe over the years we simply forgot what we knew. Perhaps we continue in a decline that has roots far deeper than we can fathom. Maybe we are just a blip on the screen of time of again slowly rising intellect. Or possibly we will again grow more powerful than we grow wise.

There is evidence of far more order in our distant past than we have been willing to accept.

The existence of the Egyptian *Book of the Dead,* translated as the Book of Great Awakening, and sometimes translated as the Book of the Mistress of the Hidden Temple,[10] has no known earliest age. According to Sir E. A. Wallis Budge,[11] possibly the foremost Egyptologist and translator of the *Book of the Dead,* the earliest known depictions are copies of earlier versions sourced far into antiquity for which no physical records exist.[12]

The *Book of the Dead,* commonly thought to be funerary rites, contains far more. The contents, attributed to Thoth, depict the trials and tribulations of initiates attempting to traverse the full realization of the essential divine nature of man and the recovery of the full knowledge and powers of his divine spiritual nature.[13] This very sophisticated knowledge, unlike cave-painting or simplistic carvings that grew into more, was an existing language of record and outpouring of knowledge, for which we have almost no understanding of its origin. Apparently, the information contained within the *Book of the Dead* came from an earlier time and place.

It is interesting to note that many of the stories, laws and wisdom depicted in the Old Testament are earlier recorded in the *Book of the Dead*. The Ten Commandments, known to have been delivered "from the hand of God" to Moses in around 1500 B.C., were far earlier referenced in the Egyptian *Book of the Dead* (Chapter CXXV),[14] as was a recounting of Noah's flood. Interestingly, the phrase "In the beginning was the Word," normally attributed to the Book of John, was far earlier recorded as the words of Thoth recorded in the *Book of the Dead*.[15] Apparently, stories and wisdom recorded in the Old Testament are rehashes of earlier times, echoing stories and myths of our ancient past.

It is apparent that the Old Testament is a recycling of the myths of antiquity as best could be done at the time. There was no way to know the lineage of stories recounted, other than to say that the authors had minimal perspective of a far earlier time. It was legend, dutifully recorded by the eyes and ears of a time that little understood its roots. Humanity was far older than it had eyes to see, and we are just beginning to glimpse.

It is from this earlier time that the long line of Mystery Schools and ancient teachings provided for the enlightenment of historical and biblical figures in our written history. After all, only approximately seven of the 33 years of the life of Jesus are known. Only in his last three or four years is he suddenly documented as having vast insight and knowledge, holding large audiences spellbound and overwhelming the leadership of his time. What he knew and taught had been on the planet for quite some time, carefully protected by the ancient Mystery Schools of Egypt and elsewhere. Though Jesus taught foundational ideas about our true divinity, it was information from an earlier time.

Many of the scholars, scientists and seekers of our past acquired their insights by the revelation of knowledge and tradition from an earlier time. Copernicus, Leonardo da Vinci, Isaac Newton, Michelangelo, Sir Walter Raleigh, Christopher Columbus, Shakespeare and many others, having heard the whisperings of ancient knowledge, had the courage to investigate for themselves at odds with the power and forces that held humanity in sway. The Knights Templar of the 12th century educated in the knowledge found within the ancient catacombs of the ruins of Solomon's temple complex, began the most spectacular developments in architecture of the time, known today as the Gothic cathedrals of Europe. This came as a result of their study of ancient texts handed down to Solomon that included mathematics, astronomy, astrology, sacred geometry, etc.

In the 12th century, a very powerful French Christian figure, Saint Bernard of Clairvaux,[16] defined God as "length, width, height and depth." Sacred geometry, as it is presently known, is a vehicle for passing knowledge from our far distant past throughout history to our present time. Sacred geometry, as mathematical formulas, defines nature, beauty, harmony and balance.

The European Renaissance of the 14th through 16th centuries was a blossoming of the underground and Mystery School teachings after a 1,000-year reign of ignorance (known as the Dark Ages) brought about, in part, by the destruction of the 700-year-old Library of Alexandra and a systematic obliteration of Pagan leadership and knowledge by fanatical Christianity.[17] As the resonance and harmonics of nature's beauty and order began to find a willing audience, eventually the Space Age and information and technology revolutions became the result. Humanity has likely risen and fallen a number of times.

The Procession of the Equinox

Ancient humanity thrived in math, science and astronomy much farther back than modern theology and science is able to understand. Evidence lies in the existence of ancient maps showing a round planet when the world was long-believed (forgotten?) to have been flat. The famous, though relatively unknown Piri Reis Map of 1513 A.D.[18] is a compilation of earlier maps showing Antarctica with mountain ranges, rivers and no ice cap, and only recently (1950s) proven to be a true and accurate rendition. Among the more interesting ancient secrets to appear before our modern gaze is the realization that the ancients mapped astronomical events of 26,000-year cycles and otherwise mapped and understood the cosmos at unparallel levels of sophistication long, long ago.

A cyclical and repeatable mapping of time encompassing a 26,000-year cycle, known by numerous ancient cultures with corresponding mathematics, is mind-boggling, to say the least. That ancient humanity, had not only an awareness of a very fine wobble in the earth's axis, but mapped this anomaly with precision and the use of the zodiac, is a very special discovery about our past indeed!

Stonehenge and other ancient astrological observatories on the planet's surface are recognized as measuring and reference points for studying this celestial time frame. Knowledge that the world is round probably has come and gone a number of times. After all, it was only 500 years ago that Christopher Columbus sailed beyond what was perceived as a flat horizon. We are not

Somehow, we have come to believe that we aren't good enough for our own possibilities.

as old as we think, or we are far older than we think. Another way to phrase it might be: "How many times have we attempted to sail beyond our limitations?"

There is substantial evidence for a mathematical interpretation of the "procession of the equinox," as it is presently called, sewn into and repeated throughout a broad range of ancient myths and legends, which modern day researchers are just beginning to recognize.[19] To realize that ancient civilizations could chart such a sophisticated scientific event and "export" this information as legend and myth is not what we expect from our "dim-witted and pagan" forbearers.

For the most part, modern recorded history does not go beyond 1700 or 1800 B.C., or earlier than the time of Abraham and Moses, and the beginnings of Judaism. As a timeline,[20] Adam and Eve existed in approximately 4000 B.C.; Egypt's Great Pyramid was supposedly built no earlier than 2500 B.C.; the time of Abraham was about 1800 B.C.; Moses lived around 1450 B.C.; Buddha lived in approximately 500 B.C. in the lineage of the ancient Hindu faith; Jesus lived in approximately the year "0," the point from which Christianity sprang; and Mohammad lived approximately 600 A.D. as the source of Islam.

According to Christianity, the beginning of modern civilization coincides with the receding of Noah's flood, in approximately 2400 B.C. While in the modern perspective of things, Egypt's Sphinx is, by the most recent estimates, at least 7,000 to 9,000 years old, and Noah's flood might be estimated at about 11,000 to 13,000 years ago.[21] It is likely that Noah's flood is tied to the most recent melting of the ice caps. On the scale of one 26,000 year cycle, not much of our history is known, though the calendar and ancient mapping of time are no doubt.

The solution is to break the chain of limitation that has been a part of our makeup for so very long.

More than 4,400 (2400 B.C.) years ago, civilization was considered to be unsophisticated and incapable of the insight and advanced mathematics that we are discovering interwoven as legend and myth in our ancient past. As we become aware of the anomalies of our history, we realize that we take a great deal for granted about our history as a species. We are discovering ancient knowledge that defies everything we think we know about ourselves. It is possible that we were far more "plugged in" than we know.

An Ancient Time Map?

For those unfamiliar with the procession of the equinox, our planet has a slight wobble in its north/south spin axis, in addition to its daily spin (and tilt creating our seasons) in its annual circumnavigation around the Sun. This slow and almost imperceptible wobble, similarly found with a spinning top, makes a complete cycle (wobble) in approximately

25,800 years. Presently the North Pole axis points directly at what is called the North Star or Polaris. But over this 25,800-year cycle, the North Pole axis swings in a very slow circle, sometimes to a different "pole" star and sometimes at none, but ultimately making its way back to a beginning point, and hence a cycle. Apparently, the ancients were also aware of the central point within the celestial circle identified by this wobble.

Furthermore, the ancients, with their awareness of the procession of the equinox, established the equivalent of a 12-month calendar, though the "months" were actually approximately 2,100 years each, for which the Piscean Age and Aquarian Age represent two of these "months," "seasons" or "ages." Stonehenge, as well as other numerous ancient astrological observatories, mapped these events, though we can only speculate as to their full intent. We do know they were able to measure and sight the sunrise at the Spring Equinox, undoubtedly representing insights into the ancient sciences of resonance, polarity, and time.

The set of stars (constellation of the zodiac) sighted in the background of the Spring Equinox sunrise told the ancients what zodiacal sign (cosmic month) they were in, which is still true today. We are presently in the Piscean Age of 2,100 years, and soon to enter the Aquarian Age, another age of approximately 2,100 years. Some suggest that we entered the Aquarian Age at the time of Sputnik and the beginnings of the space race in the 1960s. We are presently unaware of the finest details of when an age actually begins or ends. Either way, we are at the cusp of a new age[22] as identified by very ancient mathematics and knowledge brought forward as myth and legend.

The zodiac's 12 signs, as a narrow belt of constellations around our planet, create the backdrop for a calendar of 12 "ages." Without going into great detail – other than referencing the research of Graham Hancock, Robert Baval, John Anthony West, and many others – there is substantial evidence that The Sphinx, the Great Pyramid, Anghor Wat and Anghor Tom in Cambodia and others, clearly "set in stone" the date of 10,500 B.C. or 12,500 ago, as a significant date in our ancient past. Though some believe it relates to a milestone date within an ancient culture, it is my thought that the date represents the equivalent of January 1 of a 26,000-year calendar. According to this, it appears that we are coming up on the mid-point of this 26,000-year cycle within the next several hundred years.

Presently, we have little understanding of the purpose of a 26,000-year calendar. It is possible that a calendar of this magnitude gives insight into "seasonal" or cyclical comets, asteroids, ice ages and floods, or other cyclical, return events of proportion beyond our present understanding.[23] The insight of a 26,000-year calendar may become a foundational map or game board by which we are able to view what has been unviewable without perspective. Undoubtedly, a calendar and mapping of time of this proportion gives us new and additional insights about our past, and, likely, our future.

As the ancient art of astrology reveals itself to map the energetics of Universal Forces and polarity and resonance, we discover that the ancients understood its interaction with cosmic influences to a very fine degree. Today, as yesterday, we learn to merge our relationships with Innate Intelligence, and our connection with Universal Forces grows.

The ancients, who have been broadly assumed to be "dumber than a bag of hammers," to borrow a term from Ulysses Everett McGill,[24] has no merit. Ancient "pagan" humanity, prior to Christianity, probably enjoyed a far healthier and successful relationship with nature and "God" that we presently exhibit or understand.

There is evidence of far more order and knowledge in our distant past than we have been able or willing to accept as fact. According to modern science and quantum physics, it is becoming apparent that God is "everywhere," an idea we should consider looking into. A system of success that with, little review, has been attributed to a single, man-like god endowed with omnipotence and power over life and death, and, seemingly, a great deal of mischievous "decision-making," is likely far more.

A review of our surroundings and a modern interpretation of history suggests a system, an aliveness and order, that is best described as Innate Intelligence on the inside and nature, Universal Correspondency and synchronicity on the outside. And, lest we forget, around 375 A.D., the time of the Council of Nycea, the rules clearly changed. It was during this time that God took on the cloak of an authority figure that could only be reached via some sort of (male) middleman, for which substantial misunderstandings remain to this day.

As we consent to anything less than our capacity to stand on our own two feet, to know our own individuality and our own identity, we find ourselves on the slow part of the learning curve. Somehow, we were sold a bill of goods that claimed we weren't good enough for our own possibilities. Somehow we were taught that we needed to defer to another, to an authority figure outside of ourselves, to some sort of middleman, fire-keeper or priest – to someone who knew better than we. And ever since, we have been caught up in trying to understand the world as if it was outside of us rather than within – something the ancients much better knew and that we are just beginning to grasp.

It turns out "we" are the most sophisticated outlet for the Universe's creativity. Our job becomes to learn how to let the Universe flow through us, to find and maintain our connection and alignment with Universal Forces and become more – all an inside job! Humanity, out of contrast, trying to get back home, is humanity beginning to find itself.

Our life becomes a matter of releasing what we think we know. Our life becomes a matter of learning to resonate with, and become receptive to, a larger truth. It is futile to attempt to create realities with a limited perception when we have such a wide assortment of insights available to us. If we could but assume the courage to begin to access the truth, we would find a far better world ahead.

We discover that the typical conscious mind is a garbage heap of incalculable depth and dimension. Everything we have absorbed or speculated seems to be contained within the mind and its ramblings, for which we have little insight as to the truth and veracity of our held conclusions. We carry and store a great deal of useless information, and wonder why our realities and perspectives are mediocre.

As we begin to meditate and affix our mental and feeling gaze upon Universal Flow, we find that we are awash in our own background interference. We are completely full of noise and misinformation. As we attempt to understand why we are so out of sorts with nature's system of success, we realize that we have minds full of beliefs at odds with what Innate Intelligence may be offering us as insight and advice. We have chosen our beliefs without the eyes to see, the test of sensibility and Innate Intelligence's guidance.

Somehow we know that we are mystical creatures, that we spring from Source and that we are capable of being in-step with Universal Forces. Somehow we know that, in letting Universal Forces flow through our being, we find our way – the truth and the life we felt was our promise. But we seem to be in the way of our own progress. We constantly short-circuit ourselves; we constantly sabotage ourselves; and we miss the boat on a regular basis, though we grow from our mistakes. What is it about us that does not serve us in a manner to which we think we are entitled? Why so much work to become who and what we are deep inside of ourselves?

Maybe deep inside of us is the answer. Maybe deep inside of us is found the tools of our transformation into something more. Maybe in the unconscious holding of our beliefs – those that were taught to us, or beliefs that were genetically handed down to us as pain, suffering and confusion about our heritage – we became the recipients of those realities. Maybe our solution is to break the chain of the suffering, ignorance and doubt that has been a part of our makeup for so very long.

Is it possible that our nature is actually one of compassion, love and integrity and truth? And, more importantly, it is possible that we are a conduit for the love that makes up the cosmos, and that our function is give up beliefs that don't serve us? What makes this so difficult? Is it possible we carry the pain, sorrow and ignorance of a race-consciousness gone before us, and that all we need to do is allow and learn of unconditional love for our past and our present? Is it possible we were meant for more?

It is interesting to note that we drive automobiles that sometimes cost as much as houses. With paint jobs and colors that would make any artist proud, we zip around with comfortable seating and surround-sound music systems at our fingertips. We have glass as lenses at our four corners as we drive within feet of each other at sometimes startling speeds. Occasionally, we make mistakes in judging distances and stopping power, but, if we ever want to evaluate whether we are civilized and capable of compassion and love, we simply need to become accustomed to driving America's highway system.

Our automobiles are extensions of our own nature. Silently, we move along our pathway and by-way, well within our own thoughts and focus. While we meld to meet each other's needs, we maintain our focus and allow the occasional rogue, all the while with our eye on the end result – our destination. As it is with driving an automobile, we learn to tune out what does not serve us as we tune into what serves us with clarity, focus and ease.

If anything typifies our rise to becoming civilized, it is our daily use of 4,000-pound tools of steel and glass to whisk us to and fro, for which we silently acknowledge each other in countless methods of courtesy and composure. Though the middlemen would take credit for the success of the highway system and its apparent flow, a closer look suggests that each driver carries a sense of responsibility and accord that exceeds what might be perceived as a punishment system of fines "for getting caught." As we address new levels of allowing and order in our lives, we find we are capable of far more.

CHAPTER ELEVEN
MOMENTUM

*I*magine giving up resistance and moving into flow. Imagine moving into the unknown with only Innate Intelligence at your side. Initially, this might seem like a difficult choice until we realize this is the positive side of the equation. As we follow our nose (Innate Intelligence) into present time and newfound experience, we find the mind becoming receptive to synchronicities, comforts and ease and newfound order. There is no need to outsmart the mind, decide it is wrong or bad, argue with it, or even dismiss it.

Instead, we refine the mechanism that is the mind. We teach it to shoot for newer results and easier ways of accomplishing tasks, and we teach it to opt for new open-endedness in its possibilities and outcomes. Give the mind new goals to aspire to and new habitual patterns to churn out. Learn to guide the mind and train it, and put it to work in a more useful manner! Give the mind new aspirations and introduce it to infallible Innate Intelligence – after all, they are ultimately "of" the same stuff.

Who says the mind won't go where we want it to go? It is nothing but a system of habitual patterns of outpourings and beliefs, and actually a bit on the mindless side, as we are discovering. The ego, supposedly in charge, is nothing but a misdirected sense of our belief in our powerlessness and separation, for which we defer to something that doesn't really exist. The mind is no more than a "servomechanism" of our being and capacity for creation, for which we have not given much thought! It is a servo-mechanism awaiting our conscious intent and instructions.

As we experience present time based upon a conscious reckoning of input aligned with Innate Intelligence, we find feelings of gratitude and joy coursing through our bodies as old ideas melt away in the pleasure of new ideas found. It is not that we give up our traditional livelihoods and move to the beach for the perpetual tan. Instead, we accept happenstance and new experiences into our field of perception as imprints of inestimable value, while we retrain the mind for its new responsibilities. As habitual patterns have always been the dominion of the mind and its unconscious output, we feed the mind new ideas and new motivations for conscious output. As the mind begins to churn out higher quality realities and newer quality automations, we begin to experience newfound opportunities and possibilities.

Free will is at our "fingertips" as we reach and stretch for our possibilities.

As we retune our possibilities, we make way for a throughput of Universal energies that a quiet mind and refined internal circuitry make possible. As we make way for the quiet amperage of love and a newfound stillness flowing into and through our lives, our circuitry begins to hum and we become alive with the sights and sounds of Universal Correspondency. As we begin to truly live, we become truly alive. As we opt for the aliveness of Life Force coursing through our system, we realize that a stopped-up system of beliefs was the only thing in the way of our connection with Source – old wounds that seemingly never healed, resistances we couldn't overcome and minds full of attitudes and beliefs operating like a cork in a bottle – ideas and beliefs unresolved until they become resolved.

We consciously allow Infinite Intelligence to move within us and make its way through our very being. We allow more of this life-giving essence to "have its way" with us. We learn of receptivity; we learn of discretion; and we learn of allowing. We begin to understand the difference between what it was like and what we are experiencing now. We acknowledge others in their connection with Spirit as we identify their experiences as similar to our own and each important to our growth. We understand that Innate Intelligence is our partner and compatriot and that it can be no other way. We learn to allow a bit more. We become the high priests of our temples and our throughput connection with the cosmos.

As we open to gratitude and love, we create a pathway for the expansion of the Divine into newfound outpourings and order. For the most part, God/Source/Innate Intelligence and Universal Forces have been limited to our mindless reality creations, the animal, plant and mineral kingdoms and nature, for which there was limitation in the possibilities of expression available. By a conscious awareness of what we hold within and the decision to accept it as our own, nature finds a new way to express itself and we find a new way to express ourselves. It turns out free will is the key to this new system of expansion of God and Universal Forces. It turns out we are God, or at least extensions of God, and that free will is at our "fingertips" as we stretch and reach for our possibilities.

Life Force

As we become experienced in the comforts of our newfound connection with Spirit, we behold others in their expressions of Light and allowing. We experience others as whole and complete, and powerful and healthy organisms for Universal Flow and change. Moreso, we acknowledge their connection with Spirit as the power behind their growth and expansion. Namasté becomes an acknowledgment we recognize about each other to the depths of our being. We understand that the exchange of energy we hold for each other is a sacred opportunity to <u>outwardly</u> express love and gratitude. We discover that we are all the same. The Universe expands. The mind begins to get it. We begin to grow in unison.

With creation pouring though us, we realize that we are throughput vessels of unconditional love, as we understand we once had the dynamics all wrong. Where once we scavenged for Life Force from each other and under rocks, or took it by force, we now go direct for our sustenance. Where once we knew little of happiness and true power, we now know its source. Where once we distrusted our brother or sister, we now know the difference. As we come to know one another, we discover each other in "a whole new light." We discover love for ourselves and for each other.

We discover that we are each whole and complete. We play and interact with each other in newfound energetics commensurate with our newfound power and connection. Initially little different than inert objects with little identity, we become as giant redwoods stretching and following the afternoon sun, or a pair of stars encircling each other and spawning new planets in power, self-sustaining authority and reverence. Our power and authority jumps immeasurably as we come to understand and share what flows through us – all of us, each of us – directly.

We discover a newfound ability to flow energy through and among each other, sometimes called love, sometimes called joy, sometimes called gratitude, but always called ecstasy. We acknowledge and treat each other as equals as we learn to share what is part of our basic kinship. We realize that our past relationships were comprised of what we could take from each other, because we didn't know our Source. We only knew that if it was alive, we wanted, needed and required more of it. We didn't know who we were, and we didn't know our possibilities. We were mixed up, we were dysfunctional, and we had our wires crossed. We didn't know how or where to go for our sustenance, and we languished.

As we accept guidance in our lives, we put down tools and misadventures that no longer serve us. Instead, we begin to listen; we begin to learn of discretion; and we begin to learn of receptivity. We begin to learn of resonance, and we begin to thrive. We become who we really are. We become choosers in alignment with Spirit. We become more.

Who do we think is going to save us? Extraterrestrials? God? Magic? A genie? Or maybe a friendly giant?

We are responsible for what we have in our lives. Our lives are made of our choices and as we make conscious choice in alignment with Innate Intelligence, we experience new results. We experience new alignment with Source, and our reality becomes more. We realize that we are capable of conscious creating, conscious intent, conscious envisioning, and we begin to apply conscious gratitude.

Our pain and our pleasure tell us of the quality of our creations. Awareness of the quality of our creations maps our way out of our primordial ooze. We come to have gratitude for all of our experiences and begin to see what is behind them. We begin that inexorable climb toward conscious intent and a conscious unfolding of our possibilities. We begin to become more. We find that Innate Intelligence becomes more available in our lives. We become a throughput for amperage that becomes our source of energy, something we can plug into in the most prophetic of ways.

We learn that our natural inheritance is as a throughput for Life Force that flows from one end of the Universe to the other but always available to our system as we make way for it. We realize that throughput is thwarted by our resistance, wounds and a belief in what is not true. Our pain is no more than Innate Intelligence signaling that it could not flow through us unimpeded. Where we were once rooted to our beliefs, limitations and mistakes, we learn to let Life Force flow through us. We become more alive and our creations become more alive. Feelings coursing through our nervous system are enough reason to go for the experience of connection, but the power of our nature in alignment with the source of creation flowing through our systems is unmistakable. We become more; we sense "home." We set our sights higher.

> "We cannot solve our problems with the same thinking we used when we created them."
> - Albert Einstein

It is a matter of resonance and reliance on what is true and a consciousness about our choices. After all, once we begin to make conscious choice, there is nothing left but more conscious choice. Not making choice gives us little steerageway, while even poor choice is momentum toward change. We learn to choose in alignment with Innate Intelligence, vision, resonance, intent and gratitude, and we become more. Ultimately, we are always becoming more. It is as simple as that.

Faster and Faster

As we align with nature's wisdom and success, we realize that we have far more access to naturality and authenticity than we might imagine. As we compare notes, review our surroundings and discover more rhyme and reason to our existence, we are compelled to turn within for additional direction and insight. And of course, the expression, "the last place we look" is uproariously appropriate.

As we discover our capacity for visionary focus and as we accept our capacity for intentionality and responsibility, our worlds change for the better. Though a few middlemen would claim to represent our interests, it is increasingly apparent that staying on top is their survival credo. As we become more aware of the contrast, we come to a clarity about what is important to us.

As creators, we have little capacity to blame middlemen for our sorrows. By our consentience, we inadvertently nod in favor of those who would choose for us, foregoing our power and capacity as visionaries for a period of time. As observers, though powerful in our ignorance, we instead condone and create according to someone else's wishes. It is a surprisingly good use of our time, for without this contrast, we would never get clear about what is truly important to us.

We are coming to a point, similar to the new (quantum) physics replacing the old (Newtonian) physics, where a whole new order is becoming available and felt. We are achieving decision-making, choice and consentience in a whole new manner for which alignment with Innate Intelligence is our simple solution. And, of course, we reap the benefits as our world begins to become more! (Maybe "we" are the source of the "new world order"?)

Some of us partner with Innate Intelligence sooner than others in our decision-making ventures and venues. For, after all, in the nature of decision-making, if we don't know all of the variables, how are we ever going to make prudent and quality decisions? If we don't know all of the facts regarding a choice, how can we ever make a right choice and assure ourselves of rightful outcomes and solutions,[1] especially as the world moves faster and faster? Maybe this is why we have deferred to someone else, someone of seeming authority, someone claiming the answers, someone claiming to be smarter than ourselves. Maybe all we need to know is "that of ourselves."[2]

As rising and sentient beings perched upon a planet that we are about to overload with poor choices coming from poor decision-making skills, we are learning that nature, its success and know-how is becoming increasingly valuable. As a species, we are evolving, and as an aspect of our evolution, we are learning to make better decisions because the results of our thoughts and decisions are forming right in front of our eyes. As our lives move ever faster, it is becoming easier to see the results of our choices, for which we learn to choose once again!

Fast and faster is good as we race toward a time of potential global warming, destroying life in the oceans and doing irreparable damage to the myriad eco-systems of our planet. Our one saving grace is that we can now more quickly see the results of our choices and thus change our minds. New consensus is new consensus, and new consensus is new choice! As we race toward our future, it becomes obvious that our capacity for a successful resolution is a matter of conscious choice.

What would be more thought-provoking and wisdom-generating than becoming aware of our mistaken choices and making new choices in light of upcoming and inescapable apocalyptic change? After all, who do we think is going to save us? Extraterrestrials? God? Magic? A genie? Or maybe a friendly giant? Can we see that our solutions are not going to come from outside of ourselves?

We need to save ourselves; that is the design of which we are made. It is our design to come more into alignment with our own natures. This is the success of our species – the only species with free will. We are not going to be saved from outside of ourselves if our problems come from "within." This is the correction we make in our free will creation scenarios. We save ourselves, we save the whales, we save the rain forests, and we save the Earth – all by a matter of changing our minds and lining up with what works. This is well within our domain. This *is* our domain!

What would be more thought-provoking than seeing the results of our choices right in front of our eyes, for which new choices and getting clearer and clearer in our output and our prayer become our safety and our solution? After all, energy follows thought and consensus in alignment with Innate Intelligence is very powerful stuff. "Out of contrast comes clarity" is a very powerful principle and instigator of new commitment. But we must make sure we empower our focus with an underlying quality of intent endorsed by the forces of nature and our own conscious choice. Ultimately, we can use the dynamics of love and gratitude and a bit of courage to find new ways to solve problems!

As Albert Einstein illuminatively stated, "We cannot solve our problems with the same thinking we used when we created them." Our way out is onward and upward and for which nature's system of success offers plenty of options and possibilities. We need only the contrast of our past and innate signaling to know the difference. And since nature is committed to this success, it is likely we have all the time we need. All we need to do is to be sure to partner with something that works.

Moving even faster than our results, our choices are always in front of us. Our results follow our choices; effect follows our cause. Do not believe that our momentum is already dictated and that our outcomes are assured. This is the realm of observers. As soon as we make new choices, new realities fall into place. Nature has solutions and we are part of the solution. It is well within us to solve our problems. After all, we have to have someplace to play, someplace to live and

The alternative is to be reliant upon our minds, for which we are beginning to see the fallacy of that line of thinking.

someplace to grow and learn about our expansion. It is just a matter of whether we want to be responsible for the quality of our journey or get pulled through the keyhole kicking and screaming.

The Donkey and the Carrot

There are vast underlying intricacies that make up humanity and its connection to Source. After all, how can an apple decide to become a pear, or a bumblebee an elephant? It can't. The apple is innately wired to be a successful apple, and we as humanity are wired in our own similar manner. We are a successful outpouring of nature/Innate Intelligence with the added ingredient of free will. It looks like Innate Intelligence has given us wings and that our possibilities are endless. As refinements of nature's quest for expansion, we will one-day produce solutions that even nature cannot conceive nor put into place.

As a species, we have will, choice, observation, imagination and a capacity to choose our outcomes. There are no limits in alignment with Source. We come to see gratitude as another tool for our 21st century tool belt as we create realities with newfound intentionality and guidance from nature and Infinite Mind.

We find challenges set before us as essential parts of our learning curve, in far more order than we might initially understand. We find we are up to the task of knowing the difference between resonance and dissonance in our alignment and flow with Innate Intelligence. Knowing the difference is a deeply felt wisdom, ultimately indistinguishable as our prayer, our creations and our outpourings.

Our success relies upon our authentic-self in alignment with what is true and nothing less.

On the other hand, if we fail to perform in an adequate manner, nature may let us fade into the sunset without another thought. After all, Tyrannosaurus Rex and the saber-toothed tiger were each at the top of their game at some point in their evolution. The success of the system we live within is assured. We are all part of that system. The system will continue, though we may have to show up at another time to give it another try. To start from scratch, with rumors of a powerful civilization that long preceded us, is always a possibility – mythology and legends and stories long misunderstood, but threads of truth just the same.

It is my speculation that planet Earth and its inhabitants will make it to the next level of success. Ultimately, humanity as an outpouring of the cosmos is meant to blossom as a substantial part of that success. This is the nature of life and the Universe's outpourings. We will do so as a quality expression of Life Force, for which we have little to do but look to nature to reveal her secrets as we discover our own. Somewhere it was our promise.

The solution is as simple as closing our eyes and asking, listening, feeling and not opening our eyes until we experience a response that resonates in our solar plexus and gives us a great deal of clarity, sense of purpose and direction. We all know the answer, but a great many of us don't know how to put first one foot in front of another. Until we begin to create new and forward momentum in a subtlety that addresses our future in a most positive and precious manner, we are on the outside looking in. All it takes is a bit of asking, a bit of listening, a bit of courage and a bit of trust to make that first step.

Knowing what is right and doing what is right is not as difficult as we might think. After all, it is mostly a matter of changing our minds, and we can see our minds are not quite the end-all, know-all we have assumed. It turns out that "we" have dominion over our minds, and, as someone once said, "One billion connected to Source are more powerful than one trillion who are not." The alternative is to be connected to and reliant upon our minds, for which we are beginning to see the fallacy of that line of thinking. As we create from the attractor field known as courage and move up the ladder of Dr. Hawkins' calibrated Map of Consciousness, we become powered by reason, acceptance, love and alignment with Source. The world and its creations become an invaluable learning experience as we traverse our experiences, getting a handle on free will and our possibilities.

Our success relies upon our authentic-self in alignment with what is true and nothing less. It is our nature; it is our dominion; it is our promise, and maybe even our duty. We were promised a very long time ago (could be dog years, prehistoric years or cosmic months) that we could have it all. It is part of our gene pool; it is part of our nature and a part of our encoding. And, yes, we are the top rung of the many species on this planet, though we have not yet thoroughly learned of our connection. All we need is a bit of courage, a bit of love and a bit of awareness of "who we are".

Guidance

Try a simple experiment. Sit and close your eyes and try to remain still to the point of being able to feel your own balance. Relax to the point that you forget that you are sitting, and notice what happens. As you find that point of balance and relax, your body begins to topple to one side or the other. Suddenly you feel an instantaneous "alert," and your internal mechanisms immediately begin to shore you up, and you are balanced again. You have an internal guidance system and it works all the time.

You are sleeping and "you" hear a sound. Suddenly you are awake. Adrenaline is rushing to instruct motor nerves, and you feel instantaneous instructions to your body and mind. You have an internal guidance system always alert and awake. Engrossed in conversation while driving your automobile, suddenly you realize you are stopping for a red light. You have a guidance system. Chills race up and down your arms or your legs or your back when you are in resonance with something you "know" to be so, and you have evidence for a built-in guidance system. When you find yourself in fearful or unhappy circumstance or find something you know to be "not so good," you find yourself with cautionary feelings running through your system – all, in fact, guidance and communication.

We have guidance and insight available to us – all the time. The only problem is, that for the most part, it is subtle. We have to listen and preferably catch the insight and guidance early. If we catch it early, we save inestimable time over the course of our lives as we take hints, follow our nose and allow ourselves to travel the road less taken. For, as we step out of our old habitual patterns, the Universe is better able to converse and guide us, and we are better able to become more.

It is interesting to note that the purpose of self-medication is to turn our innate signaling system off, or at least to cover it up. Feelings that come from deep within, that we don't want or refuse to heed become dissonance that we instead prefer to cover up. Feelings that overeating and its discomfort are able to overwhelm. Feelings that excessive sugar, the abuse of alcohol, the violent movies that dull our senses, the television programming and the news broadcasts that grind our potential into a mal of mediocrity, the excitement and glitter of force overpowering another, do nothing but overwhelm our circuitry. It's what we do. Through self-medication, we disable our ability to listen to our innate signaling system.

We would be surprised to discover what we run from and the way we do it. We wonder why we sometimes prefer addictions and being in a self-medicated daze, and now we know. Do caffeine and nicotine overload our nervous system so that we can put our inner murmurings on hold or aside? Does pride override the solar plexus and our capacity to listen? Are we are running from ourselves, Innate Intelligence and better choices? And what is the most recent alternative to listening to our inner guidance? Fear. National fear, "they are going to get us" fear, and "we have to be ready for them" fear. Always outside of us, and never our solutions.

And what about military pride (rating 175 on Dr. Hawkins' Map of Consciousness) overriding common sense and an awareness of the commonality we all share? After all, within a military and police authoritarian perspective and prideful allegiance to "their directives," many find themselves well out of touch of useful alliance with Innate Intelligence. Oftentimes, they find themselves within the confines of one who says it is so.

You have an internal guidance system and it works all the time.

Self-Governance

We have access to Innate Intelligence. The question is: How do we merge and invest into this greater system of success with the minimalist of fuss and muss and the truest of connection? After all, we are slowly traveling in this direction anyway. It is mostly a matter of merging with where we are assuredly going. Why not do it in as conscious and intentional a manner possible? At least we know what we are getting, how we get it and the satisfaction of a job well done as our newfound realities bloom in front of us.

We become intentional in bits and pieces and trial and error, as we have done since the beginning of time. After all, someone first conceived of alternative transportation. Someone first rode horses; someone first invented bridles, saddles and horseshoes and eventually carriages, teams, wagons, commerce, freeways and autobahns. Someone invented writing and language; someone invented religion; someone invented the concept of State; and someone invented invoices. Self-governance is the act of looking "in all the right places" for insight and direction for the running of our lives. This is something that we all have in common, for which a consistency, outpouring and a capacity for success unites us into one successful, powerful and ever-expanding organism and creation.

Did we move to our next state of evolvement with a tremendous whack and a thud?

Who could imagine how to run one's affairs such that they mesh for the highest good for ourselves, our community, our nation and our planet? Isn't that why we created Church and State in the first place – to manage things that we couldn't manage for ourselves and to hold a vision we were unable to hold for ourselves? Didn't government and Church come to exist to do what we could not do for ourselves, or so we thought?

How do all of the other multiplicity of organisms, eco-systems and cultures get by and otherwise keep their act together? How do these simple and not-so-simple systems of aliveness continue to grow and expand in an orderly and consistent manner without outside help? The simple answer is that they are connected to Innate Intelligence; their governance is internal and all of their needs are met. They are simply plugged in; their intent is clear and their outcomes are clear. Is humanity's solution becoming a bit more obvious?

We are a bit different, though we come from the same place and we are going to the same place (the apple orchard in the sky?). Perhaps it is time to let what doesn't serve us go back to dust as we realign to our true nature for moving forward. After all, realignment is surely a reoccurring principle in nature, and, in our case, realignment can be seen as conscious choice and little more than a decision and a bit of perception away. It is matter of free will for which reality refines itself again and again.

If we could simply snap our fingers and shift our direction and momentum (too rapidly), we would have enormous clashes in our daily existence as old and new momentums collide with a tumultuous uproar. Better to take small steps and learn to reshape our thinking one piece at a time. Individually, and out of contrast, we make new choices. Out of those choices, we make new choices, and out of those choices we continue to make new choices. Slowly the momentum of our individual realities shift and grow. This is nature's system of success, no matter where we think we are in the scenario. As we might imagine, we are on the right track, though possibly ever so slowly. How else could it be? The changes will be subtler than we might imagine. But let's get conscious about it; let's start to do it with a bit of aplomb, a bit of awareness and a bit of grace!

There is also the matter of sudden shifts in our realties as nature lays down her cards. Paradigm shifts are how nature refines and goes about her business. Sudden shifts to newfound order out of what appeared to be chaos is nature's game as she plays her hand as necessary. The only question is: What part did we play in encouraging alignment into newfound harmony, peace and order for ourselves? Did we do it as part of our own natural refinement, or hanging on the coattails of nature's newfound clarity that we wish we had decided for ourselves?

Did we move to our next state of evolvement with a tremendous whack and a thud, or did we move with conscious intent as grains of sand through an hourglass with eyes to see? Were we rightful participants, or were we wondering what was going on, whining and complaining and missing the big picture all the while?

Receptivity

Most of us live our lives subservient to an outer directive or outside authority figure to some degree or other. It may be as simple as dodging a bossy mother-in-law or as complex as attempting to jockey the outcome of "everlasting life." Others, having side-stepped such rudimentary concerns, still believe or wonder if there is a path they "should" be living their lives according to. Still, in the guessing game of right and wrong and outside influences, they run their lives with less than optimum possibilities. And then there are those who believe they run their own lives and are responsible for their own creations, though they are still unable to manage their existences at the level they wish and hope. Somehow, most believe we are trying to live up to the perceptions of something beyond our own immediate authority and capacity.

We need to see how all of this works and begin by trying it out for ourselves. While many believe our lives are directed from "on high," or determined from outside of ourselves in some manner, they are proverbially partially right and partially wrong. As for those who believe they are the source of the determinants of their lives, they are partially right, as well.

If we are "creators," fashioned in the image of God, for which there is reasonable evidence, we need only to put the puzzle together in the correct manner. After all, if we are trying every possibility, why not try one more? Let's say that we are cognizantly refining our power for prayer/focus, for which the Universe is in a constant state of response. Let's say that we are learning to trust Innate Intelligence and, among other things, we are learning to output higher and better quality thoughts, attitudes, aspirations, intents, etc. We are consciously seeking a shifting in our inner and outer worlds. Many have come to this point in their own conscious evolution, reality creation and quest for inner peace. After all, this is one of the most profound movements on the face of planet! We are becoming aware of our thoughts, our conscious choices and our realities as a product of the quality of our newfound conscious beliefs!

But, what many fail to realize and take into consideration is that the Universe takes our requests, our output and prayer, and, in its vast system of organization, lines up a number of potential realities and delivers them back to us tied with a bow. For the most part, we don't pay attention to what the Universe has made available to us because –

- we are unaware of our output;
- we have moved on to a new variation of what we want;
- we have concluded how it should look; or
- we have decided when and how it should show up.

We miss the reflection of what the Universe has put together for us because we are not receptive to what we output. We have no problem outputting, but we have an enormous problem understanding, recognizing and receiving what the Universe parlays back to us.

Or did we move with conscious intent as grains of sand through an hourglass with eyes to see?

In step with this idea, imagine living in an interactive Universe. Imagine that the Universe's system of success is inherently more intelligent than our own (a novel idea as I poke fun at all of us) and is capable of mimicking our wishes back to us in a far more refined manner than we yet know or understand. Included with our output and prayer for a "significant other," new home, a better business or peace and pleasure in our lives, indwelling Innate Intelligence, otherwise known as our superconscious mind, is outputting a part of our prayer as well! That "still-small voice" is infused in our outgoing prayer!

We discover that we are broadcasting our subconscious mind, our unconscious mind, our conscious mind and our superconscious mind all at the same time. Our outpouring prayer, including the unconscious and subconscious noise traditionally perceived as low quality output (low), the refinement of our nature and conscious thoughts (mid), and our still, small voice (high), gives us quite a spectrum of output and prayer that the Universe reflects back to us – constantly, consistently and perfectly. It is important to note that the unconscious and subconscious mind are both capable of delivering high quality unconscious intent, and this will come as new momentum begins to take over. However, for the sake of the above example, we will assume a somewhat traditional perspective of the subconscious, unconscious and conscious mind.

Depending on our capacity for subtlety, discernment and receptivity – or expectation, hardheadedness, apathy and resistance – we perceive and we receive accordingly. We don't actually create our realities; we choose our realities. We choose them from outputs that the Universe mirrors back to us, each according to the combination of our prayer – low, middle and high. Reality creation is a matter of –
- perception,
- receptivity,
- choice, and, ultimately,
- discernment

as we review what the Universe in all of its methodologies, wisdom and success reflects back to us as our outpourings – our prayer. Our charge is to be particular about choosing from the smorgasbord of what the Universe matches back to us. We don't have to take it all. We can choose from the low, medium or high results as we assign allowing to the rest of what the Universe puts in front of us. This becomes a good analogy for visionary focus as we begin to choose our outcomes and our choices with discernment and let the rest slide by.

Even though we may wish for something and even though we may sit within arm's reach of our most fantastic aspirations, often we miss what is available to us simply because we don't understand receptivity. If we don't understand what we put out, we don't understand what is available to us. Very often we miss what is available right in front of our noses. Furthermore, we often overwhelm the circuitry that allows for our reception and discernment to identify what is right for us. Our capacity for resonance is out of whack.

Receptivity becomes an additional tool for our cosmic tool belt as we discover yet another use for the advice that is our indwelling system of guidance. Choosing from the multiples of available reality fostered by the multiplicities of our output, we have considerable choice. As we refine what we choose from the many variables that is our reality creation, we discover receptivity to be a very important cog in the "ongoingness" that becomes our momentum.

Our choices become available to us through the quality of our output, for which the Universe interfaces in its vast capacity for organization and success and places a multitude of realities right back in front of us – without judgment and often in more refinement and clarity than we can see. Based on the quality of our output, including the still, small voice and perception and listening to our inner connection, we choose our realities from a multitude of possibilities, all originally derived from our outwardly flowing prayer.

We allow and ignore many aspects of our feedback realities, similar to sand flowing through our fingers, while others we choose to merge with and make our focus as we build vision and momentum in our lives. And, depending on the choices we make, we eventually rise and grow at a speed for which we can ultimately escape what is called the human condition.

We output at a multitude of levels, and our capacity to receive is limited only by our conscious awareness of our choices. We have access to the highest quality of realities as "reality choosers," the highest quality road to travel in our momentum, the highest quality experiences to experience and the best "allowing" available. We also have access to the best quality experiences and joys for "imprinting" and refining our newfound habitual patterns of thought. This, then, becomes our vision and our momentum as we move forward in our lives. Ultimately, we wish to revise what comes from our "lower" mind, and this slowly takes care of itself as we manage first things first. Undoubtedly, we are the only source of our realities. The Universe does nothing but reflect back our outpourings, with useful tips of its own, as we have the eyes to see and the resonance to feel our way forward.

Loop and Feedback System

It turns out that we work with a middleman, an authority figure and, moreso, a benevolent and completely loving partner – what some have referred to as God. Our prayers are reflected back to us precisely as we put them out. As we become more responsible, capable and conscious, we output our prayer, and our realities are returned accordingly. No judgment – just a perfect loop and feedback system, ours to upgrade and define and refine as we wish, the price being courage and truth, alignment with Innate Intelligence and a smattering of perception, receptivity and choice.

We live in an interactive Universe for which nature's system of success delivers based not only upon our capacity to output, but to receive. What we output and what we understand is how we partner with existence in our capacity to receive what is available to us. How to pick and choose our realities becomes the game, for that is how we steer our realities and momentum into ever greater change and momentum. We are creators; we output, and we are the recipients of what we output. We have choice, and we have indwelling Spirit as our partner! As we make intentional use of our partnership with Innate Intelligence, we engender more useful momentum in our lives.

In the past, we believed we were the recipients of the bounty of God or the love of God, for which we had little or nothing to say, though some seemed to get more than others. We are discovering the subtle nature of reality creation, which says that we are each the recipients of our own creativity, our own prayer, our own output and our own good. Ultimately, we are recipients of our own love, our own gratitude, our own courage and the quality of intent that underlies our outpourings. The Universe has and always will reflect perfectly back to us. It is just a matter of learning how to "choose once again" and begin to create with a more useful momentum in our lives.

As we take our hands off the steering wheel of our accustomed methods of creating reality, we learn to harness this loop and feedback system that is such an integral part of our reality creation. Our job is to pick and choose among the spectrum of our incoming realities in our most conscious and receptive manner, for which we again output and choose our results accordingly. Ultimately, we manage our realities as a momentum and stream of receptivity and choice, not so different from cowboys directing a herd of cattle, but ultimately similar to herding a river or flow of water, already knowing where it is going.

We become receptive to the idea that our own highest good exists as a part of our output; all the while we spew a multitude of perspectives simultaneously. Imagine the idea that we have only one choice and only one reality. Not much choice there! New choices, new realities; new realities, new choices; new choices, new momentum; and on it goes. Every day we can see evidence for the quality of our realities as we make our way into new and differing choices!

CHAPTER
TWELVE
VISION

*I*t makes sense that our realities are a process of a loop and feedback system of our own making. We output and we receive; we refine our output and we refine what we receive. In all of this, we refine our choices and thus we refine our momentum. Ultimately, we wish to make our newfound momentum habitual and self-serving as we refine our drive to match the higher vibration of Universal Forces.

We wish for our habitual patterns to serve us as we wish for our momentum to serve us. And, we wish for as much of our reality creation and momentum to be on automatic as possible. Though a very great deal of it may be redundant, it can be designed to be ever-expanding, as well. As we acquire the skill to choose our momentum with clarity and ease, it becomes second nature to us. As we slip into a stream of consciousness that might be felt as a current or a river, the tuggings of the Universe make automation of our rise toward higher realms an effortless task. As we feel the flow and come to know its nature, we align more of our attention to where we want to go and less on how to get there. As we accept the tuggings of nature and the Universe, we align with the cosmic currents, and we set our sights higher.

As creators, our dominion is the place between and among the molecules of time and space. As a species with newfound free will, we chart our course into the cosmos aligned with Spirit and Innate Intelligence. After all, we are Spirit clothed in bodies beginning to consciously get it right. We learn about the tools available to us, and we adventure far out above the limitations of anger, pride, ignorance and greed. Our momentum becomes our bodies as we feed off of the newfound habitual patterns that we have set into motion for ourselves. We venture out among the stars and harmonics of the Universe that were once beyond our imaginings.

Momentum becomes our body, and vision and resonance become our navigation, as we align with Innate Intelligence and become more. Our habitual patterns of reality creation become useful, having been elevated to the positive side of the equation as we experience realms well beyond the intent of courage, as referenced by Dr. Hawkins' calibrated Map of Consciousness. As we review the map, 220 is exponentially far greater than a 20-point jump from 200; 540 is almost incalculably greater than 500; and enlightenment is far, far beyond at 700 and above. There are many realms to explore.

We swarm as individuals aligned to the Light. For at some point, it is perceived as safe to make that final journey inward and upward.

As we teach the mind to serve us and maintain reality creation in the custom of our newfound, open-ended, habitual outpourings, we experience the higher-octaves of consciousness. We become complete, carrying our "servo-mental" mechanisms along for the maintenance of our momentum, as we learn how to subtly "just add." It turns out that the journey is well worth the effort, as our visionary mode sets itself for new and distant horizons. We become comfortable with our "new skin," as well as our propulsion and navigation.

We consciously climb the scale of our own evolution and our place in the cosmos. After all, it can be assumed that enlightened masters have always had access to perceptions and values far in excess of the values of humanity with little under its hood.[1] As we discover our Divinity, we see it to be an automatic and self-fulfilling system of success, understanding and knowing. Once we usefully harness our habitual loop and feedback system, we begin to resonate with the trees melding and feeding with the sky, planets spawning from central suns and a cosmic smile that is our knowing in all of its totality. Our newfound momentum becomes our new plateau and the next step in our evolution as we review and plot our next experience, all the while climbing Dr. Hawkins' Map of Consciousness. We begin to wonder what might lie beyond 1,000.

We swarm as individuals aligned to the Light. Some first and then others, for at some point it is perceived as safe to make that final journey inward and upward. We accept that we are able to become more, and, where we once refused to step and then gingerly stepped, we gravitate with the enthusiasm of young children, for we have become young again as we lay at our side values and perceptions that no longer serve us. We become wide-eyed at the possibilities as we accept our potential as something we innately know so well. We see that we are coming home bigger than when we began our trip into descendency, alive with the awareness that we are becoming more and renewed in our true connection with Source. We master Freewill[2] and we master intentionality as we come to have dominion over our affairs. We become more.

First a few and then more, and eventually the last make that fateful realization that resistance to our true nature in no way serves us. We become what Innate Intelligence has always been telling us is our outcome – a spiritually alert, alive and awake species on Earth. We become more. Gaia has birthed a cosmic outcome in free will, exceeding anything that the plant, animal, mineral kingdoms or nature could ever produce on its own.

We see the order of creation for which we finally take our rightful place. We meld with transparency into a world of love and peace and order that knows no bounds. We become more. We become expressions and outpourings of something that is ancient, yet ever different, as we continue to refine our individuality. Yes, we are far different than we imagined but fully individual, with Innate Intelligence streaming from our eyes, our creations and our choices. We become an expanded expression of Source and free will – a new species radiating with the conscious awareness of a job well done.

We continue to expand as the most advanced outpouring of creation, marrying and integrating consciousness on a scale that is undreamt except by that still, small voice. We become that seed we carried within our genes and our unconscious mind, that potential that some always spoke and knew – something that was always innate, something our mind becomes harnessed to uncover, as we survey our horizon for our next possibilities.

We come into alignment with our true nature because it is our heritage and a promise that was always available to us. We rely on gratitude and an awareness of our surroundings in wholly newfound ways. And we trust our brothers as they sort themselves out at their own recollection and speed. We realize that in our awakening en masse – a few at first, and then more and more – our planet becomes a host and a home in all new imaginings.

Our aspirations and journeys become travels to and from our solar system for which we can always find out way back, for the resonance of our home planet is powerfully strong. Our solar system and its planets sing in a unison that is unmistakable in its clarity as we vision forth among the vistas of space and time, knowing our bearings and our way back. It turns out that the ancients knew more about comings and goings and alignment with the cosmos than we were able to discern as we toiled in the misunderstanding of our past.

The cosmos is our true home. It is ours to range within and through and above and beyond as we discover the harmonics of the space between the atoms and the planets. We are drawn to new frequencies of resonance and time and space as we discover yet another aspect of our journey. Learning and experiencing are just beginning for us. As we sense the possibilities in entirely new ways of listening and feeling, we begin a migration toward newfound order running through our nervous system and the circuitry that is our intelligence. We have learned to expand and accommodate the discoveries of our home cosmos and sphere. Eventually we discover that there are multitudes of realms and that our journeys are just beginning. And, just like in the old days, we refine our awareness of our surroundings and we head out again and again.

Yes, we are far different but fully individual, with Innate Intelligence streaming from our eyes, our creations and our choices.

We meld with benevolence and love, as well as the technologies of choice, alignment and free will, and we become more. Wherever we travel, explore and make our presence known, life blossoms. Our invisible tendrils encourage life to new experiences, as we discover we are truly part of creation. Life begets life; we accept our heritage; and the Universe expands. In our capacity to align with the harmonics of Universal Forces, we discover our very being. We discover we are an essential cog in the expansion and expression of life in the cosmic realms.

We find newfound compassion, trust and unconditional love for life – all of life. We have compassion, joy and trust for the struggles of younger and lesser experienced life forms, valiantly striving to become their own – on their own. We begin to see the mastery of truth and order, and, in its expansion and growth, we see that it continues to be truth and order. As visionaries aligned with truth, we see that we are in our rightful place at our rightful time. All is well above and below and upon Earth and our home-based connection with the cosmos.

We Define and We Refine

In its simplest form, we are all creators connected to life – streaming life, this is the only way it can be. Can you imagine the alternative – one Creator managing us all? And for what reason? What would be the point? This is not so likely as we look around to see the vast success of the countless organic[3] and inorganic systems of life that exist all around us. Innate Intelligence is built in. Luckily, with free will, we have a capacity to explore as we align with nature and true success. As we pull ourselves up from our primordial ooze, we become extensions of the nature of the Universe's outpouring and interaction in a grand new way – a new aspect of life in the Universe. Luckily, we have only ourselves to look to for our successes and our failures. Enough of the "out of alignment" middlemen and grouchy old gods and in with the intentional refinements of our cosmic natures and the Universe at our beck and call.

We are each the rivers of the momentum of our thoughts, actions and choices.

Slowly we inch ourselves out of the ooze, first one way and then another. We wriggle this way and then we try that. We use what we learn, and we learn from our mistakes. We define and we refine ourselves anew and move into more alignment. Out of contrast comes clarity, for which we seemingly have a vast and indifferent but always awesome and impartial sounding board. Never judging and never other than a perfect and true reflection of our mistakes, our learning is reflected back to us for more refinement. Could it be any other way? Could it be any better? Could we ask for more? Maybe a handbook? Maybe a guide? Oops.. we answered our own question.

What we wish to offer is a realization that the deck is vastly stacked in our favor once we see how this works. Our job becomes to look for clues as to how the Universe (nature) interprets our outbound signals and returns them back to us, for which we have a vast and constant inpouring and spectrum of choice available. We don't have to figure out the details, or how it is going to work, or how to get it done. And, we don't have to figure out the order in which it will occur (linear reality). We simply don't have the mental acuity.

Our job is to continue to refine our outpourings and then simply ride the wave that is the feedback of nature's system of success and interpretation of our wishes. We then simply choose from among the numerous strata of nature's bounty. We create momentum as an accumulation of our conscious intent as we learn how to refine our capacity for receptivity. We learn about discernment; we learn about choice; and we move forward and upward – ever upward.

My friend Sheri knew what she wanted and chose not to define how it would come or how it would look. After all, she suspected she was off to Maui. But the Universe, in its infinite wisdom and interpretation of her prayer, knew better. An increasingly larger portion of her output/ prayer included more and more of her authentic and true nature as her lower-level broadcast refined and cleaned itself up. Her choices became presented to her as more in alignment with her true wishes. She had only to refine her prayer, and refine her receptivity to the re-interpretation by nature of her wishes and then choose once again.

We are each the rivers of the momentum of our thoughts, actions and choices. As we refine our outpourings and choices ever so slightly, we steer our momentum to new heights. We become masters of an extensive and ever-expanding system of successes as we learn to rely upon what works. As we are coming to see, change is a matter of choice, well within our domain. We accept our rightful place in the cosmos.

Dissonance

During a conference call, a number of us were discussing the events and successes of the past week. One of the callers, having had recent and huge successes in her coaching business, reported that her week had slowed to a crawl and lost its "glow." Janina was shopping for a new automobile and having quite a time of it. In fact, one afternoon she bolted from the showroom floor as the process had become increasingly overwhelming. After it was decided (during the call) that she was pursuing her goal of finding a new car in a far too intellectual and linear manner and that allowing the car to come to her might be an easier way to go, she began to feel better.

As the call went on and others were discussing their breakthroughs, insights and synchronicities from the past week, Janina began to re-evaluate the number of synchronicities and flow events she had experienced, even though the auto shopping frenzy seemingly overwhelmed and overshadowed them. Although Janina claimed to have had an uneventful and even nerve-wracking week, as she relaxed and listened to the others, she began to realize that she had a fantastic and magical week. It turned out that she was missing resources and happenstances available to her because her capacity for receptivity was in a state of overload.

In the end, it became clear to all on the call that the Universe was constantly in motion on her behalf, returning creation after creation per her wishes and overall momentum. But before the call and camaraderie among friends, she seemingly missed a great deal that the Universe had put in front of her because her receptivity "had a busy signal." In the end, she was surprised to discover that she had an awesome week, though it had been masked by "getting off track" during her auto shopping frenzy. It turned out that she was missing a great deal that the Universe had in store for her.

It seems like our capacity to receive, to be receptive and to become aware of the vastness of our choices is somewhat sullied when we are not in a high state of receptivity. When we are not trusting the process, or are otherwise caught up in a dysfunctional aspect of creating or pushing or resistance, it seems that our radar antenna, sense of timing and vision are off, and we miss what might be right in front of our noses.

It is interesting to note the importance of claiming and managing our resources - not only what we put out, but, specifically, our capacity for discernment, choice and receptivity to our own good. When we get off center and out of alignment with our clarity, purpose and underlying innate guidance, we become observers instead of visionaries. We wonder why the Universe does not answer our prayer, or how we might find ourselves with train wrecks at out feet or poor decisions and momentum that has to be constantly reined in. It turns out that our state of receptivity is quite important to us.

It is not unusual to believe that we know what we want for ourselves (holding tight to the steering mechanism), holding tightly to our "vision" even though the Universe may be providing us with something entirely more appropriate if we had but the eyes to see. As it turns out, Janina's friend had just been gifted with a new automobile by her husband, and, in perfect timing and order,

As we refine our outpourings and choices ever so slightly, we steer our momentum to new heights.

the friend's "not so old" car became a perfect match for Janina. In all of its wisdom, combined with the low, middle and high spectrum of our broadcast, the Universe produces a multiple of choices as decreed by our loop and feedback system.

Individuals with useful and healthy momentum often get their heads turned as they inadvertently stray into observer mode. As they miss the bounty being delivered by the Universe, they ultimately lose sight of their healthy focus and get further off track. Potentially, this begins a cycle that only can be brought to an end by stopping all forward momentum. After all, if we are not traveling in the direction that we are wishing for ourselves and resistance is futile, we might as well bring the whole show to a stop and wait for our old (as it exists) momentum to make itself known again. Either way, becoming quiet, listening and receptivity are important aspects of our focus as we attempt to get "back on track" – back to useful momentum.

It is best to become quiet, move back to gratitude and appreciation for what we have and work toward getting our loop and feedback system back to doing us some good again. As we can see, it delivers more faithfully than we know. Slowing down is a good thing sometimes. And, often, with a bit of help from our friends, we can readily get back on track. It is always a matter of choice, a matter of receptivity and a willingness to change our mind as the terrain calls for it. Courage always plays a part in our reality creation, as steadfastness with what is true becomes our rock and stability.

Multitasking

In addition to the process of learning to align with nature's system of success and a management of our outcomes, it is helpful to understand the use of multitasking. Multitasking is a matter of putting out a number of increasingly clear prayers and focus in the most practical and capable manner and offering them the opportunity to grow at nature's behest. As nature signals us that "our project" has grown to a certain point, we become aware that our next input, upgraded focus and insight is necessary.

We learn to see the folly of ideas that the Universe does not choose to commit to in our behalf.

If we had only one wish, one prayer, one vision or only one perception available for the production of our realities, we would become reliant on only one avenue for our juice and all of our opportunities. As it is, we have a broad number of outpourings occurring simultaneously, for which they all could use the refinement that is available via a partnership with Source. And, as we often have a need or an expectation associated with our outpouring, it is best to put our expectation aside and move to another project and outpouring – something about "a watched pot never boils." For, if there is one thing that is certain, we, in our imagination and capacity for vision, are able to hold a number of visions and manage a number of flow events[4] simultaneously. And this is much moreso with the help of our partnership with nature's system of success, as well as our loop and feedback system for reality creation.

As we delegate reality creation to our partnership with Innate Intelligence, we become effective participants in multitudes of simultaneous activities and outpourings. It turns out that we do this anyway, but, without conscious intent, reality creation often leaves a great deal to be desired. As we partner with nature's system of success, our capacity for multitasking grows exponentially.

Multitasking is no different than making a list of things we need to do before jumping into the car to get them done. As we drive around checking items off of our "to do" list, usually we discover that we are doing them out of order for purposes of convenience, or adding other items that we can get done while we are out. Oftentimes, we inadvertently take a right turn when we mean to go straight and find ourselves in newfound tree-lined neighborhoods, exploring new avenues and insights, new lunch spots, new acquaintances, new opportunities, etc.

Our list exists and we will get back to it (or not), but, for various reasons, we find ourselves off track (actually more on track than we know), as we often discover something exciting and new. Pleasant or meaningful and oftentimes startlingly synchronistic, we discover new possibilities – all from breaking away from our list and our "supposed to's" (our linear reality). The list had a purpose. It just turned out to be more than we expected; it turns out to be a jumping-off place. It turns out to be the beginnings of new momentum, for which new flow takes a life of its own and events begin to unfold. Our list and multitasking skills turn out to be a place from which we can incite nature to give us input and feedback as it "wedges messages and ideas into the cracks" as we go about our day.

The list is the beginning of our momentum. Writing down what we want or what we need to do is a beginning. It is a beginning for creating focus and momentum as best we are able to describe to that point. But don't get too carried away with the list; it is only a list and it is only a launching point – similar to the initial balancing on a bicycle as we begin to pedal forward. Once we have momentum, once we are up and off, once we have created new focus and momentum, our loop and feedback system kicks in, and the Universe begins to reflect back updated information. Once we put ourselves into motion (which may include going farther down our list or new lists), the Universe is much more capable of interacting with us and we with it. It is not as easy for the Universe to interact with us when we are sitting dead in the water.

A Watched Pot Never Boils

It is important to have multiple activities, so that ones that are readily supported by the Universe can shine while new ideas wait their turn. Until they have their own momentum or a life of their own with the Universe at their back, we may be attempting to force reality at considerable expense. As we learn to let nature power our wishes and activities, we enter into a partnership with nature and its exponential power. Instead of taskmasters attempting to create change on our own, we learn to rely on momentum that only can be attained by partnership with Innate Intelligence and Universal Forces.

As "a watched pot never boils," so it is with Universal timing. We must learn to allow nature, in all of its wisdom, to support or not support our endeavors, as the case may be. It would not be unusual to have adventures and ideas in mind that the Universe never chooses to support, such that our option becomes either to continually jump-start them or let them go. Sooner or later, we see the folly of ideas that the Universe in all of its wisdom does not choose to commit to in our behalf. This is the true art of discernment and clearly a part of the nature of receptivity. To learn to trust the Universe, as well as enliven and support the events the Universe chooses to get behind, is part of being a successful creator. Otherwise, we are creating on our own, and we already know the limitations, distortions and distractions this can bring.

It is best to establish ideas and focus with a sense of resonance and guidance, while checking in occasionally to see if and when the

Universe begins to apply momentum to our differing projects. In the meantime, we can come up with a multitude of other places to focus our time and energy. Multitasking suggests we are doing a number of things simultaneously as we divide our attention between activities the Universe is supporting and activities we wish the Universe would endorse. As we wait for insight that our new projects are shaping up, we can always keep busy with hobbies and activities that promote our personal mental, emotional and physical well-being. After all, as creators, we are constantly looking to enhance our multiples of momentum!

We can divert our attention (expectation) to exercise, journaling, working on a book (writing is a marvelous catharsis and perspective for self-discovery), meditation (for bringing momentum comfortably to a stop while refining our capacity for listening), tidying up, rearranging the house or office, going to a movie in the middle of the day (great for shifting energy) or doing volunteer work. We can work on new business ideas, learn a new language, support someone else, travel, take a job and otherwise shake up our habitual patterns and open ourselves up. We can

There is something powerful about doing that which we love.

also marvel with gratitude at the quality of life consistently streaming by, all the while awaiting hints that the Universe has momentum lined up for what we perceive (there's a hint there) as the projects we wish to get underway.

These other activities are our goals as well. In the meantime, we can feed off the energy of the activities that the Universe is supporting while we attempt to subtly coax our pet projects off the ground, understanding that, if we are on track, the Universe will kick in. Lauren Holmes calls this "following our art" or finding our art, as the case may be. Needless to say, as one or another of our projects takes off, based on our clarity and focus and nature's input, they make us stronger and give us juice.[5] We will then have the satisfaction that only a knowing creator can conceive and achieve.

There is something powerful about doing that which we love, but often we have to move into it gradually as we wind down momentum or beliefs that no longer serve us. While we lay the foundation for what we wish, all the while refining our existing momentums, we watch and wait for our new activities to pick up speed. Undoubtedly, balancing a number of existing momentums is far easier than managing the end result of a huge train wreck at our feet or forcing an activity before its time. As we manage the multitude of activities that are important to us, watching and waiting on what we "know" we want, sometimes we find ourselves heading out in a new direction as something better pops up! Not to worry; the Universe has a say too.

Multitasking is easy because we do it all the time. If we wouldn't try to force outcomes out of the projects we have "already" decided upon, things would become much easier. If we could but just give up expectations and learn to rely on Innate Intelligence for our reality creation, we could contribute a bit more ease to the planet – down the street, in our neighborhoods, within our own households, and within our own natures and being. Our momentum would be something for which we become well-pleased!

Hint: Do things you wouldn't normally do. Look for where you can get the most support from the Universe.

It is always a good idea to have several sources of income. Make it a hobby to study the source of the ups and downs of the stock or currency market or dabble in a multilevel marketing company. Work on a new business idea while keeping the old alive, or research something new while maintaining something old. Always have two sources of income and numerous sources for your juice. Of course, we should all be running dozens of different and interesting facets of creativity in our lives.

Stay busy. Walk some acreage for sale in the country. Purchase some simple home design software and plan a solar-aspected home for that particular piece of property. Find another site and discover the proper design that best suits that piece of land. Find a hobby that interests you, something that gives you feedback that you are alive.

226

Learn about boats or RVs or about the National Parks or the waterfalls of the world. Dream a little. Study ancient architecture or the reasons behind the American Civil War or learn about clothes design or attend a culinary school or travel. Keep busy doing and trying different things. Adjust your habitual patterns of thinking to "open-endedness" and look for avenues supported by Innate Intelligence. Hint: Do things you wouldn't normally do. Look for where you can get the most support from the Universe. And then, watch your life unfold as you meld into a connection with Universal Correspondency and outcome.

We might even discover the joy of doing rather than having. We are ingrained with and taught that the attainment of our goals is our success. As we review what is important, we may discover that feelings coursing through our system bring us much more satisfaction than the physical end result. What difference does it make if we design a house for a lovely piece of property that may never come to exist? What if we see a kitchen we like in a movie and run to our drawing software to include it in our "flow" home? What is living about? Is it not that feeling of aliveness that comes from ideas coursing through our nervous system and the resonance of a job well done?

Which is more important? To dream and flow our juices, even if it only produces seductive and vast amperage coursing through our system, or expend a lifetime on a single ideal? Which do we prefer? Some would say that no matter, when the results are achieved and the house finally built, the juice diminishes. It turns out that the creation process is far more interesting and exciting than the end result.

How do we want to live our lives? Free will and creativity is what makes us more than the animal, the mineral and plant kingdoms. Get out there! Design another house! Court Universal Forces and learn how to allow the Universe to flow through your soul. Where do you want to go next?

If we would but disregard time, anything we put our minds to can come to us as we refine the quality of our underlying intent. It is a matter of constantly refining the momentum of our beliefs and knowings with insight from Innate Intelligence. After all, we carry a great deal of baggage that interferes with our capacity for clarity, output and receptivity. Learn to let the Universe parlay our vision into its possibilities and flow through our system as a function of creativity, knowing and living life. Discover something new about ourselves. When we decide how it should look and when it should show up, we lose sight of the possibilities. Instead, go shopping. Not that kind of shopping! Shop among our goals, activities and aspirations and see which ones offer us the most juice. In other words, multitask.

Waging Peace

As we learn to refine our vision and become more responsible for the quality of life we each have within our spheres of influence, we affect and influence the outcome of humanity in a more useful manner. As we become more powerful as individuals and come to know our relationship with Innate Intelligence, we affect the whole in a more useful, holistic (and exponential) manner. And, as we give up unconscious consentience, i.e., silently empowering the middleman through our non-participation, we begin to create change – not only for our children, not only as an influence that can be felt generationally, but also as an influence on the emerging nations of the world. As adolescents and young nations alike, their perspective and growing momentum is representative of what they have learned or not learned thus far. Ultimately, through conscious consentience (mass-mind intentional support) of human rights, justice, democracy, etc., we effectively influence the whole.

As we learn to share what we are becoming, as we learn to give up separation and a belief in man-made superiority and merge into a wholeness with each other, we realize a new world order of our own making. As we come into alignment with Innate Intelligence and a conscious consentience, we silently vote for what is right and our world slowly begins to turn our way – knowing that it can be no other way.

A good number of us carry the accoutrements of personal responsibility but use it only in the slimmest of margins or as dictated by our job responsibilities or immediate family. We use it no farther than we can consciously see and rarely beyond our immediate horizons. We all want to be, do and have more, and I suspect we are learning how. As old silent consent gives way to knowing the difference between right and wrong, we voice the values of humanity above and beyond the habits of conditioning and despair.

As the world becomes smaller, more closely knit and we recognize we are more the same, it becomes time to speak out on our own behalf. And, as we discover our true nature, we discover we have something to say. Interestingly, speaking out is not a matter of resisting what is wrong, fighting the oppressors or name calling, but a matter of putting first one foot in front of the other in alignment with what we know to be so and what we feel is right, based on our partnership with Innate Intelligence and each other. It is simply a matter of becoming conscious, in alignment with what is true and voicing the same.

When we decide how it should look and when it should show up, we lose sight of the possibilities.

Sometimes this might bring us to physical action, for, in writing the list, we begin that process of creating the focus that allows the juice to flow, reminding us that we are alive and capable of moving forward. Often it is a matter of a silent awareness and consent for what we hold to be true, as well as an awareness and vision of how we want our planet to unfold. Silently we wage peace by acknowledging only what is true for us, each other and the world. After all, we know that the quality of our underlying intent is exponentially far more powerful than the old method of solving problems through resistance.

This is not much different than the carnage of the World Trade Center and the vast pulling together of the peoples of the world. A more recent expression of unity comes from humanity arguing for peace preceding the U.S. attack on Iraq. Not that one nation is so much right and another so very wrong (and vice versa), but, as humanity begins to see momentum gone wrong for which the eventual fate is a train wreck of huge proportion, we discover we have a choice and a voice. For as we experience train wrecks in our own lives as a matter of faulty thought processes, nations do the same. As we realize that nations are ultimately made up of individuals, conscious and unconscious, we begin the transition as dictated by the formula "out of contrast comes clarity."

Never before have so many people worldwide stood tall against what they saw as injustice. Never before have people had the opportunity en masse to learn the difference between protesting war and waging peace. It is of an inestimably valuable distinction as humanity rockets into the 21st century. We become grateful for the opportunities to see the ways of the old as we become clearer about the importance of the new. Eventually we discover gratitude as the world grapples with its issues and as it creates perspective as a necessity backdrop for its birthing into the Light.

It has been said that the United Nations performed admirably in its attempts to broker a solution that did not include war. All over the world, countries were in dialogue with each other, making stands, arguing for what is right, listening to the will of the people, with concerns for justice and the human factor. Turkey turned down an offer of $26 billion in loans and aid from the United States, to position U.S. troops on Turkish soil preceding the U.S. attack on Iraq. Instead, Turkey became a leader, voting its conscience and refusing the almighty U.S. dollar. Humanity is slowly growing up. Sometimes it takes extraordinary backdrops and contrast to see right from wrong.

An e-mail began to circulate just before the U.S. attack on Iraq.[6] It introduced an individual who has been waging peace for 45 years as one of the earliest staff members of what was then a very young United Nations. At 80 years of age, he spoke before The United Nations Association of San Francisco on February 5, 2003. Dr. Robert Muller,[7] former U.N. Assistant Secretary General and presently the Chancellor Emeritus of the University for Peace in Costa Rica began his speech:

"I'm so honored to be here," he said. *"I'm so honored to be alive at such a miraculous time in history. I'm so moved by what's going on in our world today."*

"Never before in the history of the world has there been a global, visible, public, viable, open dialogue and conversation about the very legitimacy of war."

He went on to say that the whole world is now having this critical and historic dialogue – listening to all kinds of points of view and positions about going to war or not going to war. In a huge global public conversation the world is asking – *"Is war legitimate? Is it illegitimate? Is there enough evidence to warrant an attack? Is there not enough evidence to warrant an attack? What will be the consequences? The costs? What will happen after a war? How will this set off other conflicts? What might be peaceful alternatives? What kind of negotiations are we not thinking of? What are the real intentions for declaring war?"*

He ended his speech by referencing a recent *New York Times* article pointing out that up until now there has been just one superpower – the United States, and that has created a kind of blindness in the vision of the U.S. **But now, Dr. Muller asserts, *"there are two superpowers: the United States and the merging, surging voice of the people of the world.*[8] "** (Emphasis added.)

If we were to understand how loosely the illusion of reality is held together, for which we need only to change our minds, we would discover solutions undreamt. Those connected to Innate Intelligence are exponentially far more powerful than those whose quality of intent may be found as less than 200 on Dr. Hawkins' Map of Consciousness.

There is a new world order awaiting our nod as we polish our commitment to newfound responsibility, choice and decision-making. As we align with indwelling Innate Intelligence, as we learn to choose for ourselves outside the influence of the middlemen, we discover how very much alike and how very powerful we are.

On another note, regarding another e-mail that made rounds to thousands and thousands, if not millions, of people in March 2003, there was the suggestion of a prayer vigil for President Bush for a certain date. It was suggested that President Bush had an enormous decision-making load and an enormous amount of anger directed toward him. It was suggested that "we" could be of inestimable help by sending him love on a certain day. This is a very powerful example of conscious consentience and a good use of the power of conscious choice. With a conscious commitment to the issues and problems of the world, aligned with unconditional love and a sophisticated underlying quality of intent, we would see the world come to a new blossoming very quickly.

Vast opportunities await us as we refine our output and consciously choose from among our many possibilities. We discover that, in alignment with nature's system of success, we can move mountains and we can foster newfound order. And, as we align with the highest possible resources available, all we have to do is choose accordingly. We then discover that our horizons are much broader than we had imagined and our potential is the reason for the distance between the stars.

We know we have achieved visionary focus when our lives become a consistent momentum of refinement and discernment, all of which come from the conscious and deliberate choices we make. We are able to see the quality of the flow events in our lives as rivers of momentum, for which we learn to pick and choose, carefully discerning our choices and what I like to call "just add."

CHAPTER THIRTEEN
LUCIDITY

*W*e see rhyme and reason in our actions, thoughts and desires, and we see how we power our realities. Our loops of habituated patterns of thinking become our servant and we its master, rather than the manner of a bulldozer without a driver. We glimpse possibilities of personal responsibility in a new light as we defer to a part of us that we did not know existed – that part of us that is God, that part of us that is connected to God and that part of us that allows us to become more.

We map the intricacies of the mind. We see that "we" are cause, that effect is our outpouring and that the Universe offers an obliging hand. We no longer fear what is around the bend or beyond our immediate perspective because we are whole and complete. We accept our circumstances with grace and knowing because they are extensions of ourselves. We have become one in our relationship with outside circumstances as our identity in separation falls by the wayside. We become a voice in unison as we discover our samenesses and share our splendors among each other. We are more.

Reality becomes little more than feedback for the quality of our alignment with Source. Finally, we realize that alignment with Source is more important than reality itself! Wholeness feeds our outpourings as we refine our momentum to ever finer distinctions. The world was not created in a single day, and we continue to refine ours, as well. This is not so difficult as we get the hang of being intentional creators in partnership with Universal Forces. We build upon our successes and we align with our growing resonance. We refine our natures and become recipients of the bounty that is the cosmos. We thrive. This is life. This is creation expanding. This is humanity expanding. We continue to become more.

As we become aware of our give-and-take relationship with nature, we ride our momentum to conclusions that only a partnership can deliver. The wisdom and authority of the Universe is at our beck and call as we become accustomed to our possibilities. After all, we have been making choices for quite some time and we have quite a bit to show for it. We see that refinement is a major part of the process.

The wisdom of the Universe is at our beck and call as we become accustomed to our possibilities.

We broadcast from a multiple of perspectives as we learn to decipher reality creation and extend ourselves. We refine our incoming and outgoing messaging systems while flow events, synchronicities and higher-octave happenstances light our way. Our momentum becomes distinct and self-serving as we realize it is up to us. As we shift and refine our output, we establish new and significantly more appealing outcomes. Momentum becomes our primary creation and the vehicle for the attainment of our possibilities. We steer our momentum as we learn how to "just add." Our momentum becomes our being.

Flow

Our circumstances automatically flow out in front of us as evidence of the quality of our momentum. By definition, "flow" is a series of events that are linked in clarity and healthy momentum of its own, for which we experience feelings of exhilaration and knowing that we are on a rightful track – a track in alignment with our inner nature. Flow produces a deep comfort as we accept solutions offered by Innate Intelligence that are felt as lift under our wings. Flow may be further defined as the release of the experience of polarity and duality as we merge into a simple oneness. We become one with the nature of Universal energies. Flow becomes one with our surroundings.

I can remember only years ago holding momentum and carrying vast amperages of energy though my system for what seemed like weeks at a time. I was able to experience flow and I was experiencing expanded energies coursing through my body, something I was not soon to forget. After one exhilarating three-week period, I was worn out as the experience came to a completion. Somehow I thought I was holding the experience together by the sheer use of will because I was exhausted at its conclusion.

I now understand that I did not have sufficient alignment with Universal Forces flowing though my system. Portions of my deeply held beliefs were counterproductive to the maintenance of the opening I had created for myself. This was six or seven years ago and I remember it well. Elusive alignment with flow becomes easier as our beliefs line up with new input and possibilities. My experiences encouraged me to continue to refine my nature while Innate Intelligence encouraged me with its nudges and insights. I continued to quest for my Holy Grail.

Our realities are not only a matter of what we output and receive, but also of learning to decipher and align with Universal Correspondency effortlessly carrying the ball – our ball. It is not so much different than the lift of an airplane wing in its harnessing of the forces of nature. What we are looking for is momentum, synchronicities and happenstances that mesh to produce extended periods of flow in our lives. Ultimately, we might describe the experiences as similar to what it must feel like to be a flower blooming or the subtleness of the onset of a light rain shower - something for which we give up control and instead happens in splendor, synchronicity and effortlessness.

Connecting the Dots

As we release what does not serve us, we make room for more in our lives. There is no way to experience flow while under the influence of grudges, expectations, anger or resentment. A cleaning and clearing of our system, our hang-ups and our limitations must be replaced with a knowings of our connection and innate capacity for amperage coursing through our system. Allowing and gratitude are key as we refine our systems of belief, for which guidance becomes indispensable as we choose once again.

It behooves us to review our synchronicities, happenstances and flow events in a more useful manner. As comfort and ease infiltrates our experience, we move forward with newfound ease and grace. We decipher resonance for events drawn into our lives as guidance propelling us toward "finding the groove" of our beliefs, our momentum and our choices. As we consent to and partner with inner guidance, we see synchronicities, flow events and otherwise resonance and harmony populating our accumulating reality. Eventually, we get a clear picture for what nature "nods for" in our thoughts and choices.

Initially, these events are fleeting and our "observer" mode strong, returning us to our old style realities all too quickly. It would be our intent, then, to see hints in our successes (i.e., synchronicities, flow events, resonances) and line them up as breadcrumbs toward what the Universe supports and for which our visionary focus becomes a valuable tool and directional device. As we recognize synchronicities and flow events as reflections of what nature is supporting, we refine our vision accordingly. At the same time, we allow the results of our old momentum, to simply stream by, as we sift our way toward conscious intent, newfound focus and alignment with Universal Forces.

It is not for us to decide what we want and push forward come hell or high water, though this has been a popular method for getting things done in the past. It is ours to try on ideas, to try visionary models and to look for hints of the Universe's support. As we look for resonance suggesting the amount of support we might be able to attain, we refine our visionary focus and we continue to make choices. We watch for what the Universe suggests, and, lining up the dots, we find clarity in our momentum. Seeing the difference between what we want and what the Universe supports is an interesting opportunity to learn to trust and accept a bigger picture. It is a part of our cosmic adolescence.

As we refine our capacity for alignment with our inner nature and outward circumstances, we experience more and more synchronicity and order in our lives. As we delve further into the innateness of life, we find our paths crossing with others of like vibration and outpouring. We begin to meld with the momentum of others, and our sense of wholeness continues to expand. We enter and become one within a shared matrix of wholeness.

As we release what does not serve us, we make room for more in our lives.

In clarity and momentum, there are others who live their lives in octaves of flow similar to our own. As we increase our capacity to accept the biddings of Universal Correspondency, we find our paths crossing and our flows and synchronicities interlinking. It could be said, then, that we are not only the recipient of the grandeur of Universal Forces in our own lives, but a participant in the synchronicities of others, as well. After all, who says that being a recipient of the intent of the cosmos is our only function?

As our momentum aligns and blends within a matrix of synchronicity and wholeness, we fill in the cracks and provide happenstance for each other, all the while extending our own momentum and outcomes. In our correspondency with nature, as we rise through the calibrated Map of Consciousness, we meet other visionaries plying the forces of nature in each their own way. We feel compelled to experience activities that become a blending of our wishes with the flow of others. In a new level of correspondency and flow, we scratch each other's backs and deliver to each other gifts as we inadvertently mesh with each other's wishes and outcomes. It turns out there is more to flow than simply being a wide-eyed recipient of Universal Forces.

A Matrix of Wholeness

By way of example, I attended a conference in Victoria, British Columbia, for which Barbara Marx Hubbard was one of the main speakers. Certainly, in preparing for her presentation, she had been gathering her forces, directing her staff, arriving at her destination, and concluding momentum toward what would become her talk. As her momentum headed toward its culmination, others were caught up in the intent of her thought and focus. It is likely she was unaware of many incidental events that ultimately lent to the overall support of her speaking engagement.

It is ours to try on ideas and to look for hints of the Universe's support.

In step with my own synchronicities, happenstances and delicious periods of flow, I became a player in her synchronicities and momentum without my knowing. Plans were dashed as nature better sorted outcomes and gently placed me into circumstances other than I might have chosen, as I attempted to act out my itinerary and travel plans for the conference. My Seattle rental car failed to materialize, and instead offered me the opportunity to take a 6-hour bus shuttle to Victoria. Furthermore, because of the failure of my rental car to materialize, I was unable to take advantage of the beautiful harborside hotel I had planned for myself.

So much for the convertible and hotel that boasted the best seafood restaurant on the waterfront, or my intent to tour Vancouver Island after the conference. Nature in its alignment with my true wishes and underlying quality of intent instead delivered me to a campus dorm room right in the center of the event I was attending. Had I stuck to my linear list and progression and plan, I might have found myself sprinting through morning traffic to get to the conference hall for events that started as early as 8 a.m. and ran as late as 10 p.m. As it was, I had use of a tiny dorm room and walked through the campus on my way to the multiple events at the Prophets Conference in comfort and ease and with time on my hands.

How could I have known that my perceived momentum as I studied airfares, rental car arrangements and hotels would fade to dust as the Universe, in its all-knowing, rearranged my trip and my capacity to be an outpouring for others. Had I stood my ground and demanded my rental car, though none were available, I might have missed some serious synchronicity that brought whole new experiences to light.

There was some talk that our conference at the University of Victoria was somehow perceived as radical and that we were not getting the favorable press to which we were surely entitled. After all, we were a bubbly group and not a bunch of misfits or revolutionaries – well, maybe not misfits. But somehow, our somewhat unusual crowd coursing across the border into Canada put a strain on immigration, as attendees spoke of an event with speakers James Redfield, Tom Robbins, Norman Shealy, M.D., Ph.D., Huston Smith, Ph.D., Robert Anton Wilson, Brook Medicine Eagle and others. Somehow there had been suggestions that we were part of an uprising of some sort and that local newspapers were supposedly in discontent of our gathering.

As it was, I made a fateful spin on my heels and ended up in the cafeteria on a relatively quiet Saturday noon hour. I had picked up a lunch tray, and as I walked into the sparsely filled eating area, I choose to sit by a window and not too distant from a woman rummaging through her notes. As I sat and we eventually spoke, it became apparent that she was a reporter preparing to interview Barbara Marx Hubbard.[1] Barbara hails from Santa Barbara, California, and as a visionary over the past 30+ years, eloquently beholds a world in a transitory state and "birth in progress."

As I began to interact with Therese, a journalist from Canadian Public Radio, I began to understand my position within the momentum that is Barbara Marx Hubbard. Therese had drawn Barbara to interview among the many journalists who were covering the event. But Therese was at a disadvantage because she was out of the loop, did not know Barbara or her books or influence and only had several hours to get ready.

Without my car and fancy hotel, I was aligned to new flow as my projected outcomes evaporated into something nature better had in mind. Instead, I found myself at the beck and call of Universal Forces as this reporter made the decision to prepare as best she could for her interview. I arrived right on cue and was able to lay down a bit of foundation about the purpose of the Prophets Conference and why we had come together. After all, we had Dr. Edgar Mitchell, former astronaut, Moon walker and founder of the Institute of Noetic Sciences; James Redfield of *The Celestine Prophecy* fame; Gregg Braden, a past senior aerospace computer systems designer turned researcher, author and visionary; several other highly regarded scientists, researchers and Ph.D.s; a Mayan Elder "Day Keeper" from the Yucatan; and so on.

In an apparent eddy of Barbara's momentum, flow and underlying quality of intent, I was able to offer Therese a 12-page document I had, for some reason, printed off of Barbara's Web site[2] before I left on my trip. I was happy to share, because it became apparent that I was helpful to Therese's preparation for her interview. I also felt my timely arrival was a source of information as to the conscious nature and intent of our gathering. As it turns out, Therese had drawn Barbara's name only hours earlier and she was undecided about a mad dash to the city for information, or to prepare for her interview in a more useful manner. As it was, sitting in the cafeteria on a relatively quiet Saturday and apparently open for solutions, we each arrived in a similar manner of quality of intent and openness and expectation of the possibilities. I was able to deliver a solution that ultimately lined up with the momentum that was both Barbara's and Therese's, as well as my own.

It was exciting to be a participant in a synchronistic and electrifying coincidence of this magnitude. This was not in the usual vein of receiving of the bounty of the Universe. This was instead Universal Forces flowing through me seeking completion authored by the intent of another! Somehow I had elevated my vision, my possibilities and my quality of intent, allowing me to mesh with "others" in a similar rampage of synchronistic flow and outcome. I became enlivened to offer my participation in "another's" dance that I could never have conceived, much less acted out on my own. In other words, I delightfully found myself not only the pawn of Universal Forces, but a cog in the machinery of the momentum and underlying intent that is Barbara Marx Hubbard!

As we refine our vision, we align with others operating within a similar octave of resonance and synchronicity.

For Therese's part, she chose to become receptive and chose the cafeteria as an alternative to a mad dash to town to prepare for her interview. Certainly a multitude of possibilities came together illustrating the exponential authority available as we refine our underlying qualities of intent, for which the Universe has a ready response. Therese decided that "collecting her thoughts" was more useful than action, for which she instead achieved newfound flow and results.

Somehow, within Universal Correspondency and a holistic matrix of connection, we respond within the spectrum of each other's quality of intent. I was in resonance to my own momentum, and I was apparently in flow to the momentum of "others." Therese was in alignment with order in her life and preparation for her interview, all the while "open to the possibilities." And what seemed to be momentum foreign to my own instead became the fulfillment of the wishes of others in a whole new and healthy way. I, of course, had an electrifying experience that I would be happy to host again and again!

Somehow, as I released the way it was supposed to be, took hints from Innate Intelligence and my feeling nature and followed my nose, I found myself synchronistically bounding through life fulfilling and supporting the happenstances and synchronicities of "others." It was a powerful and telling experience, especially upon realizing that "my sense of a plan" had begun to fall apart soon after I arrived.

It turns out that we are all part of a vast matrix of experiences and flow events intertwined and enmeshed with each other. As we refine our vision and our capacity for momentum and corresponding flow, we align with others operating within a similar octave of resonance and synchronicity. As we climb the Map of Consciousness, it becomes increasingly apparent that our interactions feed and support not only ourselves, but also each other. It turns out we are all in this together. As we have the eyes to see and the vision to elevate the quality of our intent, what once was perceived as separation is now perceived as wholeness. We relax. It gets better.

As we let ourselves expand into the flow and possibilities, our worlds just naturally get better.

To relate some of the other synchronicities during the event would be beyond the scope of these pages, other than to say that I walked the three-day conference feeling my way through it. Within my own cocoon of experience, I reviewed the activities, the speakers, the audience and the love that was coursing through the event. As I considered the rapt attention and participation of the audience and the intent of the speakers and staff, I began to gauge how my message might be accepted within such a conference. I began to "try on" how my material (for which this book was just beginning) might blend within the group experience and the questions and answers being bandied about. I measured how effectively I might interact as a speaker offering a piece of the puzzle explained from the numerous perspectives of the different speakers.

As I melded, merged and matched my sense of the conference over several days, as well as evaluated whether "my message" might offer a cohesive value to this "uprising," I was mistaken for one of the speakers. This was an interesting turn of events. In yet another example of synchronicity, clarity and feedback from the Universe, I was approached by several individuals who began to question me about the Shroud of Turin, which was part of the presentation by the featured speaker Gregg Braden.

As I sat during lunch, on yet another day in that magical cafeteria, several individuals walked up to me, not asking if I had a minute or if I was Gregg, but simply launching into their questions about the Shroud as if I were Gregg. To me, this was an interesting experience. Certainly Gregg and Barbara were both peers and associates, as were all of the speakers aligned as one cohesive group. After all, they had camaraderie among themselves because of their similar masses of momentum and similar underlying qualities of intent – they were in the same boat (on the same stage?) and obviously of a "similar vibe." But, I found it profoundly interesting to be mistaken as the featured speaker and identified as part of that momentum.

I don't even think I look like Gregg, but I must have been doing "something" that aligned me with this group! I suspect it was my underlying quality of intent as I wandered the pathways and byways of the conference perceiving myself as a future speaker with solutions and insights. Nevertheless, I had the experience of gently bringing the questioners to a stop as I expressed to them that I was not whom they were looking for.

It is interesting to note that as we climb the scale of conscious intent, we merge into our possibilities, our awarenesses and our similarities – as well as our capacity to "scratch each other's back." Maybe I should have let them continue with their questioning. Maybe I would have had a reply that might have been useful to them. As we see things as more whole, we see and share with each other in more correspondency and similarity. As we move in a similar direction as peers, not so different from the resonance of animals in migration or a school of fish in motion, we awaken to our possibilities. We become more together.

We see each other in a new light as we discover that we match each other vibrationally and in intent as the Law of Attraction weaves it magic. We interweave within each other's lives as we realize that we don't have to supply all of our own solutions, supply all of the facts or even build all of the momentum ourselves. As we get the hang of Universal Flow and Universal Correspondency, we find we are all in the same dance. We are part of a holistic and cosmic matrix whole, a matrix that is the opposite of a matrix of separation.

Yes, we operate at many different octaves, for which we share among those of a similar vibration and underlying quality of intent. It is not that we are not all equal or entitled to the same circumstances, but that our vibrational correspondency attracts "soul level" group experiences, all the while climbing Dr. Hawkins' Map of Consciousness. We each dance to our own drummer, and, within our own octave, we find similar souls in correspondency, and thus our worlds exist and are held together in similar manners.

Separate, in alignment, or the differing states of refinement – we each experience our realities as outpourings of our capacity to refine our underlying qualities of intent, for which we then share accordingly. Ultimately, we find correspondency within everything we do. It is a basic principle of the Universe. Eventually we find wholeness. Eventually we find each other.

Strife begets more strife; allowing begets more allowing; and our momentum, whether we understand it or not, begets more of the same. It is sometimes difficult to understand that we are all capable of outpourings and receptivities that far exceed what our linear perceptions are able to imagine. It becomes ours to release how specific realities "should" turn out and instead focus on refining momentum that takes us to the other side of the equation and beyond.

How Did That Happen?

To cap an otherwise fully eventful trip and conference, I had somehow lost the brochure that indicated the shuttle bus with departure times for a key part of my journey back to Seattle. After all, there were taxis, ferries, shuttles and hotels to line up as I was well off of my preordained "flight plan." Scheduling my checkout to match up with shuttles and ferries to end up at my hotel on the mainland for a business meeting on my final day was another activity I had to sort out. Somehow I had lost the name of the shuttle service that would match my hotel in Vancouver (on the mainland) with my flight out of Seattle.

I discovered that information on campus was suited to locals and regulars and left me without the name of the shuttle I needed to piece together my return and take best advantage of my time. Asking at the lobby for the dorm services, nobody knew of the shuttle I was attempting to discern. As I walked back to my dorm room in the rain, I stooped to pick up a brochure to discover it

As we refine the quality of our intent, our prayer reaches deeper into Universal Mind.

was precisely what I was looking for! Somehow the schedule I needed showed up as a soggy brochure at my feet in the twilight dark. Anybody got any ideas how that happened?

It seems that as we learn to build momentum and let ourselves expand into the flow and possibilities, our worlds just naturally get better. I can vividly remember the SeaTac Airport car rental agency mishandling my reservation, giving me no option but to start from scratch by standing in a new rental agency line sans reservation, or asking and listening for what was next. As it was, I saw a sign that said "Information" – which to me is an acceptable method for beginning to access hints as to one's new direction. I discovered that I had about 25 minutes to decide on a new course of action that included several shuttle busses that would take me more than 180 miles and still deliver me that same evening. As I settled down on the shuttle bus heading out of Seattle in bumper-to-bumper traffic, I decided to relax and let nature do the driving.

As we climb the scale of correspondency with Universal Forces, what once was separation, becomes unity, oneness and wholeness. As the quality of our intent rises, there is a whole other world, a whole other correspondency to which we become enabled – a whole new world of happenstance and synchronicity that becomes our existence and momentum and something we become accustomed to.

As we refine the quality of our intent, our prayer reaches deeper into Universal Mind. As our underlying quality of intent drives us into further correspondency with Universal Flow, we recognize our connection with wholeness. In other words, we become active nodal points in a matrix of wholeness that knows no bounds. It turns out that we are all one. What ties us together is our output and our refinement and our alignment. What makes us more is what we do with what we have.

We have to give up what we have in order to have more.

It is interesting to think of the possibilities as we raise the quality of our conscious intent. It is true that we have to let go of existing realities, or let existing realities flow into newfound realities, though, ultimately, we have to give up what we have in order to have more. And as we are beginning to see, having the synchronicities of flow and alignment in our lives is worthy of our time and effort. As we break away from the tried and true methodologies and as we give up fight and resistance and discover allowing in combination with a bit of newfound vision and intent, what replaces our existence becomes something wholly beyond our imaginings – something we flow into, rather than march into. It becomes something we need help to accomplish, for which Innate Intelligence is ready, willing and able.

As we grow in the awareness of what fuels our realities, we see how this might turn out – vast systems of life fighting and scrapping for limited resources and the taking from each other for survival, or an alignment with Innate Intelligence that brings our truest possibilities, abundances and potentials. As we discover realities held together by substantially and exponentially more powerful glue, our invisible tendrils more capable influence the whole.

As we invisibly join forces (our momentum) with those whose connection with Innate Intelligence becomes their primary drive, our worlds begin to spin in a different manner, conjuring delicious octaves of corresponding reality. Dr. Hawkins tells us that one individual rating 540 on the Map of Consciousness "neutralizes" and offsets, many hundreds of thousands that are operating at far lower levels. In other words, as we discover our vision, hold our vision and merge our vision with others of like mind and qualities of intent, we enhance a vibration that is substantially and exponentially far more powerful than the volume of those whose allegiance is toward force, raucous output or victimhood.

Although they do not know of the dissonance they create, it is of little matter, as visionaries aligned in refined vibrational output and corresponding realities counter their influence. As the exponential power of our possibilities rise to offset the raucous nature of those forcefully holding sway in world affairs or naively offering unconscious consentience, our world revolves toward its possibilities. This is the divine plan, the second coming and assuredly what we are becoming in our conscious evolution of life on Earth. After all, we are a species powered by free will and our partnership with Innate Intelligence. It is only by the blossoming of the flower within each of us, that the world's bounty increases. It turns out it is an inside job!

Digital Influence

As we discover our wholeness and our oneness, we become cognizant of new possibilities and outcomes. By way of example, we are becoming digital voters and digital swayers of momentum. As we become connected to each other in the Information Age via computers, the Internet and the communications revolution, and more connected through the bridge that is each our quality of intent, the world begins to shift for the better. In December 2002, a group of Hollywood actors spoke out against the United States war-mongering against Iraq. Their initial message was that it was patriotic and responsible to speak out against U.S. policy that seemed to be at odds with the greater good.

These actors began what has grown into a huge waging peace movement within the U.S.A. and around the world. Hundreds of thousands of individuals across the planet were expressing themselves, and even a U.S. congressman or two. But the general American population had muffled itself into a silent support (silent consentience) for leadership, even though leadership was a bit murky in its interpretation of the issues.

Out of the initial 100 or so actors who signed a statement decreeing that there were better solutions available has come a huge surge of response that is exciting in its possibilities. Several groups, including Hollywood's Win Without War Coalition,[3] and MoveOn.org,[4] created a series of Web sites that initiated the first virtual march on the planet. On February 6, 2003, Washington senators and other top U.S. officials were systematically bombarded with phone calls, faxes and e-mails in opposition to the U.S. war effort. Approximately one million calls and faxes were received by elected officials in one day, and a huge new momentum was initiated. The first virtual march for peace was a meteoric success.

All that was required was to register on a Web site in response to several broadcast e-mails that were in circulation. Registration was quick and easy: your name, your time availability, zip code and a statement if you wished. What came back in a matter of one day was an auto-generated e-mail informing you of the time of your calls and whom to call. Another auto-generated e-mail was sent the day before your call, reminding you of your commitment and the time of your calls, which were spaced four minutes apart.

With the help of the Electronics Age, participants, with telephones in hand and computer screens to light the way, were advised about their local representatives and phone numbers, and the first virtual march began. The computer screens also reminded "the marchers" of their earlier statement, should they care to use them, as well as a reminder that the recipient offices were staffed by individuals and that kindness and diplomacy would be useful tools in getting the message across.

As it was, the phone lines and circuitry of Washington, D.C., reverberated to a new part of America speaking up. A digital part of America had found its voice – a nonviolent response with minimal expense and time commitment, had come to exist. The virtual march contained no anger nor rising emotion, for which common sense sometimes goes out the window, as participants physically merge into sometimes angry groups. Instead, within the privacy of our homes, using desks and computers and telephones, we made our voices heard.

Making new choices and choosing for new outcomes is all that is ahead for Team HomoSapien™. No raucous behavior, mindless milling or tempers flaring; only quiet, caring and knowing powering conscious reality creation. Telephones and digital expression become extensions of what we know to be so.

Can a corporation be designed with courage and flexibility within its underlying intent? I think so.

We Move in New Ways

Institutions and authority models shift to mirror our newfound outpourings. Existing authority morphs into matrixes of connection, expansion and service in keeping with a waking population finding its place in existence. Similar to our own experience of finding new outcomes and synchronicities as we lift our vision to the possibilities, institutions of learning, the Church, government, and business corporations echo new growth as Team HomoSapien's™ values expand throughout the human sphere. As we begin to revel in our newfound self-governance, corporations and institutions created to serve us revise themselves into matrixes reflective of nature's resonance and our own. Wholeness begets wholeness as we begin to have newfound influence over long-standing societal structures. Corporate institutions, the epitome of feudal role models, begin to feel the heat, as Team HomoSapien™ makes good on its connection with Source. Centralized, trickle-down authority models contain little circuitry to support themselves as the world spins ever forward toward wholeness. Centrist structures merge into self-organizing and ever-evolving networks of wholeness and order, fulfilling their purposes subservient to humanity's growth, or they go broke.

Outwardly, difficult transition is seen as no more than the toppling of top-heavy authoritarian structures that no longer serve useful functions. Not so much different from a tree falling in the forest, its function having been fully performed, outmoded authority returns to dust, as well. Centrist structures revise themselves as they meet the exacting standards of nature's system of success as adopted by humanity, or they fail. Those who are open to flow thrive in this transitory and birth-like phase of existence on Earth. This would be the case for humans and artificial entities alike.

Institutions become matrixes of wholeness as they express newfound allegiance to common purpose and core concentric principles reflective of humanity's aspirations. Nature has found yet another method of expressing itself, as has humanity. Artificial entities, designed from the ground up to serve Team HomoSapien™, are imbued with circuitry that aspire for alignment with nature's system of success. Artificial entities, catalyzed and carrying the underlying qualities of intent that initially fed humanity, begin to pick up the pace. Humanity soars far ahead of its creations.

Team HomoSapien™ learns to design institutions and structure society in a manner that allows Innate Intelligence to flow through and inhabit its circuitry. We design artificial entities (corporations, government, non-profits, etc.) in alignment with our bidding, feeding our growth, all the while "keeping the red lights red and the yellow highway stripes yellow." Although we have learned our lessons the hard way, we plunge into artificial entity creation again and again, for the values we gain are essential to our existence. By the infusion of Innate Intelligence within the "servo-mechanisms" of the artificial entities we create, we imbue that entity with safety, expansion and repeatability as we go on about our business. After all, nature can keep the apple tree on track!

Consider an Example

Visa International, known for the Visa card, was founded by Dee Hock in the late 1960s. As a futurist, student of nature and America's founding documents (hint), he designed and produced an artificial-entity business platform that successfully emulates nature's success. It is designed from the center outward to align with fundamental principles of expansion and flexibility and therefore a capacity to welcome change and new direction as it morphs to accept growth and challenge. This is a business structure in which the aspirations and goals are clear and evolve to meet their circumstances. This is a company where the employees and managers know their responsibilities at they relate to the overall whole, and internal competition is a clear-cut and daily directive. Visa was designed as the opposite of a feudal, trickle-down authoritarian role model (already a failure at its core), as reality moves faster and faster.

It turns out that Dee Hock copied the best of nature by creating a business matrix of nodal points, each greased with the flexibility of "chaordic intent." To paraphrase Dee –
> *Chaordic* describes the behavior of any self-governing organism or system to harmoniously blend what were previously conceived to be opposites, such as chaos and order, or cooperation and competition.

He merged the best nature had to offer, and, on that knife's edge, ran what has become a huge business platform with an infinitely flexible outcome and potential.

It turns out that the "damn hippies" were right. They challenged a rigidity in the world and a trickle-down authority structure of black-and-white beliefs that made no sense to them. Through the use of delving within and access to Innate Intelligence, they discovered that they were on the wrong track and went about finding new models to role their lives after.

Black-and-white reality has been breaking down ever since. Single-minded, rigid, linear authority gives way to a matrix of flexible wholeness that is the pathway and byway through which nature extends itself, expansion occurs and we become more whole. Any system that does not include flexibility as its primary ingredient at the cusp of the 21st century has "doom" duct-taped across its forehead. Centralized authority gives way to self-governance aligned in partnership with Innate Intelligence. There is no other way. Centralized authority matches the momentum of the carrier pigeon – extinction.

An interview with Dee Hock (fully printed with permission as Appendix A and an important review), fully illustrates this point. Mankind is moving ever faster since the invention of the wheel, which may have taken 1,000 years to become widely accepted. While the smelting of iron might have taken 100 years to become widely known, we knew of the Moon landing almost instantly. Electronic gadgets gain worldwide acceptance and appeal within weeks, and, most recently, digital photos reach around the world in minutes. Everything is moving faster and faster, except for the lowly, feudally inspired, top heavy, centralized authority model heading toward its ultimate fate.

Wholeness begets success in all aspects of life.

Corporations and business models built on foundations of centralized authority are beginning to crack and many are failing. This can be seen as we watch corporations (governments and churches included) operating with huge expenses, huge liabilities, red ink, dysfunctional decision-making and surprising disorganization. Wholeness begets success in all aspects of life, and institutions out of alignment with wholeness beget wreckage. There are no exceptions. Inwardly structured and ever-expanding mechanisms replace centralized authority models in the care and feeding of the modern society.

It becomes clear that centralized authority does not work as it ultimately fails the litmus test. A true test of the efficacy of a product, truth, momentum or authority would be its capacity for expansion. Would it remain the same in its expansion? Would it show signs of failure as it moved away from its centralized base or, in enough expansion, does it simply collapse? Truth begets truth, no matter the amount of expansion, no matter how finite the detail. Even in the finest details of the expansion of truth, there is no weakness and no fault. As centralized authority attempts to rise to the occasion, we see a multitude of dysfunctional and telltale signs that its capacity for expansion is exhausted. In its inflexibility, we hear groans, complaints and whistle-blowing, as well as the sound of life savings lost and stolen.

Not so different from humanity initially failing to take advantage of its partnership with Innate Intelligence and nature's systems of success, we learn to manage our creations with more care. Corporations and trickle-down authority schemes amend their "flow techniques" lest they fail the oncoming tide of humanity discovering itself.

Existing structures expand or fail to meet the challenge. Entrepreneurs and those who no longer fit within the traditional stifling corporate structure take on the challenge. As centralized authority dissolves into newfound expansion and hope, individuals empowered by holistic ideas take up the reins in new ways. Centralized authority falls away as empowered choice melds into new ways of accomplishing tasks and Team HomoSapien™ comes into its own. Humanity creates choice where it does the most good – in partnership with Innate Intelligence.

Comparing notes among ourselves, we stretch and we grow as we discover how powerful we are. We share solutions with each other, and Team HomoSapien™ moves beyond its doubts, fears and faulty perceptions. We accept self-governance and partnership with Innate Intelligence as we learn to know the difference. Always taught to rely on outside authority, we turn within and generate new outcomes that are solid at their foundation and stable in their expansion. As with any birthing process, it begins with a spark and a bit of commitment. For what we envision begins to take hold and have a bit of momentum of its own.

Humanity, by gathering its exponentially more powerful momentum and making new choices in resonance, rules with righteous tools. These are tools of choice, tools of vision and tools of partnering with a system of success that is far grander than we can imagine, unless we were to look to the stars on a moonless night. There is something in the vastness of nature that tells us success has been here for quite some time and will be likely be here for quite a bit longer.

Even though aspects of humanity with free will might be perceived as getting out of hand, we are immersed in far more order than we understand. And, though with our unconscious foot on the gas, our unconscious hand at the wheel and the possibility that our disorder may result in vast destruction, nature's system of success sees it in a different way. Nature sees it as learning and choice, and out of contrast comes clarity, for which we will surely get it right. Ultimately, our lessons and contrasts beget wisdom, a good forerunner and partner of our true success as a species.

And being a reasonably benevolent system of success, nature allows humanity (the fruit of its vine) as much room as possible. This process of refining our commitment to life, our commitment to growth and our commitment to love and acceptance of the world around us does not happen overnight. After all, what would be the point, other than the multitude of possibilities that make up the vast collection of perceptions and choice-makers ever allowed under one sun? What would be the point of not letting each of us argue our own argument until it becomes crystal clear as to the clarity of our choice?

Underlying all of our peerings, wanderings and mistaken assumptions is a system of success whereby the outcomes of humanity is assured. We don't know precisely what it will look like because "what would be the point?" But surely Mother Nature, not so dissimilar from a human mother, assures us of outcomes of the highest and best possibilities available. Or not. Ultimately, it is still up to us.

Some will be first. Some have already been first. The way has been established and the path described over the eons. Though it has become garbled by continuous rewrites, interpretations and re-interpretations, the path is ever in front of us – the path daily traveled by those in search of what might be called enlightenment, consciousness or the quest for the Holy Grail. Though it has been assumed to be beyond the reach of most, it has also been assumed to be beyond the capacity for choice, and this is not the case. We express our creative outpourings in a myriad ways, and, as we do, each time we let a little more creativity and a little more juice flow into our existence. We get a little bit closer.

It is of a momentum that most recently began with Christopher Columbus and the European Renaissance, the Industrial Revolution, the Information Age and the Space Age that brings mankind to the brink of its jumping off place en masse. For, after all, far more than ever before, we have access to choice, and choice begets a growing perception of our possibilities. Choice begets and fosters a new sense of personal responsibility and self-governance. As we discover how our neighbors across the street or across the planet overcame their obstacles, the rest of mankind eventually follows. With just a bit of comparing note and a bit of courage, we all grow.

Slowly, at first, and increasingly, we become more as we assume the authority of our own individuality. As we make new choices, new choices become available. Solutions come from a different type of thinking than the problems they begat. Our vision overcomes our beliefs in limitation and injustice. Subsequently, we discover there is more order than we thought.

As we consciously and intentionally align with a system of success that has always been there (dare I say patiently?), we attune ourselves, align ourselves, and become more. After all, anybody with any sense knows that the bit of fanaticism lurking in the shadows of mankind is not of what we are made. It is the smallest of deterrent to this thing called humanity getting its act together and joining a system of success that gives rise to our possibilities. Luckily, with the simplest of choices over the next one-half generation or so, we will see startling results as humanity makes more conscious and intentional choices partnered with Innate Intelligence.

Hell, if Visa can do it, we can do it.

EPILOGUE

The pleasure has been all mine. I don't know when I last accomplished something more satisfying and thought-provoking than writing this book. Clearly, I have discerned and clearly, I have discovered. Write what you know and you will discover what you don't know, and you will then be presented with what is next. My path has become illuminated before me, and what is next in my life has become open-ended and crystal clear at the same time. It is my hope that you, too, will discover an open-endedness and outpouring in this extravaganza called life.

Visionaries Thrive In All Times began as a journaling experience and catharsis and ended up as so much more. Initially, I journaled for about two years immediately after my daily meditations, and eventually my journaling began to take on a life of its own – not only writings that defined what I knew to be true for myself and a newfound clarity about what was important to me, but a lucidity about how to get to what I wanted to know about and practice next. Writing became a vehicle for self-discovery, a method of exploration and a method of "getting to and over the rainbow," so to speak. I brought myself to the edge of what I knew, and I was then presented with the unknown out of a format that was an outflowing of my truths thus far. My new pathway and excitement was beckoning; I was ready to go forward, and the written word was the vehicle.

Supported by my daily momentum, I found a perspective from which to flow my outcomes with clarity and ease. And as I have discovered, the writing is a reflection of what is inside of me as I have been able to let it out, and to view and review of what I am made with an eye toward discovering my authenticity and grace. In fact, my purpose has become to discover what is the truth of my nature and to let it out. I have discovered my loftiest goal, and my loftiest goal is me – letting the inner me out. My expansion, my self-discovery and the release of my inner nature is my purpose and my highest aspiration. To find out what is inside of me and to let it out - to expand and become more – is my life's work.

In the end, I discovered that writing and defining what I knew, and refining what I thought I knew, by attempts at descriptions and assigning words to ideas, brought me to the boundaries of the world in which I live and prepared me for what was next. From discovering and elucidating what I knew and standing on the precipice of that boundary/edge, I began to surmise what was obvious as my next bout of learning and discovery. I began to glimpse the possibilities and considered the act of soaring sans training wheels.

Based on the richness and inherent stability I discovered about myself (and my connection with Source), I began to explore what my momentum told me I would find. And, not so distant from my old boundaries, I find myself living an exploration of what I don't yet know, sometimes tethered to familiarity and oftentimes soaring far above my old limitations and rule. Clearly, I am exploring my life and its potential, having left my limitations far behind. Life and synchronicity comes to me faster and faster as I refine my alignment with the formula that aligns me with Universal Forces in step with the Universe's expansion. I embrace the richness of my partnership with Innate Intelligence, which I have come to know and trust. I am an explorer of a new magnitude, and my sidekicks – trust, innate guidance, and Infinite Intelligence – are ever present.

As I allow the experience of trust and knowing, without a need for cataloging the new, I let go and soar. Some might think my experience "ought" to be a heart-fueled experience and flight, and, to a very large degree it is. But I find the intellect leads the way and clears the path (to the heart). In fact, I am not so sure that what is perceived as the Heart and Innate Intelligence are any different.

Trust and knowing find and refine the pathway that releases me from the daily grind, but in a manner that is thoroughly grounded and safe. The mind and the intellect are, in fact, vast reservoirs (as tools) for receptivity, courage and choice, ultimately to be released to Universal Mind. As I clarify my identity in traveling beyond my known boundaries, I discover that the heart finds a home in the comforts of the momentum I have achieved intellectually, with a bit of insight from Spirit. It is from this blending that I wish you the best and offer my bit of experience as a perspective and a perch for you who are contemplating the leap.

For it was written, by no lesser than a fellow just like myself, "Just add" and you will become more..."

Namasté

J.Hamilton
Sedona, Arizona

Visionaries Lab Press
2675 W. Hwy 89A, #1101
Sedona, Arizona 86336

www.visionarieslabpress.com
jhamilton@visionarieslabpress.com

APPENDIX

Transformation by Design
An interview with Dee Hock
by Melissa Hoffman

You don't have to understand chaos theory to appreciate the new species of corporate organization that Dee Hock has unleashed on the planet, an organizational paradigm that could very well represent the next step in the collective evolution of the human family. You don't even have to know anything about corporate structure, nor do you have to nurse a secret passion for institutional reform. All you have to do is take a long look at a snowflake, reflect on a forest, ponder the neurons in your brain—or use your Visa card—and you will begin to appreciate the intricate, manifold hive of pulsing impulses and multidimensional parleys of information that give rise to everything in the created universe. Sound perplexing? Well, as a group of scientists are discovering, this orderly chaotic buzz is the way of the world, and if you just sit down and think about it, really think hard about it, or take long walks in the woods like Dee Hock did, you might find yourself surfing waves of miraculous and intricate order foaming at the narrow edge of chaos. Look deeply enough and you will discover the true nature of all of evolution's architecture, which is what this issue of What Is Enlightenment? is all about: living transformation.

Dee Hock is the founder and former CEO of Visa International, the most successful business venture on Earth. Could this former bank manager with a conscience be evolution's unlikely hero? Visa owes its success, according to Hock, to its structure, which is nothing less than an evocation of nature's "cha-ordic" laws. Hock coined the term chaordic to describe that perfect balance of chaos and order where evolution is most at home. Yes, that's right. A business venture that takes its cues from Mother Evolution, whose "trademark" dynamism, changing change, and explosive originality are forever groping to innovate, prosper, and extend creation's euphoric reach further and further into manifestation.

· If you don't think that something as common as the plastic Visa credit card in your wallet could be part of evolution's plan, consider this: Visa International

> ... espouses no political, economic, social or legal theory, thus transcending language, custom, politics and culture to successfully connect a bewildering variety of more than 21,000 financial institutions, 16 million merchants and 800 million people in 300 countries and territories. Annual volume of $1.4 trillion continues to grow in excess of twenty percent compounded annually. A staff of about three thousand people scattered in twenty-one offices

in thirteen countries on four continents provides ... around-the-clock operation of two global electronic communication systems with thousands of data centers communicating through nine million miles of fiber-optic cable. Its electronic systems clear more transactions in one week than the Federal Reserve System does in a year.

Hock has chronicled Visa's spectacular emergence along with his philosophical and personal odyssey in a book called *Birth of the Chaordic Age*. Therein he deftly disassembles assumptions you didn't even know you had; assumptions about how we have come to order, organize, and configure everything, from our desktops to our institutions to the very pattern of our thinking.

Hock wrote *Birth of the Chaordic Age* in the late nineties, years after walking away from the thriving Visa. He had spent the better part of ten years in retirement, restoring the degraded acreage around his ranch to vibrancy. Then, as the story goes, one night while reading Mitch Waldrop's *Complexity* (a book about chaos theory), he found illuminated in its pages an uncanny echo of the very principles he had invoked to bring Visa into being. His bucolic retirement was soon to come to an end (a fascinating story which you'll have to read about in his book).

You may be wondering what a chaordic organization looks like, and if you ask Hock, he would likely point you in the direction of a snowflake or a bee's wing. But fortunately his book, along with the website of the nonprofit organization he helped found (The Chaordic Commons, www.chaordic.org), explains this phenomenon in captivating detail. Principally, a chaordic organization is a self-organizing and self-evolving entity, which ends up looking more like a neural network (like the Internet) than a hierarchically-organized bureaucracy in which decision-making power is centralized at the top and trickles down through a series of well-regulated departments and managers. Chaordic organizations do not fear change or innovation. They are, by their very nature, supremely adaptive. They also tend to be inclusive,

263

multicentric, and distributive and, ultimately, strongly cohesive due to their unshakable focus on common purpose and core principles. If you can't quite visualize it, there's a good reason, which Hock will explain in the following interview.

So the reason that this issue of What Is Enlightenment? had to include Dee Hock—a corporate innovator whose personal risk taking and conscientious peeling of life's onion has led to the emergence of a new collective life-form—is this: our spiritual canon, while replete with examples of personal transformation, has rarely addressed the intricacies of real collective transformation. And since the ability of the many to communicate, coalesce, and coordinate as one may be the only hope for humanity's future, we thought that what Dee Hock had to offer was nothing less than a profound example, wrought out of his own sweat and experience, of just where we humans might be heading for our next evolutionary leap. Hock has proved that a very large group of individuals can come together under the cohesion of a unifying purpose while enhancing—rather than swallowing—the autonomy of each participating individual. To say that the individual and collective benefit each other in this arrangement would be an understatement, for, ideally, the intricate dance between part and whole endlessly releases new creative capacities in both. Hock talks a refreshing brand of truth and proves that it's possible for a unified yet diverse group of people to wend its way through tumultuous change while continuously growing and transforming itself as it embraces the hidden potentials of an unknown future.

Finally, Hock's own odyssey made us wonder: What would it take to be fully chaordic in this crazy, fomenting world, teetering on dual brinks of salvation and disaster? Must we, as Hock suggests, consistently sweep our minds of their old, beleaguered Newtonian concepts, which act as an invisible lens through which we behold a mechanistic and controllable world? What manner of dedication on our part would be needed to cast aside our old ways of thinking so that we might even begin to directly perceive the ever-present genius of evolution's design? In the following interview, Dee Hock talks to WIE about the mind-stopping implications of the "chaordic age," an age that may have begun more than thirty years ago, in part, with this ordinary bank manager, who looked around, saw what was happening, asked a heck of a lot of questions, and took action.

WIE: In your book *Birth of the Chaordic Age*, you describe how you combined the first syllables of chaos and order, inventing the term chaordic to describe a dynamic form of organization modeled on the fundamental organizing principles of evolution and nature. Your work, the underpinnings of which have much in common with the science of chaos theory, involves reconceiving organizations according to these fundamental chaordic principles and represents a departure from the traditional, relatively rigid, mechanistic model that characterizes most organizations today.

DEE HOCK: Yes, and to add to the definition a little more, chaordic simply describes the behavior of any self-governing organism or system that harmoniously blends what were previously conceived to be opposites, such as chaos and order or cooperation and competition. But most importantly, this is a way of thinking. And in fact, everything I could say about it, you already know. It's already there because you are chaordically organized. It's the way nature has been organizing things since the beginning of time, including you—your brain, your immune system—and every living thing. So in terms of a chaordic commercial, political, or social organization, the question becomes: Can you evoke it, or bring it into being?

WIE: What inspired you to become involved in organizational transformation?

DH: Well, years and years ago, I started to ask myself three very simple questions, which dominated my life for many years. One of them was, "Why are organizations everywhere, whether commercial, social, or religious, increasingly unable to manage their affairs?" The second question was, "Why are individuals throughout the world increasingly in conflict with and alienated from the organizations of which they're a part?" And the third was, "Why are society and the biosphere increasingly in disarray?" When I asked these questions to audiences a few years ago, they didn't have that much meaning to most people. But with such recent events as September 11 and the collapse of Enron and WorldCom, it's all pretty obvious now. So if all those things are true— and to me they're just as obvious as the nose on anybody's face—there has to be some deep, universal, underlying thing we're not getting at. There has to be.

WIE: How do you help people understand chaordic principles in relation to the current forms of organization that are so much a part of our lives?

DH: An illustration I use to get people to understand it is this: I'll ask major corporate audiences: Why don't you just take all your traditional beliefs about organizations, and apply them to the neurons in your brain? Organize the neurons in your brain, the most complex, infinitely diverse organ that has ever emerged in evolution, as you would a corporation. The first thing you've got to do is appoint the Chief Executive neuron, right? Then you've got to decide which are going to be the Board of Directors neurons and the Human Resources neurons, and then you have to write an operating manual for it. Now, if you could organize your brain on that model, what would happen? You would instantly be unable to breathe until somebody told you how and where and when and how fast. You wouldn't be able to think or see. What if your immune system were organized on this basis? First you'd have to do some market research to determine what virus, if any, was attacking you, right? Then you'd have to write a business plan for how you were going to deal with it. And you'd have to get it approved by the senior executive neurons in your brain. Then you'd have to have marching orders for all the various aspects of your immune system. Okay. So why in God's world do we think we can use something like the brain, which is organized on this beautiful set of chaordic principles to organize society in a superior manner? That's an exercise in arrogance and ego.

WIE: So, basically, what you're saying is that it just doesn't make sense for us, as part of evolution's intricate design, to think we can organize society in a manner that is superior to the way in which nature has so perfectly organized us?

DH: Exactly. It's unbelievably arrogant and foolish.

THE COLLAPSE OF FLOAT

WIE: Before we talk further about why our old models need to be abandoned, I'd like to ask you about the current climate of change surrounding the emergence of chaordic systems. We just interviewed Don Beck, a leader in large-scale systemic transformation, and he emphasized how our climate of rapidly accelerating change and increasing complexity is generating the need for new organizational forms. This is how he put it:

> We know what's happening everywhere on the planet within ten minutes after it happens, and it's on the TV news live. The complexity has been there in the past, but it didn't arrive here until the ship came in six months later or by telegraph maybe twenty-four hours later. Now all these things that are happening on the planet are suddenly right in our face in real time. And that's one reason why there's so much stress on us, which also means that we might be looking for new organizational forms—more ensembles of people—because no single person is going to be able to keep all these things in mind.

Now, you have actually brought a new organizational form into being. Does what Beck describes here match your experience?

DH: Well, I agree completely with what he's saying, except I think he's understating the case. I use two different examples to try to get people to understand this: one called "float" and one called "CRUSTTI," which is an acronym for the Capacity to Receive, Utilize, Store, Transform, and Transmit Information. You can probably remember the days when a check would often take weeks to find its way through the banking system. That was called "float." This float was used as an early form of venture capital. Now, stop and think about other kinds of float. Think about information float (this is what Beck is speaking about): if you go back just a few centuries, it took, for example, almost a century for the knowledge about the smelting of iron ore to cross one continent. That brought in the Iron Age. When we landed on the moon, it was known and seen in every corner of the world in 1.4 seconds. Think about technological float: it took centuries for the wheel to gain universal acceptance. Now any microchip device can be in use around the world in weeks. Think about cultural float: it used to take centuries for one culture to even learn about or be exposed to a tiny bit of information about another. And now anything that becomes popular anywhere in the world can sweep through other countries in weeks. Consider space float: in just one long lifetime, a hundred years or so, we've gone from the speed of the horse to interstellar travel. People and materials now move in minutes when they used to move in months. And even life float—the time it takes to evolve new life-forms—is collapsing with genetic engineering.

What all this means is the loss of change float—the time between what was and what is going to be, between the past and the future—so the past then becomes ever less predictive, the future ever less predictable, and everything is accelerating change with one exception: our institutions. There has been no truly new concept of organization since the ideas of nation-state and corporation emerged several centuries ago.

Now even more important—and you have to think hard about this—is the history of what I call the "capacity to receive, utilize, store, transform, and transmit information." If you go back to the first single-cell form of life, it clearly possessed the capacity to receive, to utilize, to store, to transform, and to transmit information. This capacity even precedes the cell, for that's the very definition of DNA. So the key to understanding what Beck is speaking about is that the greater the capacity of any entity or organization to receive, utilize, store, transform, and transmit information, the more diverse and complex the entity. You can track this capacity from particle to neutrino to nucleus to atom to amino acid to protein to molecule to cell to organ and to organism. Or the phrase I like to use: from bacteria to bee to bat to bird to buffalo right on through to the baseball player.

And evolution went on, and in time this ability to receive, utilize, store, transform, and transmit information escaped the individual entity and became shared—as the song of birds, the sonar of bats, the pheromone of ants, or the language of humans. With the capacity to communicate, immediately came the evolution of complex communities of organisms: hives, flocks, tribes, herds, whatever. Language was a huge expansion of that capacity to deal with information. And immediately you had a huge leap in societal complexity. With mathematics, the first global language, you had the same thing—a huge increase in societal diversity and complexity. With the printing press came the capacity to include that which can be mechanically recorded and transported. Then the telegraph brought electronic capacity, and the telephone brought phonic capacity, and television brought visual capacity. Every single one of those expansions was immediately followed by a huge leap in societal complexity.

All of a sudden, just within the last three decades with the emergence of microtechnology, we have on the order of a thousand times better algorithms, five hundred thousand times more computing power per individual, and five hundred million times more mobility of information. As I like to say, the entire collective memory of the species—that means all known and recorded information—is going to be just a few keystrokes away in a matter of years. Now, what does that explosion in the capacity to receive, utilize, store, transform, and transmit information mean for organizational forms and for the complexity and diversity of our problems?

But that's nothing. Take nanotechnology—which in simple language is the engineering of self-replicating computers and assembly machines so tiny they can arrange atoms as though they were bricks—that's the way that we're going to be constructing organs, organisms, products, and services within three or four decades. With nanotechnology, information will move in speed and quantities hundreds, perhaps thousands, of times greater than it moves today, okay? And equally important, each such change brings an equal increase in our power to alter and destroy nature. That's where we are. So unless evolution has totally changed its ways, we're going to face an explosion of societal diversity and complexity, and a disruption of biological systems, enormously greater than we now experience or can yet imagine. The essential question then becomes: Can we deal with it with the same old seventeenth-century mechanistic command-and-control forms of organizations? There's not a snowball's chance in hell. I always tell my audiences, if you think this change isn't going to happen, or isn't happening, or that you can prevent it, or that you can operate in the old way and not deal with it, just try to remember the last time evolution rang your telephone number and asked your permission. It is going to happen. But there are two ways it could happen. We can continue to perpetuate these old forms and try to make the world behave in accordance with our old mechanistic internal model of reality, or we can change our internal model of reality. The first is not only foolish, it's futile. The second is difficult, but it is essential if we are to have a livable world.

WIE: The way you're describing it, our individual and collective willingness to change our internal model of reality is fundamental to meaningful transformation. But what you seem to be saying is that what we're replacing the old model with isn't merely a new substitute model. What we're actually attempting to do is to align our perception and behavior with the essential nature of evolution.

DH: Yes. We don't have to remain in this radically destructive mind-set and institutional-set. We can change, and the natural order of things could emerge in all of our societal organizations—government, commerce, religion—it's right there, waiting to happen. I often tell people that every mind is like a room in an old house, stuffed with very old furniture. Take any space in your mind and empty it of your old conceptions and new ones will rush in, good or bad. So change is more a getting rid of rather than an adding to or an acquiring.

BEYOND THE MECHANISTIC MINDSET

WIE: At the end of your book you emphasize that you hadn't anticipated the power of individuals' resistance to change. You noticed this phenomenon throughout your experience with Visa. Since then, how have you come to understand this resistance to change?

DH: The reason people have so much trouble with change, I think, is a matter of conditioning. It arose many thousands of years ago, but essentially, this mechanistic way of thinking came into dominance about the time of Newton and Descartes, when Newtonian science postulated that the universe and everything in it could only be understood as a clocklike mechanism, a machine, with each part acting on the other part with precise linear laws of cause and effect. So when this way of thinking came into being through science, we began to try to apply it to everything. Starting about four hundred years ago, we tried to organize every aspect of society based on this mechanistic, scientific perspective. The Newtonian way of thinking has marvelous uses. For example, if I go in the hospital for eye surgery, I don't want a chaordic operating room. If you're going to build a perfect silicon chip, you need a totally controlled, very clean, highly organized, almost mechanistic environment. But that doesn't mean it's a good way to run Intel, or a good way to run a health care system.

So for four hundred years we've been trying to build all our organizations as though the Newtonian mechanistic internal model of reality were universally applicable. You know, this person reports to that person who reports to that person. Planning comes from the top and is distributed down. Everything else—money, power—is distributed up. Everything has linear cause and effect, which leads to endless manuals of rules and regulations.

If you think about it, you realize that every institution you have experienced in your lifetime is consciously or unconsciously based on that metaphor and that model. Your school operated that way, and your church, and your community, and your state. Your internal model of reality is the machine. So it doesn't surprise me at all that it's difficult to think otherwise or even to really understand that you are thinking in a mechanistic way. Stress arises out of having this internal model of reality at a subconscious level, literally in your genes, without knowing you've got it, and without asking how you've got it, and why you've got it, and whether it's useful any longer. And it's enormously more difficult, even if you can intellectually understand it, to literally get it in the bone.

So it's just not surprising at all that people should have such difficulty after so many years of conditioning, and given the fact that even if they start thinking in a different way, they are immediately head-to-head with a society in which virtually every institution and situation is operating on the old Newtonian model. That's why it's difficult. I think it will take several or more generations to break completely free of the Newtonian mechanistic mindset.

WIE: In light of the enormity of this conditioning and our reluctance to let it go, what do you think actually provokes the leap out of the old system? You were incredibly motivated to do this. What do you think it's going to take for individuals to be willing to endure the discomforts of leaving the old model behind?

DH: Well, first of all, you really need to open your mind to try to understand what your existing internal model of reality is and how it functions. And then you need to familiarize yourself with it. Emerson had a wonderful line. He said, "Everywhere you go you take your giant with you." So you have this giant unconscious thing, this internal model of reality, against which you judge and measure everything. You're never going to get rid of it, so you might as well turn around, introduce yourself to it, and say, "We're going to be together the rest of our lives, but I'm not going to let you drive my thinking any more. You have to live with my ability to think in a different way." You just confront it. I often tell audiences, "Lord, I was raised to command and control. I'm a sort of command-and-control-a-holic." I may never get it out of my system. But unless I understand it, I can't begin to deal with it.

272

PURPOSE AND PRINCIPLES

WIE: How can a group of people learn to think in a different way on a collective level?

DH: Well, you really have to go deep. I spent months and months asking myself, "What is an organization?" If I'm talking about institutional and organizational change, what am I really talking about? What is an organization in the deepest sense? It surely isn't just a set of bylaws, because I can write a set of bylaws and shove it in a desk drawer, and it just becomes an old moldering piece of paper. And if you really think deeply about it, you discover that every organization and every institution, without exception, has no reality save in your mind. It's not its buildings. Those are manifestations of it. It's not its name, it's not its logo, and it's not some fictional piece of paper called a stock certificate. It's not money. It is a mental concept around which people and resources gather in pursuit of common purpose.

Now let's follow this just a little further. If that institution has no reality save in your mind and the minds of all your associates and the people who deal with it, then what is its real nature? What's its real strength? And that led me to believe that the heart and soul of every organization, at least every healthy organization, is purpose and principles. What is the purpose that brought you together and what is your system of beliefs about how you intend to conduct yourself in pursuit of that purpose? If your beliefs are based on the old model of top-down command and control, specialization, special privilege, and nothing but profit, your organization will, in time, turn toxic. It will become antithetical to the human spirit and destructive of the biosphere. The evidence is everywhere around us.

Your organization needs to be absolutely clear about purpose and principles and must be very careful to know what a purpose and a principle is—you know, a purpose is not an objective, it's not a mission statement—a purpose is an unambiguous expression of that which people jointly wish to become. And a principle is not a platitude—it is a fundamental belief about how you intend to conduct yourself in pursuit of that purpose. You have to get very precise about these things. If the purpose and principles are constructive and healthy, then your organization will take a very different form than anything that you ever imagined. It will release the human spirit and will be constructive of the biosphere. Natural capital and human capital will be released in abundance and monetary capital will become relatively unimportant. To put it another way, I believe that purpose and principle, clearly understood and articulated, and commonly shared, are the genetic code of any healthy organization. To the degree that you hold purpose and principles in common among you, you can dispense with command and control. People will know how to behave in accordance with them, and they'll do it in thousands of unimaginable, creative ways. The organization will become a vital, living set of beliefs.

I've found that it's very difficult to lead people through enough metaphors and enough thinking about this—you can only think about it so much and your circuit breakers just go out. You have to rest, reset them, and come back to it. And you go over and over it. But what I find is that once you get a group of people who really begin to understand this, then energy, excitement, and enthusiasm literally explode out of them—they know what to do. You know, it's just in their nature. You can't stop it.

So to go back to the question of change—you can see that because of these four hundred years of intense conditioning, we've been taught to fear change. If you're in a rigid, mechanistic, cause-and-effect society and/or organization, then any change becomes a crisis in self-esteem. It destroys our identity, our sense of being, our sense of time and place. And we're never sure we're going to be of any value in the new order of things. We falsely see this as terrifying. But my God, this might be the greatest, most exciting adventure for the species that ever occurred.

WIE: You're pointing to a strong relationship between an individual's willingness to change and the emergence of new organizational forms.

DH: Once you understand that you and your organization are inseparable (since every organization exists only in your mind), then the idea that it's about individual change or it's about organizational change, and that one can proceed independently of the other, is utter nonsense. It takes both. I was working with one group—and this always happens in one way or another when people truly begin to understand chaordic concepts—one woman stopped the meeting to say, "Wait a minute, wait a minute. I thought we were here to work on changing our organizational structure. This is about changing me. I'll have to change my consciousness, my spirit, my way of thinking, in order to function in this new organizational form." She said, "I'll probably have to withdraw. I don't think I'll be capable of making that kind of personal change."

Individual and organizational change go hand in hand. It takes openness and a strong will to make such a change. And this comes back to why I started doing this work and what it takes to create an organization that's more harmonious with nature, and based on, the same concepts around which nature organizes every living thing and, in fact, organizes the inanimate functioning of the universe as well. When you start thinking this way, the distinction between animate and inanimate begins to vanish, and you can't be sure that the universe is not a form of life, a different manifestation of a living organism.

ETERNAL BECOMING

WIE: So for individuals to really go somewhere with this work requires that they embrace the evolutionary dynamics of the universe in a very personal way. This sounds like a thrilling prospect that, by its nature, provokes constant transformation.

DH: I wrote in my book about one of my deepest beliefs, which is that life is not about doing, it's not even about being. Life is eternal becoming, or it's nothing. It can't exist without eternal becoming. Fundamentally, the whole story of evolution is a story of experimentation and change, is it not? So if you think you can freeze that, if you think you can create a controlled environment, you are living a life of total illusion. And you are going to be full of angst and conflict, because you are essentially trying to live contrary not only to nature and evolution but to your own nature. So change is not a strange thing. It's the very essence of life.

But the bigger question people always ask is, "But, gee, so if I'm embedded in these huge command-control organizations—in the school it's the same, and my church is much the same, even the city operates this way—what can I do? Where do I begin?" And my answer is very obvious. I say, "Right now, right where you are, with what you've got—and don't hesitate for a moment." If you start pursuing these concepts, you're going to find dozens and dozens of people within your own organization and in other organizations who support these concepts. And if you don't get the support and understanding from your own organization, then cross the boundaries and link with people in other organizations who are moving this way.

WIE: You're describing quite a high level of individual commitment, the kind that has the power to create sweeping change.

DH: At one time I got interested in trying to understand how great leaders created enormous social change—take Christ, take Muhammad, Gandhi, Mother Teresa, Joan of Arc, Martin Luther King, Jr. When you look back at their history, almost without exception they were nobodies. Nobody! Gandhi was just a mediocre attorney who got thrown off a train into the dust by the British because he was Indian. Mother Teresa—just an ordinary nun. And so I studied—what made their ideas so compelling? Their ideas weren't that unique. In fact, they were often pretty traditional. Why, then, did their articulation of their beliefs have such profound effect? What I discovered was something that I think is almost universally true. They really examined what was happening around them, and examined all the existing institutions, and saw with clearer vision. They didn't delude themselves about it. Furthermore, they had the capacity to project themselves into the future and deal with the four aspects that I think are essential to understanding anything: how things were (history), how they are today, how they might become or where they're heading, and how they ought to be. They had the capacity to take that larger question of "how things ought to be" into the future and decide how they ought to be.

Now, the interesting thing is that almost without exception, they didn't start by preaching it. They started by living as though it were already true. They profoundly changed their way of living and said, "I don't have to live the way I am now." Mother Teresa said, "I can pick up a beggar in the street and tell him God loves him and help him die with respect and dignity. That I can do." Right? So once they began to live as though what ought to be was true, they had an authenticity that was just compelling. Complexity theory would call it a strange attractor, a legitimacy, an authenticity. And then they talked about it. They never wavered, no matter what the obstacle, or what the condemnation. And many of them died because they couldn't live any other way. Some of them were killed. I don't think they were unique. I think that capacity is in every single living human being. We just have to get in touch with it. And begin.

WIE: Your work calls on people to stretch and grow tremendously, in part because you're evoking something at a collective level. By definition, what a group can accomplish is beyond what any one individual can imagine or encompass. This seems to be calling for a release of something in our nature over which we fundamentally have no control.

DH: What gets released, and what is arising, is what complexity theory would call an emergent phenomenon. Something starts to emerge in multiple thousands of places and nobody can figure out what caused it to happen. The kind of consciousness I've been describing is an emergent phenomenon. These kinds of organizations are going to happen. There is no alternative. The question becomes: Are they going to happen by the old Newtonian model of collapse, destruction, and reconstruction—tear the building down, build another one—or will they move in a totally different direction? For example, there are architects who say a building should be a living thing that evolves in total harmony with nature. And they're doing it. This way of thinking is emerging almost everywhere in surprising places. But it's not yet emerging as fast as the change in societal complexity and diversity that I described. It may catch up, but it's not there yet.

ON THE KNIFE'S EDGE

WIE: Where would you say we are on a global scale? Are we poised to move in a different direction?

DH: I think we're on the knife's edge where we're going to undergo cataclysmic institutional failure. We have it all over the world. Look at some of the countries that are in a state of perpetual starvation and revolution; there's just no present institutional structure capable of dealing with societal complexity and diversity with anything other than more centralization of power and increasing violence and force. So we'll have one of two possible scenarios. The first would be that we'll have a massive series of institutional failures, social anarchy, and enormous societal and biological carnage—far more than we now experience— and then maybe out of that will emerge these new concepts. But I think if we do experience massive institutional failure, the first thing that will emerge, before we see the new forms, is almost total centralization of power and control, which will result in a widespread loss of liberty and freedom. That will last for a while, but it ultimately will not work, much like the Soviet Union. And when that collapses, then we're in for a second period of social carnage that will be unbelievable.

WIE: So you're talking about a double cataclysm?

DH: Yes. And out of that, right from the ashes, may emerge the new forms of organization.

WIE: What's the second scenario?

DH: The second scenario is that enough momentum can be put behind more chaordic ideas of organization, and there can be enough interconnection and enough actual examples of these organizations built so that as the old institutions are failing, the energy of the people goes into the emerging new forms. Existing organizations can even come to realize that transformation is essential for their health and continued existence. You would then see people's energies and resources move away from destructive behavior toward constructive behavior. If that happens, it's going to be the emergence and rebirth of a community in harmony with the human spirit and biosphere, such as we've always dreamed of.

Because of the collapse of change float, either one of these scenarios can happen in a fraction of the time we would ever expect. As I said before, we can change and allow the natural order of things to emerge—it's right there, right now, waiting to happen—

WIE: —if we choose to go along with the natural order of things.

DH: Yes, but we don't have to go along. I also believe in free will. Within us as a species for the first time is the capacity to say, "Yes, I want to go along. I want to affirm this, to consciously choose it." It's an affirmation of where we came from, what we are, and it is totally compatible with every living thing, with the living Earth, and with the universe. We have the possibility of a regeneration of these natural characteristics that will bring us totally in harmony with the human spirit and the biosphere. I see it as the greatest opportunity that I can imagine in history.

WIE: And it seems that through your work you're attempting to create the very conditions whereby this regeneration can occur now.

DH: You said the magic words. You cannot cause such things to happen. You can only create the conditions by which they can emerge and realize that they're already there. Everything I described already exists in the universe, in the Earth, in every individual, in every collective of individuals. It's just waiting to be evoked. So you create the conditions and you try to evoke it, and that's the most you can hope to do.

WIE: Perhaps that's what real transformation is.

DH: Yes. It's an evolutionary approach. And if our societal institutions and our consciousness are contrary to the fundamental organizing principles of evolution and nature, we're on a collision course. They represent the ultimate in arrogance and ego. What we need is a huge dose of humility. By the way, all those great leaders I mentioned were invariably quite humble people. But that humility did not prevent them from being very pragmatic and practical about getting things done. I'm fond of saying that we don't have any idea what the Earth could produce if we came into harmony with it.

WIE: Maybe by its very nature it's impossible to imagine.

DH: Well, is it so far-fetched to believe that somehow something wonderful and incredible beyond our present imagining could occur? I don't think so. I think that's what's been going on in evolution since the beginning of time. So let's give it a chance.

END NOTES

CHAPTER ONE

[1]"All You Need Is Love," written by John Lennon (Lennon/McCartney), was live broadcast by the BBC to approximately 350 million viewers on June 25 1967. Interestingly, this was the first global TV program, beamed via satellite, and available over much of the planet. www.beatles.com/html/allyouneedislove/

[2] The identity of that famous student seems to be unknown. http://en.wikipedia.org/wiki/Tank_man

[3] www.chrisgriscom.com/

CHAPTER TWO

1 A medical term I borrowed from the movie "Tin Cup," uttered by a "real" psychologist.

CHAPTER THREE

[1]Universal Declaration of Rights as adopted by the United Nations. www.un.org/Overview/rights.html

[2] Inalienable rights, also pronounced un-a-lien-able, are rights that come from God. Inalienable rights are different from civil rights which are privileges extended by government. Inalienable rights, identified by America's founding documents include Life (the right to exist), Liberty (the right to move about freely) and the Pursuit of Happiness (the right to the ownership of property to the exclusion of all others). According to America's founding documents, inalienable rights are rights for which no real or artificial entity may trespass.

[3] An artificial entity is one who may have a bank account in the same bank as you do, the right to sue you in court, earn money and pay taxes, but is not flesh and blood. An artificial entity is defined as a "legal fiction" and "person" as defined in the law. An artificial entity includes any corporation, or legal entity including the church or government, that is or was created for a specific purpose. They can exist for hundred's of years.

[4] www.indigochild.com, www.indigothemovie.com

CHAPTER FIVE
[1] Resistance is focus.

CHAPTER SIX
[1] The average human being has about 37 miles of nerves in his/her body. This potentially exceeds the gathering power of any man-made sensing device including the largest telescopes or the finest electron microscopes. - *Alive To The Universe*, by Robert Massy pg. 24

[2] I owned a Pearson 39 centerboard yawl built in Portsmouth, Rhode Island in 1975. I had completed the sale in February and was bringing it down the Intercoastal Waterway during the height of Jimmy Buffett's "Cheeseburger in Paradise" hit song in May of 1978.

[3] www.abraham-hicks.com

[4] Insight on Dr. Flanagan can be found at: www.phisciences.com/lifemagazine.html.

Chapter Seven

[1] Throughput is a computer term and means how much information a computer can process. In my use, throughput is defined as information, insight, etc. "processed" through our nervous systems.

[2] This was the identification of a feeling from Innate Intelligence for which I responded.

[3] This is how it works.

[4] I attribute this expression to Abraham. I heard it in a live seminar and have molded it to my own use.

[5] www.carlysimon.com

Chapter Eight

[1] Could be multiples of lifetimes.

[2] Commonly used Abraham concept.

[3] www.spacepix.net/earth/earth_apollo_17.htm

[4] Miscreation is a word used by Abraham to describe creation produced unconsciously or with little or no conscious intent. Miscreation is poor quality creating – missing the mark.

[5] "Missing the mark" is an Aramaic definition of sin. Aramaic was the language of Jesus.

Chapter Nine

[1] Dr. Hawkins indicates that the scale does not stop at 1,000. He states that Archangel Michael is in the range of 50,000, well beyond the human potential of 0 – 1,000.

[2] According to Dr. Hawkins, the measure of planetary-scale humanity bumped from just under 200 to 207 in 1986 or so.

[3] Comes from the expression "Leaving a Trail of Leadership™."

[4] Finally a useful definition for Karma. It is the experience of coming into life and becoming the recipient of all the thought forms and habitual patterns of existence that have come before us. To break away from unhealthy human momentum, is to break away from Karma.

Chapter Ten

[1] The word "naturality" comes from the book *Peak Evolution*, authored by Lauren L. Holmes.

[2] www.naturality.net and www.frontiering.com

[3] The term "naturality mode" comes from *Peak Evolution* by Lauren L. Holmes.

[4] According to an early Egyptian priest named Manetho. Reference: *Fingerprints of the Gods*, by Graham Hancock, Trade Paper, Chapter 43, pg. 383

[5] Ibid., page 385

[6] *The Sign and the Seal*, by Graham Hancock, Trade Paper, Chapter 13, pg. 314

[7] Thoth, known as Hermes to the Greeks, is perceived to be the author of the ancient (*The*) *Hermetica* which was likely portions of *The Book of the Dead* available to the ancient Greeks at the time.

[8] The Incan, Aztec and Mayan cultures are readily discernable. But, they represent only the tip of the iceberg of civilizations that extend thousands of years into antiquity in Central and South America. Reference: *Fingerprints of the God*, by Graham Hancock, Parts 2 and 3.

[9] www.flem-ath.com/ and many others.

[10] *The Secrets of the Great Pyramid*, by Peter Tompkins, pg. 260.

[11] Former Keeper of Egyptian Antiquities at the British Museum and renowned Egyptologist.

[12] In the Introduction of *The Egyptian Book of the Dead* written by E.A. Wallis Budge, he states that the *Book of the Dead* "long" predates the first king of Egypt king Menes, estimated to have reigned in 5800 B.C. Clarification: Budge wrote *The Egyptian Book of the Dead* as a translation of the ancient *Book of the Dead.*

[13] *Secrets of the Great Pyramid*, by Peter Tompkins.

[14] *The Sign And The Seal*, by Graham Hancock, Trade Paper, Chapter 13, pg. 313 (footnote 3).

[15] Ibid.,

[16] Ibid., page 102.

[17] The burning of the Library of Alexandra took place in 389 A.D. on the orders of the Christian Emperor Theodosius. Reference: *Secrets*

of the Great Pyramid, by Peter Tompkins, pg. 3.

[18] *Fingerprints of the Gods,* by Graham Hancock, Chapter 1.

[19] *The Mill of Time – Celestial Cycles And Ancient Mythological Science,* by Terry Alden, and *Fingerprints of the Gods,* by Graham Hancock.

[20] *Ryre Study Bible.*

[21] *Fingerprints of the Gods,* by Graham Hancock, Trade Paper, Chapter 27, pg. 213

[22] It is interesting that many identify with the term "New Age." Procession is the likely underlying source of this popular term.

[23] There is an interesting holographic depiction of the purpose of a calendar of this magnitude in the film "Mission to Mars" (2000).

[24] An expression lifted from the movie "O Brother, Where Art Thou?" uttered by Ulysses Everett McGill.

CHAPTER ELEVEN

[11] A nod to Arnold Patent for the work he had done. www.arnoldpatent.com

[2] An acknowledgment to Dhyani Wahoo. Dhyani is a Cherokee medicine woman and Tibetan Buddhist teacher. She can be found at the Sunray Meditation Center in Vermont.

CHAPTER TWELVE

[1] This is a 20th century colloquialism referring to having a lot of power (large engine) under the hood of one's automobile versus a small engine.

[2] A new term is born – Freewill. Divinity and free will combined.

[3] Organic means carbon based life. Inorganic includes much of the mineral kingdom.

[4] Acknowledgment of Lauren L. Holmes for this term and concept.

[5] Juice might be defined as amperage running through our nervous system telling us to the degree that we are on track.

[6] The e-mail was taken from the article "Waging Peace: A Story About Robert Muller," by Lynne Twist. www.westbynorthwest.org/artman/publish/article_340.shtml

[7] www.wagingpeace.org/articles/wca/robert_muller_bio.htm

[8] As reported by Lynne Twist with copyright permission. www. soulofmoney.org

Chapter Thirteen

[1] Barbara Marx Hubbard is an effervescent, esteemed "elder" and keen representative of the consciousness movement. Her new book at the time was: *Emergence: The Shift from Ego to Essence.*

[2] www.evolve.org

[3] www.winwithoutwarus.org

[4] www.moveon.org